ISLAM

MUHAMMAD AND THE KORAN

A Documented Analysis

Second Edition
Revised and Expanded 2002

Dr. Labib Mikhail

ISLAM

MUHAMMAD AND THE KORAN

A Documented Analysis

Unless otherwise noted all Scripture quotations are from the King James Version of the Bible.

Unless otherwise noted all verses of the Koran are from Mushaf Al-Madinah An-Nabawiyah King Fahd Holy Koran printing complex. Verses denoted as MPT are from the Marmaduke Pickthall Translation of the Koran. Verses denoted HK are from the Dr. Muhammad Al-Hilali and Dr. Muhammad Khan Translation.

Hardcover ISBN 1-890297-05-4
Paperback ISBN 1-890297-06-2

First Printing 1996
Copyright© by Dr. Labib Mikhail
Second Printing 2002
Copyright© by Dr. Labib Mikhail
Blessed Hope Ministry
PO Box 2581, Springfield, VA 22152

DEDICATION

I dedicate this book
to those who want to know the truth,
all the truth, and nothing but the truth
about Islam, the religion of the Muslims.

TABLE OF CONTENTS

Introduction 7

**Part One: Muhammad, the Founder of Islam,
from His Birth to His Death**

1. The Beginning 15
2. Khadija 23
3. The Call 27
4. Muhammad's Prophethood 43
5. Muhammad in the Bible? 67
6. The Wives 73
7. The Hijra 85
8. The Sword of Islam 89
9. The Death of the Prophet 99

**Part Two: The Koran,
The Holy Book of Islam**

10. The History of the Koran 105
11. The Koran is Not a Miracle 115
12. The Doctrine of Abrogation 123
13. The Koran is Not Divinely Inspired 127
14. Contributions of the *Jinn*............................141
15. Discrepancies in the Koran 147
16. The Koran does not Satisfy Spiritual
    Needs of Mankind 157
17. The Koran Teaches Polytheism 171
18. The Bible and the Koran 195

4

19. Contradictions Between the Bible
   and the Koran 211
20. The Fruit of Believing the Koran 239

Part Three: Understanding Islam

21. Islam is Not a Religion of Peace 271
22. Islam is Not a Divine Religion 295
23. Jihad 303
24. Major Differences Between
   Christianity and Islam.............................321

Appendix A: Major Sects of Islam 349
Bibliography 359

5

INTRODUCTION

Muhammad is one of the most controversial persons in the history of mankind. Muslims believe he is the greatest prophet, the seal of the prophets, and that no other prophet will come after him. Christians believe Muhammad is a self-proclaimed prophet, or in other words, a false prophet.

More than one billion humans around the world confess Islam, the religion Muhammad founded over 1400 years ago. Therefore it is important to study the life of Muhammad and his teachings in the Koran, the Holy Book of Islam.

Thomas Carlyle, a Scottish historian who lived between 1795 and 1881, wrote concerning Muhammad:

> Can it be possible that so many creatures have lived and died for something which must be regarded as a tragic fraud?

Carlyle assumed that because of the great number of people who follow Muhammad and his religion, Islam, that Muhammad was sincere and original. Carlyle did not realize that the rapid growth of Islam is related to polygamy. Muslims in many Islamic countries marry more than one wife, and consequently have many children, this being one reason why Islam has become the fastest growing religion in the world today.

In addition to growth by birth rate, there are indeed converts to Islam. We must, however, take into consideration that many Christians in Islamic countries have been driven to convert to Islam to escape persecution.

Some Christians have also actually chosen to convert simply in order to be able to divorce their spouse. For example, in Egypt divorce is not allowed between Christians. Once a partner converts to Islam, however, they come under Islamic religious law which allows for divorce. The large number of Muslims in the world, therefore, does not necessarily indicate the integrity of the religion.

We cannot judge any religion by the number of its adherents. The Lord Jesus Christ said:

> Enter by the narrow gate; for wide is the gate and broad is the way that leads to destruction, and there are many who go in by it. Because narrow is the gate and difficult is the way which leads to life, and there are few who find it. (Matthew 7:13,14 NKJ)

The Apostle Paul said:

> Now the Spirit expressly says that in latter times some will depart from the faith, giving heed to deceiving spirits and doctrines of demons. (1 Timothy 4:1 NKJ)

Alighieri Dante, the Italian poet who lived from 1265 and 1321 A.D., wrote *The Divine Comedy*. In it he describes Muhammad, with his body split from the head down to the waist, in the twenty-eighth sphere of the inferno. It shows him tearing apart his severed breast with his own hands because he is the chief among the damned souls who have brought schism into religion.

To the medieval mind, Muhammad's claim to deliver a divine revelation, superseding Judaism and Christianity, could only be regarded as an implausible fraud. Yet Anis Mansoor, a well-known Egyptian journalist, wrote a book in 1985 entitled *The Distinguished Personalities in History are One Hundred, Muhammad is the Greatest of Them.*

8

The Koran declares that Muhammad's contemporaries in Arabia said he was a sorcerer (Surat Yunus 10:2). They said they could write a book like his Koran because it was nothing more than the tales of the ancients.

> And when our verses (of the Quran) are recited to them, they say, 'We have heard (the Quran); if we wish we can say the like of this. This is nothing but the tales of the ancients'. (Surat Al-Anfal 8:31 HK)

They said that a human being was teaching him:

> And indeed we know that they say, 'It is only a human being who teaches him (Muhammad) the tongue of the man they refer to is foreign, while this (the Quran) is a clear Arabic language.' (Surat Al-Nahl 16:103)

How can there be such diverse and extreme opinions regarding one man such as there are about Muhammad? Let us study the life of this man Muhammad. Let us also study the Koran, and let us clearly understand Islam.

This book is different from any other book written about Islam because it compares the Bible and the Koran and exposes the radical differences between them. It has been written after many years of research to reveal to the English-speaking people of the world the truth about Islam, about Muhammad, the prophet of Islam, and about the Koran, the Holy Book of Islam.

Following the distribution of the first edition of this book, many who read it wrote to me, and in revising the book for the second edition, I thought it might be helpful to include some of their comments:

> The book, *Islam, Muhammad and the Koran* by Dr. Labib Mikhail is 'must' reading for all, be they of the Jewish, Christian or Muslim faiths.

The author has done us all a service by analyzing and comparing the books on which each faith stands; and from which each faith teaches each new generation; also comparing the lives and lifestyles of their respective founders, Moses, Jesus, and Muhammad. As a Christian pastor in Egypt for some thirty-four years, he has experienced not only the theological differences, but the results of these teachings on the minds, and conduct, and world view of each adherent. While scholarly, it is not pedantic, but very well organized and easy to read.

It is the one and only book you will need to read in order to understand Islam, the Middle East today, and the danger facing a world complacent about the world's fastest growing religion... ISLAM.

And knowing the facts you will no longer be confused or intimidated by the many faces of Islam!

(Alan C. Lazerte, B.A., LL.B. Executive Director, Canadian Friends of the International Christian Embassy, Jerusalem).

Dr. Campbell Millar, MD, a medical missionary in the Middle East, wrote a lengthy letter in which he stated his findings and highly recommended the book as a source of information about Islam.

Dr. Robert Morey, Christian apologist and author *of The Islamic Invasion* wrote:

Islam, Muhammad and the Koran analyzes the life of Muhammad and the Koran. It is a fascinating look at the details of the life of the 'prophet,' and a critical analysis of the Islamic Holy Book.

Mr. Mark Nelson, an M.A. in Public Administration and Social Work wrote:

10

In I John 4:1, we read that 'we are to test the spirits to see whether they are from God.' And in what many believe are the last days, it seems that we Christians have plenty of testing to do. New false prophets are multiplying and the old ones are making a comeback. I believe your recent book, *Islam, Muhammad, and the Koran*, is an excellent resource for scrutinizing the ambitious claims of this sixth-century man, but it is also an example of the important fruit that can come from a methodical review of comparing the claims of any man with the truth in God's word, or in other words - to test the spirits. To that end, I hope your book can find its way into church libraries everywhere.

Patricia Emard Sidhom wrote:

After having read your most recent book, *Islam, Muhammad and the Koran*, I felt I must write and thank you for this most informative work. I found it to be a thorough and scholarly analysis of a complex subject matter. Yet because of your presentation and writing style, it could be easily understood by this lay person. Your technique of juxtaposing the text of the Holy Bible with the Koran provided me with an opportunity to see for myself the shortcomings of the latter.
Upon completion of *Muhammad from His birth to His death, The Koran,* and *Testimony and Decision,* I came away with an understanding of precisely why the Koran cannot contain the inspired Word of God and His message of love and salvation.

Dr. Richard Gross, an engineer, his wife Ginny and his daughter Martha wrote lengthy comments. I will only mention what Dr. Gross and his daughter Martha wrote. Dr. Gross commented: "Very penetrating book! Contained hundreds of new revelations for me, and I would also think for many others. It will be mightily used."

Martha commented: "This book educates Christians about the grim realities of Islam and strengthens their own faith thereby. It also forces Muslims to face their religion's contradictions."

Rev. Elmer R. Gerbrandt, Missionary with Euro-Team in Germany, wrote:

> A fellow missionary lent me a copy of the volume, *Islam, Muhammad and the Koran*. Although I have a number of brochures and a few books on Islam, none are so well documented as yours. I would like to translate some parts into German, put it on folio, and by means of an overhead projector let the audience read it while I give further explanation, but I need your written permission.

My written permission was granted to Rev. Gerbrandt.

Shandal Publishing Mission in St. Petersburg, Russia, wrote: "We have seen the advertisement of the book, *Islam, Muhammad and the Koran*, by Dr. Labib Mikhail of your publishing house. We are very interested in this book and we would like to publish it in Russian."

Finally, I would like to suggest to the English speaking reader to buy an English translation of the Koran and read it carefully to see the great contradictions between the Koran and the Bible. At the same time you will discover the discrepancies in the Koran itself as well as with some of the English translations. As a native Arabic speaker, I have provided English translations in this book which are true to the original wording in Arabic for that particular verse. Not all translations are as accurate or as honest.

This volume required a lot of research over a period of many years. It is written with sincerity, honesty, and much prayer.

July 2002   Dr. Labib Mikhail

PART ONE

MUHAMMAD

The Founder of Islam
From His Birth to His Death

Chapter One

The Beginning

The first thing I looked for when I began to seriously study the Koran more than twelve years ago, was to find Muhammad's origin. I wanted to read in the Koran about his father, his mother, and the tribe he came from. To my bewilderment, I did not find such information there. All that I found were a few scattered verses in the Koran about Muhammad himself.

In Surat Al-Duha, I learned that Muhammad was a poor, lost orphan:

> Did He not find you (O Muhammad) an orphan and gave you a refuge? And He found you lost [Author's literal translation of the Arabic word *dallan*] and guided you? And He found you poor and made you rich.
>
> (Surat Al-Duha 93:6-8)

In Surat Al-Sharh I read that Muhammad was burdened by a heavy load of iniquity that weighed down his back:

> Have we not opened your breast for you (O Muhammad) and removed your iniquity [Author's translation] which weighed down your back.
>
> (Surat Al-Sharh 94:1-3 HK)

15

The only ones who are mentioned in the Koran from Muhammad's family are his first wife and his uncle, Abu Lahab. In Surat Al-Massad both were destined to hellfire. His first wife and uncle ridiculed Muhammad and rejected his Islam:

> Perish the two hands of Abu Lahab (an uncle of Muhammad) and perish he. He will be burnt in fire of blazing flames. And his wife, too, who carries wood (thorns which she used to put in the way of Muhammad, or used to slander him). In her neck is a twisted rope of Massad (palm fiber).
> (Surat Al-Massad 111:1, 3-5 HK)

In vain I searched for the origin of Muhammad in the Koran. In contrast, the Judeo-Christian Bible is clear about the origins of both Moses and Jesus Christ.

In the book of Exodus we read about Moses' father and mother and all the details of his birth (Exodus 2:1-10). Moses was born into a family of strong faith in God as we read in the letter to the Hebrews:

> By faith Moses, when he was born, was hid three months by his parents, because they saw he was a proper child; and they were not afraid of the king's commandment. (Hebrews 11:23)

Moses' father's name is Amram from the tribe of Levi:

> The name of Amram's wife was Jochebed, the daughter of Levi ... and to Amran she bore Aaron and Moses and their sister Miriam. (Numbers 26:59 NKJ)

The New Testament of the Bible also gives the details of Jesus' birth and how it fulfilled the prophecies concerning him (Matthew 1:18-23; Luke 1:26-38 and 2:1-13). Jesus Christ was born of the

Virgin Mary to whom the angel Gabriel was sent from God to announce his birth:

> And the angel came unto her, and said, 'Hail, thou that art highly favored, the Lord is with thee: blessed art thou among women. . . behold thou shalt conceive in thy womb, and bring forth a son, and shalt call His name Jesus. He shall be great, and shall be called the Son of the Highest: and the Lord God shall give unto Him the throne of His father David; and he shall reign over the house of Jacob forever; and of His kingdom there shall be no end.' (Luke 1:28, 31-33)

To know Muhammad's origin, I had to read the Arabic book entitled *Alsera Alnabawia* (The Biography of Muhammad) written in 758 AD by Ibn Ishaq and edited in latter years by Abdelmalik Ibn Hesham. I also read the Arabic books entitled *Fatrat At-Takween Fi Hayat Al-Saddik Al-Amin* (Genesis of Muhammad's Life and Training) written by Sheik Khalil Abd-AlKareem, *Al-Hezb Al-Hashemy WaTaases Al-Dawlah Al-Islamiah* (The Hashemite Party and the Establishment of the Islamic Nation) written by Dr. Said Mahmmoud Al-Kemny, and *Fe Alsher Al-Jahily* (Poetry in Jahilia) by Dr. Taha Hussen.

The prophet Muhammad's biographies indicate that Muhammad was born in Mecca in the Arabian peninsula in the year 570 AD to a pagan family who worshipped idols, and had no faith in the true God.

Muhammad's full name is Muhammad Ibn (Ibn means son) Abdullah, Ibn Abdul-Muttalib, Ibn Hashim, Ibn Abdmanaf, Ibn Qussai. Ibn Hesham mentioned in his book that Qussai, the great grandfather of Muhammad, was the governor of Mecca and the Guardian of the Kaabah where 369 idols were worshipped by the different Arab tribes.

History tells us that there was a great conflict between the tribes in Arabia concerning who would govern Mecca. The

17

conflict went on until Muhammad's great grandfather, Qussai Ibn Kolabn of the tribe of Quraysh, became the governor.

Massouli, the historian, wrote that Qussai built the Kaabah. The word "Kaabah" means a building in the form of a cube. Qussai invited the other tribes in Arabia to place their gods and idols in the Kaabah of Mecca to increase traffic to the city and therefore enhance trade.

However, the Koran says that the Kaabah in Mecca was built by Ibrahim (Abraham) and Ishamael:

> And remember when Ibrahim (Abraham) and (his son) (Ishmael) were raising the foundations of the house (the Kaabah at Mecca), (saying) 'Our Lord! Accept (this service) from us. Verily! You are the All-Hearer, the All-knower.' (Surat Al-Baqarah 2:127)

The late Dr. Taha Hussen, a great professor and author, and Dean of the College of Arts at Cairo University, wrote in his book, *The Poetry of Jahelia:*

> Mecca was searching for old historical roots to connect the Arabs to these glorious roots mentioned in legends, so they accepted the myth which says that Ishmael and Abraham built the Kaabah.
> (*The Poetry of Jahelia*, 28-29)

To say that Abraham and Ishmael built the Kaabah in Mecca is a myth. Abraham never trod Mecca or the Arabian peninsula. It is clear that Qussai, the great grandfather of Muhammad is the one who built the Kaabah at Mecca.

It is interesting to note here that **freedom of religion was granted to all religions before Islam. When Islam subdued all Arabia, freedom of religion was eliminated, and Islam became the only religion there until this day.**

Muhammad was raised in this pagan atmosphere. Since the Quraysh tribe worshiped the god Allah, Muhammad was dedicated to him as a child. Muhammad's mother's name is Aminah Bint Wahab. Muhammad's father's name is Abdullah, which means "slave of Allah."

Was that Allah the same God of the Bible, or was he, as Dr. Robert Morey wrote in one of his books, the Moon God? The God of the Bible, whom Jews and Christians worship, is not called "Allah" but "Jehovah," as we read in the book of Psalms:

> That you may know that Thou, whose name alone is JEHOVAH, are the Most High over all the earth.
>
> (Psalm 83:18)

Abdullah, Muhammad's father, died before Muhammad's birth. When he was born, his mother Aminah could not breast feed him, so she gave him to a woman by the name of Halima to nurse him along with her son.

Muhammad's mother died when he was six years old, and his grandfather, Abdul Muttalib, assumed responsibility for him. After the death of his grandfather, his uncle Abu-Talib cared for him.

Traumatized by his mother's death, Muhammad suffered from a neurological disease, a special kind of epilepsy. Muhammad's childhood was difficult. Loneliness took its toll on him. Because his uncle Aub-Talib was poor, Muhammad was hired as a shepherd when he was a child.

Arabian Society in Muhammad's Time

Muhammad's uncle Abu-Talib was a merchant, and he used to take Muhammad with him on trading caravans across Arabia. Muhammad was introduced to the surrounding world and many different kinds of people during these journeys with his uncle.

H.A.R. Gibb, professor of Arabic at Oxford University, wrote in his book, *Muhammadanism*:

Mecca at this time was no sleepy hollow, remote from the noise and bustle of the world. A busy and wealthy commercial town, almost monopolizing the entrepot trade between the Indian Ocean and the Mediterranean, it recalls Palmyra without the flashy Greek veneer. Its citizens, while preserving a certain native Arab simplicity in their manners and institutions, had acquired a wide knowledge of men and cities in their intercourse, commercial and diplomatic, with Arab tribesmen and Roman officials. Amongst their leaders these experiences had stimulated intellectual faculties and moral qualities of prudence and self-restraint rare in Arabia. (*Muhammadanism*, 24-25)

The geographical position of Mecca, away from the power of the Persian and Roman Empires, helped it become a powerful trade center. In 570 A.D., the year Muhammad was born, the Christian King of Ethiopia, Abraha, sent his army to Mecca intending to destroy the Kaabah and take over the city. However, his army, known as the Army of the Elephant, was defeated.

Mecca's prominence, along with the defeat of the army of Abraha, in the year of the elephant, gave Mecca and the Quraysh tribe the greatest authority in the Arabian peninsula. According to their legend, the Arabian people believed in the god of the Kaabah in Mecca, who protected the Kaabah by sending birds to strike Abraha's army with stones and defeated them.

Believing this legend, Roya Ibn Al-Ajaj wrote the following poem:

They were touched as the owners of the Elephant, which were struck with stones, by flocks of birds, and were made like an empty field of stalks.

When Muhammad proclaimed himself as a prophet, he recited the same words of Al-Ajaj, claiming that he saw the invasion even though he was a baby at the time. Here are the words of the Koran:

> Have you (O Muhammad) not seen how your Lord dealt with the owners of the Elephant? Did he not make their plot go astray? And He sent against them birds in flocks, striking them with stones of sijel (baked clay). And he made them like empty fields of stalks.
>
> (Surat Al-Fil 105:1-5)

We must remember that during Abraha's invasion of Mecca, the Kaabah was a shrine which contained 360 idols. Would the true God protect a pagan shrine containing all these idols?

Certainly, the Koran in Surat Al-Fil was not talking about the true God.

Chapter Two

Khadija

This chapter is dedicated to Khadija, the first woman Muhammad married. Her complete name was Khadija Bint Khowalid Ibn Assad Ibn Abd Al-Auza Ibn Kusai Ibn Kolab. She had two previous husbands: Ateek Ibn Abed, and then Abu Halah. Muhammad was the third. Khadija and her cousin, Waraka Ibn Nofal Ibn Assad Ibn Abd Aluzza Ibn Kusai who was the Ebionite Bishop of Mecca, played a great role in preparing and training Muhammad to be a prophet.

We read about the first marriage of the prophet Moses in the Bible when Moses went to Midian, and Reuel, the priest of Midian, took him into his house:

> Then Moses was content to live with the man and he gave Zipporah his daughter to Moses.
>
> (Exodus 2:21 NKJ)

But we do not read anything in the Koran concerning Muhammad's marriage to Khadija or any of his other wives.

We have to think about Khadija for a moment. Here is a woman who lived before Islam. She was very wealthy and educated, and she even hired Muhammad to go with her caravans. Khadija used to prepare good food for Muhammad and the other men who escorted him in his commercial journeys. She would spend time talking to him, and she even met her hired men without *hejab* (traditional Muslim head covering for women). After some time she fell in love with Muhammad and sent her maid, Nafisa, to propose marriage to him on her behalf. He was twenty-five years old and she was forty. Some other sources recorded that Muhammad was twenty years old and Khadija was forty-five. Muhammad accepted her proposal of marriage as her wealth was more important to him than her age. Muhammad's marriage to Khadija transformed his life from poverty to great wealth. The Koran refers to this in the following verse:

And He found you poor and made you rich.

(Surat Al-Duha 93:8)

Muhammad's marriage to Khadija assured him of prestige among his tribe, the tribe of Quraysh (*The Mind Crises in Islam, p 89*). Khadija's marriage to Muhammad was an Ebionite marriage. The Ebionites were a Christian cult, and her cousin, Bishop Waraka Ibn Nofal, officiated at the marriage ceremony. So Muhammad's first marriage was in a way a Christian marriage.

From studying Khadija's life, we must conclude that women enjoyed high esteem before Islam. Here is a woman who was very wealthy, educated, free even to propose marriage to a man and hire men to manage her business. She had total control over her life. All that freedom was eliminated by the *Shariah*, the laws of the Koran and the Hadith.

We might ask, "Why was Muhammad content with Khadija and did not marry any women beside her?"

♦ First of all, Khadija was to him as a mother, she gave him compassion and much love, and he was as an obedient son.
♦ Secondly, the Ebionites did not permit polygamy.
♦ Thirdly, she was very wealthy and Muhammad did not want to lose this wealth.

24

However, after Khadija died, he degraded women and stripped them of their freedom and privileges. To say that Islam gave women a better status is a lie and deception. I will elaborate on that important issue in chapter six.

Chapter Three

The Call

At the time of Muhammad, Arabia was largely paganistic, but both Judaism and Christianity were present. Jewish tribes had lived in Arabia for hundreds of years by the time Muhammad was born. They were established, prosperous, and well respected.

There were also many Christian cults in Arabia: the Ebionites, who denied the deity of Christ; the Docetic Gnostics, who emphasized His deity but denied His humanity; the Arians, who attributed to Him a subordinate deity; and the Nestorians, who denied the proper union of His two natures.

Here I have to repeat that freedom of religion was granted in Arabia <u>before</u> Islam. These various religions and cults lived side by side in relative peace.

Religious Influences on Muhammad

Muhammad's prosperous union with Khadija gave him enough time to mingle with the people in the market places and know their ideas and beliefs. It also gave him time for solitude at the cave of Mount Hira in a suburb of Mecca where he used to go with Khadija. It was there that Khadija and her Ebionite cousin, Bishop Waraka Ibn Nofal, trained and prepared him for prophethood.

The Ebionites did not believe in the deity of Christ. They kept the law of Moses and believed in the Torah, but they denied the apostleship of Paul and rejected his letters. Besides the Torah, they

27

only used the book of Psalms and a distorted copy of the Gospel of Matthew as their Bible.

They were a cult, but they firmly believed in the virgin birth of Jesus Christ. Bishop Waraka handed down all of these teachings to Muhammad, who in turn recorded it in his Koran. Concerning the denial of the deity of Christ, the Koran says:

> Surely, those who say that Allah is the Messiah, son of Maryam, are infidels.
>
> (Surat Al-Maida 5:17, Author's translation)

The virgin birth of Jesus Christ is mentioned in the Koran in many verses and in more than one surah (Read Surahs Maryam 19:16-33 and Surat Al-Imran 3:42-51). However, the story in the Koran is different from the story of the gospels. The Koran also only mentions one gospel, which was the Ebionite gospel.

Bishop Waraka taught Muhammad many of the stories of the Torah and the gospel of Matthew. These stories are mentioned in the Koran with great distortion.

Muhammad was also influenced by a Nestorian monk named Buhaira. He met Buhaira on one of the trade caravans he went on with his uncle. Ibn Hesham, Muhammad's biographer, recorded that Buhaira looked at Muhammad's back and saw a mole on it, which he thought was a sign of prophethood. Buhaira told his uncle Abu-Talib about Muhammad's prophethood and told him to protect his nephew.

When the time came for Muhammad to proclaim his prophethood, Arabia was ready for his proclamation. Ibn Hesham mentioned in his Biography of Muhammad that pagan priests declared:

> Satan's *Jinn* told them of the soon appearance of the prophet, whom they await.
>
> (*Alsera Al-Nabawia*, Part Two, 27)

After proclaiming himself as prophet, Muhammad had a special relationship with the *jinn*. *The Reader's Digest Illustrated Encyclopedic Dictionary* defines the word *jinni* as follows:

> Jinni: (*plural* Jinn) In Muslim legend, a spirit capable of assuming human or animal form and exercising supernatural influence over man.

The Koran declares:

> And (remember) when we sent towards you (Muhammad) a group (three to ten persons) of the *jinn*, listening to the Quran. When they stood in the presence thereof, they said, 'Listen in silence!' And when it was finished, they returned to their people as warners.
> (Surat Al-Ahqaf 46:29)

The Koran dedicates a whole surah to the *jinn* under the title Surat Al-Jinn (Surat 72). In the Bible, however, God commanded His people:

> Give no regard to mediums and familiar spirits (*jinn*); do not seek after them, to be defiled by them: I am the LORD your God. (Leviticus 19:31 NKJ)

Again God said to the Israelites:

> When you come into the land which the LORD your God is giving you, you shall not learn to follow the abominations of those nations. There shall not be found among you anyone... who practices witchcraft, or a soothsayer, or one who interprets omens, or a sorcerer, or one who conjures spells, or a medium, or a spiritist (who ask the jinn), or one who calls up the dead. For all who do these things are an abominations to the

LORD, and because of these abominations the LORD your God drives them out from before you.

(Deuteronomy 18:9-12 NKJ)

The Koran declares:

... Iblis (Satan). He was one of the jinn....

(Surat Al-Kahf 18:50)

That means the *jinn* belong to Satan's ranks. But knowing all that Muhammad had a special relationship with the *jinn* who announced and confirmed his prophethood.

Muhammad's Alleged Call

It is important to notice that the call of Muhammad to be a prophet is not recorded in the Koran. It is only recorded in the biographies of Muhammad by Ibn Hesham and others.

One night when Muhammad was forty years old, and after almost twenty years of training by Waraka Ibn Nofal and his wife Khadija, he was asleep in the cave of Hira when a spirit appeared to him and commanded him, saying, "Read." "I cannot read," Muhammad answered because he was illiterate.

Then the spirit squeezed him until he thought he would die and commanded him again, "Read." "I cannot read," he answered. The spirit tightened his grip and pressured him more and said for the third time, "Read." Afraid that he might die, Muhammad said, "What shall I read?" The spirit said:

Read: in the name of thy Lord who Createth. Createth man from a clot. Read: and thy Lord is the Most Bounteous, Who teacheth by the pen, Teacheth man that which he knew not. (Surat Al-Alaq 96:1-5 MPT)

Then the spirit disappeared. Muhammad returned to his wife, frightened and in great distress. He worried that what had happened to him was a hallucination or the appearance of a *jinni*. Muhammad asked Khadija to cover him for he was shivering. Khadija covered him, surprised by his fear, his shivering, and his pale face. According to Ibn Hesham, Muhammad told Khadija what happened to him. Kahdija said to Muhammad, "Be of good cheer, and do not be moved, by Allah I hope that you would be the prophet of this nation."

This indicates that Khadija was the first to assure Muhammad he was the prophet of Arabia. Then Khadija went to Bishop Waraka Ibn Nofal and told him what had happened to Muhammad. Waraka said,

> Holy, Holy, Holy, by Allah. If you have told me the truth, Khadija, the greatest being who used to come to Moses came to Muhammad. Muhammad is the prophet of this nation, tell him, 'do not be moved.'
>
> (Ibn Hesham, Part Two, 73-74)

Therefore it is clear that it was an Ebionite Bishop who declared that Muhammad was a prophet.

The spirit who squeezed Muhammad was not the angel Gabriel.

The Bible admonishes us to test the spirits:

> Beloved, do not believe every spirit, but test the spirits, whether they are of God; because many false prophets have gone out into the world.   (1 John 4:1 NKJ)

Dr. H. A. Ironside commented on this verse:

31

The Holy Scriptures recognize the fact that there is an unseen spirit world, and that in that world there are spirits both good and evil. Of the elect angels it is written, 'He maketh His angels spirits, and His ministers a flame of fire' (Hebrews 1:7). That these spirits have a certain ministry to the people of God here on earth is perfectly clear, for we read, 'Are they not all ministering spirits, sent forth to minister for them who shall be heirs of salvation?' (Hebrews 1:14). Their ministry has to do with temporal mercies rather than with the unfolding of spiritual truths, for there is another Spirit greater than all created spirits, to whom it is given to guide us into all truths, that is the Holy Spirit of God, and we as believers look not to the angels for guidance and understanding, but to the Comforter, the Holy Spirit, the divine Person who came into the world to take of the things of Christ and open them to us.

On the other hand, there is a realm of evil spirits. We are told in Ephesians 6:12 that 'we wrestle not against flesh and blood, but against principalities, against powers, against the rulers of the darkness of this world, against spiritual wickedness in high places.' It is possible for a man to be under the control of the Holy Spirit to such an extent that He is free to use that man to spread the truth of God in a mighty way, but it is just as possible for a man to be under the control of the evil spirits, and teach lies instead of truth. When under their control he will seek to turn people away from the revealed message that God has given in His Word, and bring them into bondage to some form of error. It is important, therefore, that we should be able to distinguish between the spirit of truth and the spirit of error.   *(The Epistles of John and Jude: 133-134)*

Was the spirit who squeezed Muhammad at the cave of Hira the spirit of truth or a spirit of error? In other words, was that spirit the angel Gabriel?

It is of great importance to identify the spirit who squeezed Muhammad at the cave of Hira near Mecca. After his encounter with the spirit, Muhammad was afraid that what happened to him was from a *jinni*. After his migration to Al-Madina, Muhammad declared in the Koran that the spirit who squeezed him was the angel Gabriel. We read in Surat Al-Baqarah 2:97:

> Say: Whoever is an enemy to Gabriel - for he brings down the [revelation] to thy heart by Allah's will, a confirmation of what went before, and guidance and glad tidings for those who believe.

Was the spirit really the angel Gabriel? The answer: Absolutely not!

First: Had the spirit been Gabriel, he would have calmed Muhammad and relieved his fear. But the spirit left him scared and in extreme distress.

Gabriel appeared to many people before his alleged visit to Muhammad and each time the first thing he did was to allay that person's fear. Gabriel appeared to the prophet Daniel. Daniel was afraid, but Gabriel only touched him and did not squeeze him:

> And I heard a man's voice between the banks of Ulai, which called, and said, 'Gabriel, make this man to understand the vision.' So he came near where I stood: and when he came, I was afraid, and fell upon my face . . . but he touched me, and set me upright. . . .
> (Daniel 8:16-18 NKJ)

Gabriel appeared to Zacharias, the father of John the Baptist, who is called Yihia in the Koran; he identified himself and said to Zacharias:

> Do not be afraid, Zacharias . . . I am Gabriel that stands
> in the presence of God.   (Luke 1:13, 19 NKJ)

Gabriel appeared to Mary, the mother of Jesus. Mary was greatly troubled, but Gabriel said to her "Do not be afraid, Mary" (Luke 1:30 NKJ).

But the spirit who squeezed Muhammad left him quite frightened and disturbed. Therefore, the spirit could not have been the angel Gabriel.

Second: Had the spirit been Gabriel, he would not have contradicted his former revelations.

Six hundred years before Muhammad, Gabriel appeared to Mary and said:

> The Holy Ghost shall come upon thee, and the power of
> the Highest shall overshadow thee: therefore also that
> holy thing which shall be born of thee shall be called
> the Son of God.   (Luke 1:35)

But the spirit who appeared to Muhammad said to him:

> . . . and the Christians say: The Messiah is the son of
> Allah. That is their saying with their mouths. They
> imitate the saying of those who disbelieved (literally
> those who are infidels) of old. Allah [Himself] fighteth
> against them. How perverse are they.
> (Surat Al-Tawbah 9:30 MPT)

So Gabriel said to Mary that Jesus would be called the "Son of God." But the spirit who gave the revelations to Muhammad said that this is the saying of the infidels. This spirit declared that Allah Himself fights against the Christians who confess that Jesus is the Son of God.

Was the spirit really the angel Gabriel? Could Gabriel contradict himself in such an important matter?

Third: Had the spirit been Gabriel, Muhammad would have believed what he heard from him with no further need for Khadija to test that spirit the way she did.

Ibn Hesham recorded in his biography the words of Muhammad after his encounter with the spirit:

> I was in the midst of the mountain, when I heard a voice from heaven saying, 'O, Muhammad, you are the Messenger of Allah and I am Gabriel.' I looked toward heaven, I saw Gabriel as a bright figure in the horizon. I looked to the horizon, and wherever I looked I saw him. I stood there until Khadija sent to call me.

But Muhammad did not believe what he saw and heard.

We are told by Ibn Hesham that Khadija tested the spirit who squeezed Muhammad to make sure that he was a holy angel. She said to Muhammad:

> 'Would you please tell me when the spirit comes to you?' When Muhammad told her of the spirit's arrival, Khadija said, 'Muhammad, sit on my left thigh.' Muhammad sat on her left thigh. 'Do you see the spirit?' she asked. 'Yes.' 'Then sit on my right thigh.' Muhammad sat on her right thigh. 'Do you see the spirit?' 'Yes,' he answered. 'Then sit on my lap.' Muhammad sat on her lap. 'Do you see the spirit?' she

asked. 'Yes,' he answered. Khadija uncovered a feminine part of her body while Muhammad was sitting on her lap. 'Do you see the spirit?' 'No,' he answered. Then Khadija said, 'Muhammad, that spirit is an angel, not a devil.' (Ibn Hesham, II: 74-75)

What a strange way to test a spirit! It is amazing to notice that Muhammad acted as an obedient son to Khadija and that a woman succeeded well in training Muhammad.

Fourth: Had the spirit been Gabriel, he would have taught Muhammad to read and write.

The Koran declares that Allah taught Jesus how to write. In Surat Al-Imran 3:48 it is said concerning Jesus:

> And Allah will teach him the book and wisdom, the Torah and the Gospel.

Ibn Katheir, in his exposition of the Koran (Vol. 1: 344), says, "The book mentioned here means writing."

We would expect that Muhammad, who calls himself the seal of the prophets, would be taught to read and write. The spirit said in his revelation to Muhammad:

> Read; and thy Lord the Most Bounteous, who teaches by the pen, teacheth man that which he knew not.
> (Surat Al-Alaq 96:3-4)

The question is, if God teaches man that which he knew not by the pen, why did He not teach Muhammad how to read and write instead of leaving him illiterate all his life?

There came a time when Muhammad was in doubt concerning the revelations he received from the spirit. The Koran records:

36

If thou wert in doubt as to what we have revealed unto thee, then ask those who have been reading the Book from before thee: The truth hath indeed come to thee from thy Lord; so be in no wise of those in doubt.

(Surat Yunus 10:94)

The "Book" mentioned in this verse is the Bible, and that shows very clearly that the Bible was the final authority for Muhammad even when he was in doubt. If Muhammad had been a learned man he would have known the truth directly from the Bible. But the spirit left him illiterate.

Muhammad had the right to be in doubt of the revelations given to him by the spirit which appeared to him at the cave of Hira, for that spirit was not the angel Gabriel. If he had been a learned man, he would have known what the New Testament says concerning Satan:

And no wonder! For Satan himself transforms himself into an angel of light.   (2 Cor 11:14 NKJ)

It is obvious that Muhammad was totally deceived, for he was illiterate and could not search for the truth as it is recorded in the Holy Scriptures which were available in his time.

Fifth: Muhammad was the only one who saw that spirit. One witness is not acceptable in substantiating his testimony.

God said in the book of Deuteronomy 19:15, "By the mouth of two or three witnesses the matter shall be established." Jesus Christ said to the Jews of his days:

If I bear witness of Myself, my witness is not true. There is another that bears witness of Me, and I know that the witness which He witnesses of Me is true. You

37

have sent to John, and he has borne witness to the truth. Yet I do not receive testimony from man, but I say these things that you may be saved. . . But I have a greater witness than John's, for the works which the Father has given me to finish - the very works that I do - bear witness of Me, that the Father has sent Me. And the Father Himself, who sent Me, has testified of Me . . . You search the Scriptures, for in them you think you have eternal life; and these are they which testify of Me.

(John 5:31-39 NKJ)

Christ has four witnesses:

♦ The testimony of John the Baptist
♦ The testimony of the miracles He performed
♦ The testimony of the Heavenly Father
♦ The testimony of the prophetic word

Muhammad is the only witness for himself. We cannot accept his sole testimony.

Sixth: Had the spirit been Gabriel, he would have passed the biblical test of the spirit of truth.

There are three biblical tests by which we may discern between the spirit of truth and the spirit of error.

♦ The test of the inspired Word
♦ The test of the cross of Christ
♦ The test of demonstrating God's love

The test of the inspired word

Here is what the inspired Word says:

In the beginning was the Word, and the Word was with God, and the Word was God. The same was in the beginning with God. All things were made by him; and without him was not any thing made that was made. In him was life; and the life was the light of men. And the light shineth in darkness; and the darkness comprehended it not. There was a man sent from God, whose name was John. The same came for a witness, to bear witness of the Light, that all men through him might believe. He was not that Light, but was sent to bear witness of that Light. That was the true Light, which lighteth every man that cometh into the world. He was in the world, and the world was made by him, and the world knew him not. He came unto his own, and his own received him not. But as many as received him, to them gave he power to become the sons of God, even to them that believe on his name: which were born, not of blood, nor of the will of the flesh, nor of the will of man, but of God. And the Word was made flesh.... (John 1:1-14)

Every spirit that confesses that Jesus Christ has come in the flesh is of God and every spirit that does not confess that Jesus Christ has come in the flesh is not of God.
(1 John 4:2-3 NKJ)

Therefore I make known to you that ... no one can say that Jesus is Lord except by the Holy Spirit.
(1 Corinthians 12:3 NKJ)

Any spirit who does not confess that Christ was from eternity with the Father and that he became flesh in due time is a spirit of error.

The test of the cross of Christ

> For the message of the cross is foolishness to those who are perishing, but to us who are being saved it is the power of God.　　　　　　　　(1 Corinthians 1:18 NKJ)

Any spirit that denies the crucifixion of Christ is a spirit of error. The spirit who appeared to Muhammad denied the crucifixion of Christ.

The test of demonstrating God's love

> But God demonstrates His own love toward us, in that while we were still sinners, Christ died for us.
> 　　　　　　　　　　　　　　　　　(Romans 5:8 NKJ)

> For God so loved the world, that he gave his only begotten Son, that whosoever believeth in him should not perish, but have everlasting life.　　　(John 3:16)

> . . . for God is love.　　　　　　　　(I John 4:8b NKJ)

God was never called "love" in the Koran which was dictated by that spirit. Therefore, that spirit could not be the angel Gabriel; he was a spirit of error.

We can make a few observations at the conclusion of this chapter:

First of all, even though Muhammad claimed that he was escorted by the angel Gabriel for twenty-three years hearing his revelations, he was at the same time under the sway of Satan. Satan assailed Muhammad's mind with suggestions. Here are the words of the Koran:

> If a suggestion from Satan assails thy (mind), seek refuge with Allah.　　　　　　　(Surat Al-Araf 7:200)

Satan caused Muhammad to forget the verses of the Koran:

> And when you (Muhammad) see those who engage in a false conversation about Our Verses (of the Koran) by mocking at them, stay away from them until they turn to another topic. And if Satan causes you to forget, then after the remembrance sit not you in the company of those people who are the Zalimun (polytheists and wrongdoers).
>
> (Surat Al-Anam 6:68)

Muhammad Fareed Wagdy recorded in his exposition of the Koran:

> It is said that a Jew bewitched Muhammad, that he caused him to forget what he did, so Allah gave him two surahs. When he recited them he was healed.
>
> (*Al-Mushaf Al-Mufassar*, 827)

It is hard to believe that Allah would assign Gabriel to escort Muhammad for twenty-three years. Gabriel has more important things to do.

The second important observation is that Gabriel did not reveal any new revelations to Muhammad concerning the ancient patriarchs. The stories of Adam, Abraham, Joseph, Moses, David and all the rest were recorded wonderfully in the Old Testament. All we read concerning these great men in the Koran is totally distorted.

The third, and very crucial observation is that there came a time in Muhammad's life when the spirit's revelations stopped coming to him for a period of more than two years. He was so depressed that he thought of committing suicide because his message was interrupted.

Ahmad Abd-Elwahab recorded this in his book, *Prophethood and Prophets in Judaism, Christianity and Islam*:

> The revelations came to Muhammad to declare Islam in his home. Suddenly a surprise Muhammad never imagined.... Revelations stopped. Nights and days passed, and no revelation came from heaven. The news spread and the infidels said Allah forsook Muhammad. The prophet was in distress; he suffered so much from this spiritual experience that he thought to commit suicide by throwing himself from the top of Abu-Kubais mountain, after he saw himself hanging between heaven and earth. (first edition, 177-178)

Contrary to that terrible experience Christ declared:

> He who sent Me is with Me. The Father has not left Me alone, for I do always those things that please him.
> (John 8:29 NKJ)

Since the revelations that were given to Muhammad by that spirit contradict the message of the gospel of Jesus Christ, then we must apply the words of the Apostle Paul:

> But even if we, or an angel from heaven, preach any other gospel to you than what we have preached to you, let him be accursed. (Galatians 1:8 NKJ)

42

Chapter Four

Muhammad's Prophethood

Before we discuss Muhammad's prophethood, we have to realize that there are three kinds of prophets:

The first type are those chosen by God to establish a religion, like the prophet Moses who established Judaism.

The second type are those chosen by God to warn the people and urge them to repent of their sins and at the same time to utter prophecies of things to come. There are many prophets of this kind such as Isaiah, Jeremiah, Ezekiel, Daniel, and the rest of the Jewish prophets.

The third type are false prophets. The Apostle Peter describes those false prophets in the following words:

But there were also false prophets among the people, even as there will be false teachers among you, who will secretly bring in destructive heresies, even denying the Lord who bought them, and bring on themselves swift destruction. And many will follow their destructive ways, because of whom the way of truth will be blasphemed. (2 Peter 2:1-2 NKJ)

So the main characteristic of the false prophet is denying the truth of the sacrificial work of Christ on the cross. Chapter 23 of the book of Jeremiah speaks about those prophets and warns the people of God not to listen to them.

> Thus says the Lord of hosts: 'Do not listen to the words of the prophets who prophesy to you. They make you worthless; they speak a vision of their own heart, not from the mouth of the Lord.'   (Jeremiah 23:16 NKJ)

The Prophet Muhammad Does Not Meet The Qualifications of a True Prophet.

What are the qualifications of a true prophet?

First: A true prophet chosen by God to establish a new religion must receive a direct call from God.

Moses, the prophet of Judaism, received a direct call from God. Here is the story of his experience and call.

> Now Moses kept the flock of Jethro his father-in-law, the priest of Midian; and he led the flock to the backside of the desert and came to the mountain of God, even to Horeb. And the angel of the LORD appeared unto him in a flame of fire out of the midst of a bush; and he looked, and, behold, the bush burned with fire, and the bush was not consumed. And Moses said, 'I will now turn aside, and see this great sight, why the bush is not burnt.' And when the LORD saw that he turned aside to see, God called unto him out of the midst of the bush, and said, 'Moses, Moses.' And he said, 'Here am I.' And he said, 'Draw not nigh hither: Put off thy shoes from off thy feet, for the place whereon thou standest is holy ground.' Moreover he said, 'I am the God of thy father, the God of Abraham, the God of Isaac, and the God of Jacob.' And Moses

hid his face; for the was afraid to look upon God. And the LORD said, 'I have surely seen the affliction of my people which are in Egypt, and have heard their cry by reason of their taskmasters; for I know their sorrows; And I am come down to deliver them out of the hand of the Egyptians, and to bring them up out of that land unto a good land and a large, unto a land flowing with milk and honey; unto the place of the Canaanites, and the Hittites, and the Amorites, and the Perizzites, and the Hivites, and the Jebusites. Now therefore, behold, the cry of the children of Israel is come unto me: and I have also seen the oppression wherewith the Egyptians oppress them. Come now therefore, and I will send thee unto Pharaoh, that thou mayest bring forth my people the children of Israel out of Egypt.' (Exodus 3:1-10)

The Koran declares:

And to Moses Allah spoke direct. (Surat Al-Nisa 4:164)

Muhammad did not receive a direct call from God but rather a call from the spirit who squeezed him in the cave of Hira. Muhammad claimed in the surahs he uttered at Al Madina that the spirit was the angel Gabriel. But he did not claim that in the surahs given him in Mecca:

Say (O Muhammad) whoever is an enemy to Gabriel - for he brings down the (revelation) to thy heart, by Allah's will. (Surat Al-Baqarah 2:97)

No matter who the spirit was, God did not give a direct call to Muhammad.

45

Second: A true prophet must perform miracles to authenticate his call.

Moses performed many miracles. Concerning Moses' miracles, the Bible says:

> Israel also came into Egypt, and Jacob dwelt in the land of Ham.... He sent Moes His servant, and Aaron whom He had chosen. They performed His signs [miracles] among them, and wonders in the land of Ham. He sent darkness, and make it dark; and they did not rebel against His word. He turned their waters into blood, and killed their fish. Their land abounded with frogs, even in the chambers of their kings. He spoke, and there came swarms of flies, and lice in all their territory. He gave them hail for rain, and flaming fire in their land. He struck their vines also and their fig trees, and splintered the trees of their territory. He spoke, and locusts came, young locusts without number, and ate up all the vegetation in their land, and devoured the fruit of their ground. He also destroyed all the firstborn in their land, the first of all their strength.
> (Psalms 105:23, 26-36 NKJ)

The Koran declares:

> To Moses We did give nine Clear signs [miracles].
> (Surat Al-Isra 17:101)

The Bible recorded more than nine miracles performed by Moses.

The New Testament recorded the miracles of Christ and they proved that he was sent by God. Here is what Christ said to the Jews:

But I have greater witness than that of John: for the works (miracles) which the Father hath given me to finish, the same works that I do bear witness of me, that the Father hath sent me.   (John 5:36)

In his Gospel, the Apostle John recorded many miracles Jesus performed. At the end of his Gospel he says:

And truly Jesus did many other signs in the presence of his disciples which are not written in this book; but these are written that you may believe that Jesus is the Christ, the Son of God, and that believing you may have life in His name.   (John 20:30-31 NKJ)

The Koran also declares that Jesus Christ performed many miracles. Here are the words of Jesus according to the Koran:

I have come to you, with a sign from your Lord, in that I make for you out of clay, as it were, the figure of a bird, and breathe into it, and it becomes a bird by Allah's leave: And I heal those born blind, and the lepers, and I bring the dead into life by Allah's leave; and I declare to you what ye eat, and what ye store in your houses. Surely therein is a sign for you if he did believe.
                              (Surat Al-Imran 3:49)

But Muhammad did not perform any miracles. He never healed a sick person, cleansed a leper, commanded a demon to come out of a possessed person, or raised a dead person.

Christ responded to the plea of a blind man, Bartimaeus, the son of Timaeus, and gave him his sight (Mark 10:46-52). But when the blind man Abdullah Ibn Umm-Maktum came to Muhammad when he was preaching to some of the Quraysh's chiefs, Muhammad "frowned and turned away" (Surat Abasa 80:1). He could not give that blind man his sight.

Muhammad's contemporaries challenged him to perform a miracle to authenticate his claim as a prophet, saying:

> Why are not signs (miracles) sent down to him from his Lord? Say: (O Muhammad) 'The signs (miracles) are only with Allah, and I am only a plain warner.'
>
> (Surat Al-Ankabut 29:50)

Again they challenged him saying:

> We shall not believe in you (O Muhammad) until you cause a spring to gush forth from the earth for us... Say (O Muhammad) glorified (and exalted is the Lord (Allah): Am I anything but a man, sent as a messenger.
>
> (Surat Al-Isra 17:90, 93 HK)

As a result of Muhammad's inability to perform any miracles, his contemporaries said:

> ... These (revelations of the Koran) are mixed up false dreams! Nay, he has invented it! Nay, he is a poet! Let him bring us an ayah (miracle as a proof) like the prophets that were sent before (with miracles).
>
> (Surat Al Anbiya 21:5 HK)

Muhammad failed to meet their challenge. He could not perform a miracle and therefore his call was not authenticated.

Third: A true prophet must utter accurate prophecies that are fulfilled to the letter.

The prophecies of Joseph, Moses, Isaiah, Daniel and the rest of the true prophets recorded in the Old Testament were perfectly fulfilled. The rest of their prophecies will certainly be fulfilled.

The only so-called prophetic utterance Muhammad recorded in his Koran is Surat Al-Rum. It says:

> The Romans have been defeated - in a land close by:
> But they, [even] after [this] defeat of theirs, will soon
> be victorious within a few years, with Allah is the
> command in the past and in the future: On that day shall
> the believers rejoice. (Surat Al-Rum 30:2-4)

This surah cannot be considered a prophecy in any sense, for it does not mention who defeated the Romans, where they were defeated, or who would be defeated by them.

The surah declares that on the day of the Romans' victory Muslims shall rejoice. Romans were Catholics at that time. So why would the Muslims rejoice?

The reader of the Koran will not find in any of the 114 surahs detailed signs of the last days as we find in the books of Daniel, Zechariah, Isaiah, or The Revelation.

Muhammad did not utter any prophecies.

Fourth: A true prophet must be consistent with the former revelations given by the holy prophets of God.

Jesus Christ confirmed all that the Old Testament prophets had said:

> Do not think that I came to destroy the law or the
> prophets. I did not come to destroy but to fulfill.
> (Matthew 5:17 NKJ)

When He rose from the dead and met the two disciples on the road to Emmaus, He said to them:

> 'O foolish ones, and slow of heart to believe in all that
> the prophets have spoken! Ought not the Christ to have
> suffered these things and to enter into His glory?' And

49

beginning at Moses and all the prophets, He expounded to them in all the scriptures the things concerning Himself.   (Luke 24:25-27 NKJ)

Muhammad declared in his Koran:

The religion before Allah is Islam.(Surat Al-Imran 3:19)

Again in verse 85 of the same Surat:

If anyone desires a religion other than Islam, never will it be accepted of him; and in the hereafter he will be in the ranks of those who have lost.

In Surat Al-Ahzab 33:40 we read:

Muhammad is . . . the Messenger of Allah and the Seal of the Prophets.

In addition to these verses, the Koran clearly denies the death and crucifixion of Christ:

That they said, 'We killed Christ Jesus the son of Mary, the Messenger of Allah.' But they killed him not, nor crucified him.   (Surat Al-Nisa 4:157)

With verses like these in the Koran, Muhammad contradicted Judaism and all the books of the New Testament from the Gospel of Matthew to the book of Revelation, because all these books confirm the crucifixion of Jesus Christ. He claimed Islam as the only religion accepted by Allah and declared himself to be the seal of the prophets.

Muhammad was not consistent with the divine revelations that came before him; the Koran contradicts many revelations written in the Old and New Testaments of the Bible. We will mention specific contradictions in Part Two.

Fifth: A true prophet must have a definite mission assigned to him by God.

When God called Moses to be a prophet, He gave him his mission. God said to Moses:

> Come now, therefore, and I will send you to Pharaoh that you may bring My people, the children of Israel, out of Egypt. (Exodus 3:10 NKJ)

Moses' mission was to liberate the children of Israel from the bondage of Egypt. Later on He gave him the law: "For the law was given through Moses."(John 1:17 NKJ)

When Jesus Christ began His ministry, He went to the synagogue at Nazareth and opened the book of Isaiah where it is written:

> 'The Spirit of the LORD is upon Me. Because He has anointed Me to preach the gospel to the poor. He has sent Me to heal the brokenhearted, to preach deliverance to the captives and recovery of sight to the blind, to set at liberty those who are oppressed, to preach the acceptable year of the LORD .' Then He closed the book, and gave it back to the attendant and sat down. And the eyes of all who were in the synagogue were fixed on Him. And He began to say to them, 'Today this Scripture is fulfilled in your hearing.' (Luke 4:18-21 NKJ)

This was Christ's mission which He sealed by His death on the cross.

What was Muhammad's mission? The spirit who appeared to him while he was asleep or awake and squeezed him so hard that he thought he would die did not give him any mission. Rather he said to him, "Read." Later we read in the Koran that Muhammad preached monotheism, but monotheism was known thousands of years before Muhammad. Moses said to the children of Israel:

Hear, O Israel: The LORD our God is one LORD.

(Deuteronomy 6:4)

Muhammad brought no new revelation. On the contrary, his Koran permitted:

♦ Polygamy instead of monogamy,
♦ War and bloodshed instead of peace,
♦ Revenge instead of forgiveness,
♦ Salvation by good deeds, instead of salvation by the grace of God through the shed blood of Jesus Christ, and
♦ A sensual paradise after death where the Muslims will have rivers of wine, women with wide lovely eyes and beautiful boys (Surat Al-Tur 52:17-24) instead of a new heaven and new earth in which righteousness dwells (II Peter 3:13).

What Muhammad proclaimed and practiced is in total contradiction with the New Testament principles and commandments.

Sixth: A true prophet according to Islamic theology must be infallible.

In a leaflet printed by the cabinet of Islamic affairs in Saudi Arabia's kingdom under the title *Prophethood in Islam*, it is written that:

After receiving the message he (the prophet) is infallible. That is, he would not commit any sin.
(Islamic Series No. 7)

If we apply this qualification to Muhammad we will find that he is not a true prophet because according to the Koran he committed many sins after he proclaimed his prophethood. In many verses of the Koran Allah commanded Muhammad to ask for forgiveness of his sins:

Patiently, then, persevere (Muhammad) for the promise of Allah is true: and ask forgiveness for thy sin.
(Surat Ghafir 40:55, Author's literal translation)

And seek (O Muhammad) the forgiveness of Allah, Allah is ever oft-Forgiving, most Merciful.
(Surat Al-Nisa 4:106)

Dr. Khan and Dr. Al-Hillali commented on this verse in the margin of their translation of the Koran:

The prophet seeks Allah's forgiveness by daytime and at night.

Abu Huraiah was one of Muhammad's friends and is quoted extensively in the Haidth. The Hadith is the sayings of Muhammad as quoted by witnesses and is the second authoritative source for Muslim clerics. Abu Haraiah is quoted as follows:

I heard Allah's Messenger saying, 'By Allah! I seek Allah's forgiveness and turn to him in repentance for more than seventy times a day.'
(Sahih Al-Bukhari, Vol. 8, Hadith No. 319)

So glorify the praises of your Lord, and ask His Forgiveness. Verily, He is the One who accepts repentance and Who forgives. (Surat Al-Nasr 110:3 HK)

Verily, We have given you (O Muhammad) a manifest victory. That Allah may forgive you your sins of the past and the future.... (Surat Al-Fath 48:1-2)

Muhammad was not infallible after he proclaimed himself a prophet, therefore, according to Islamic theology, he is not a true prophet because he lived a sinful life.

Seventh: A true prophet must be like Moses.
Muhammad was not a prophet like Moses

God gave Abraham two sons, Ishmael and Isaac, but he declared clearly that His covenant would be with Isaac:

But my covenant will I establish with Isaac.
(Genesis 17:21)

We have mentioned before that the Koran declares:

We... grant to the children of Israel the Book (Old Testament), the power of command, and prophethood.... (Surat Al-Jathiyah 45:16)

Who switched prophethood from the Jews and gave it to the Arabs? Prophethood was granted only to the Jews, so that there would not be any confusion in knowing who is the true God, who is the true prophet, what is the plan of God for the salvation of mankind, and what is the will of God. The Apostle Paul says:

54

What advantage then hath the Jew? Or what profit is there of circumcision? Much in every way; chiefly, because that unto them were committed the oracles of God.   (Romans 3:1-2)

The Koran declares:

It was We who revealed the Torah (to Moses): therein was guidance and light, by its standard have been judged the Jews, by the prophets who bowed to Allah's will, by the Rabbis and the Doctors of Law; for to them was entrusted the protection of Allah's Book, and they were witnesses thereto....   (Surat Al-Maida 5:44)

Jewish people according to the Koran are the protectors of Allah's Book. God would never entrust His book to dishonest people.

Muslim clerics claim that the prophecy of Moses concerning the coming prophet was fulfilled in Muhammad. Let us read Moses' prophecy and analyze it, and see for ourselves if the prophet like Moses is Christ or Muhammad. Here is the prophecy of Moses:

The LORD your God will raise up for you a Prophet like me from your midst, from your brethren. Him you shall hear according to all you desired of the LORD your God in Horeb in the day of the assembly, saying, 'Let me not hear again the voice of the LORD my God, nor let me see this great fire anymore, lest I die.' And the LORD said to me, 'What they have spoken is good. I will raise up for them a Prophet like you from among their brethren, and will put My words in His mouth, and He shall speak to them all that I command Him.'
                                        (Deuteronomy 18:15-18 NKJ)

First: The prophet like Moses must be an Israelite "from your midst, from your brethren." This is the same condition God set for the Jews when they wished to have a king:

> When you come to the land which the LORD your God is giving you, and possess it and dwell in it, and say, 'I will set a king over me like all the nations that are around me,' you shall surely set a king over you whom the LORD your God chooses; one from among your brethren you shall set a king over you; you may not set a foreigner over you, who is not your brother.
>
> (Deuteronomy 17:14-15 NKJ)

The prophet Muhammad was an Arab. That prophecy does not apply to him. It certainly applies to Christ, for He was an Israelite.

Second: The prophet like Moses must be sent to the children of Israel: "The LORD your God will raise up for you..." (Deuteronomy 18:15-18).

Muhammad is a prophet to the Arabs. It says in the Koran:

> A book, whereof the verses are explained in detail; a Koran in Arabic for people who understand.
>
> (Surat Fussilat 41:3)

> And thus We have revealed to you (O Muhammad) a Quran in Arabic that you may warn the Mother of the Towns (Mecca) and all around it, and warn (them) of the Day of Assembling of which there is no doubt; when a party will be in paradise, and a party in the blazing fire.
>
> (Surat Ash-Shura 42:7)

But Christ came first to Israel:

56

I have not been sent except to the lost sheep of the house of Israel.   (Matthew 15:24 NKJ)

When the Jews did not receive Him, the Gospel was given to all nations:

He came to His own, and His own did not receive Him. But as many as received Him, to them He gave the right to become children of God.   (John 1:11-12 NKJ)

Third: The prophet like Moses must be like Moses. Now, let us see clearly the similarities between Moses and Christ, none of which can be applied to Muhammad.

When Moses was a baby He was destined to be killed by the command of the King of Egypt but was rescued by God's intervention.   (Exodus 1:22, 2:1-10)

When Jesus was a baby He too was to be killed by the command of King Herod, yet He was rescued by God's intervention.   (Matthew 2:1-15)

Nothing like this happened to Muhammad when he was a baby.

Moses was learned in all the wisdom of the Egyptians.
          (Acts 7:22 NKJ)

The Bible says about Christ: 'In Whom are hid all the treasures of wisdom and knowledge.'   (Colossians 2:3)

Muhammad was illiterate his whole life. (Surat Al-Araf 7:157)

♦ Moses was a miracle worker (Exodus 4:1-9 and 17:3-7).

Christ also performed many miracles throughout the gospels.

Muhammad did not perform one miracle (Read Surat Al-Ankabut 29:50 and Surat Al-Isra 17:90-93).

♦ Moses received a direct call from God (Exodus 3:1-10).

Christ was proclaimed by God the Father in heaven (Matthew 3:17).

Muhammad's alleged call came from the spirit who met him at the cave of Hira.

♦ Moses liberated the children of Israel from the bondage of Egypt (Exodus 14:30 and 15:1-21).

Christ liberated and still liberates sinners from the bondage of sin and Satan: "Therefore if the Son makes you free, you shall be free indeed" (John 8:36 NKJ).

Muhammad adopted all the customs of the Arabs and sanctified them and put all of Arabia under the bondage of his Islam.

♦ The face of Moses shone while he talked with God (Exodus 34:28-30).

Christ's face shone like the sun when he was with Peter, James, and John on the mount of transfiguration (Matthew 17:1-2).

Nothing like that ever happened to Muhammad.

♦ God spoke to Moses face to face (Exodus 33:9-11). The Koran even says, "And to Moses Allah spoke directly" (Surat Al-Nisa 4:164).

God spoke audibly from Heaven concerning Christ when he said "This is My beloved Son in whom I am well pleased" (Matthew 3:17).

God never spoke to Muhammad face to face.

What about the death of Muhammad? In June 632 A.D., death came to Muhammad in the room of his wife Aisha as he rested on her lap after being poisoned by a woman whose father, uncle, and brother had been killed by Muhammad.

It is said that a grave was dug in that very place, and in it the prophet of Islam was buried. Later a mosque was built there, and Muhammad's grave became a place of pilgrimage in Al-Madina.

Now we realize a great difference between Muhammad's death and burial and Moses' death and burial. The Bible says:

Moses was a hundred and twenty years old when he died, yet his eyes were not weak nor his strength gone.
(Deuteronomy 34:7 NIV)

Muhammad died when he was sixty-three years old with four of his front teeth broken. His wife Aisha was only sixteen years old.

Moses died according to the word of the Lord. His funeral was an angelic funeral (Jude 9). God attended Moses' funeral and buried him in a grave and to this day no one knows where his grave is located.

So Moses the servant of the LORD died there in the land of Moab, according to the word of the LORD. And He buried him in a valley in the land of Moab, opposite Beth Pe'or, but no one knows his grave to this day.

(Deuteronomy 34:5-6 NKJ)

Concerning the Tomb of Jesus Christ, we read the words of the angel to Mary Magdalene and the other Mary who came with her to see the tomb:

> He is not here; for He is risen as He said. Come see the place where the Lord lay. (Matthew 28:6 NKJ)

Here is the great difference between Jesus Christ, who died to save those who believe in Him and rose victorious over death, and Muhammad, who was poisoned and defeated by death. The Koran records the death of Muhammad and his followers:

> Lo! thou wilt die, and lo! they will die. (Surat Al-Zumar 39:30 MPT)

Jesus Christ says to His followers, "Because I live, you will live also" (John 14:19 NKJ). Christians believe in a living Savior.

Moses appeared after his death on the mount of transfiguration, escorted by the prophet Elijah. Together they talked with Jesus. Peter, James and John also saw him at that time (Matthew 17:1-8).

When Muhammad died, his death was the final chapter of his life, and no one has seen him since his death. Jesus Christ arose from the dead and appeared after His resurrection to more than five hundred brethren (1 Corinthians 15:4-8).

The final and authoritative word concerning Moses' prophecy about the coming prophet was uttered by the Apostle Peter on the day of Pentecost to the Israelites:

> Men of Israel... the God of Abraham, Isaac, and Jacob, the God of our fathers, glorified His Servant Jesus, whom you delivered up and denied in the presence of Pilate, when he was determined to let Him go. But you denied the Holy One and the Just, and asked for a

murderer to be granted to you, and killed the Prince of life, whom God raised from the dead, of which we are witnesses. Yet now, brethren, I know that you did it in ignorance, as did also your rulers. But those things which God foretold by the mouth of all His prophets, that the Christ would suffer, He has thus fulfilled. Repent therefore and be converted, that your sins may be blotted out, so that times of refreshing may come from the presence of the Lord, and that He may send Jesus Christ, who was preached to you before, whom heaven must receive until the times of restoration of all things, which God has spoken by the mouth of all His holy prophets since the world began. For Moses truly said to the fathers, 'The Lord your God will raise up for you a Prophet like me from your brethren. Him you shall hear in all things, whatever He says to you. And it shall come to pass that every soul who will not hear that Prophet shall be utterly destroyed from among the people.' Yes, and all the prophets from Samuel and those who follow, as many as have spoken, have also foretold these days. You are sons of the prophets and of the covenant which God made with our fathers, saying to Abraham, 'And in your seed all the families of the earth shall be blessed.' To you first, God, having raised up His Servant Jesus, sent Him to bless you, in turning away every one of you from your iniquities.

(Acts 3:12-15, 17-26 NKJ)

We can conclude therefore that there are no similarities between Moses and Muhammad. Christ was the awaited Messiah (Daniel 9:26), who was also the awaited prophet (compare John 1:19-21 with Daniel 9:26 and Deuteronomy 18:15-19).

Certainly Muhammad was not a prophet like Moses.

No Necessity for Muhammad's Prophethood

Why would Christians reject the alleged call of Muhammad to be a true prophet of God and consequently reject Islam **First and foremost because God's plan was made perfect by the coming of Christ, His death on the cross, and His resurrection. Nothing needs to be added to perfection.**

When an artist paints a beautiful colorful picture and puts his last touches on it, any addition to that picture will ruin it. God in His wisdom planned the salvation of man through the shed blood of Jesus Christ before the foundation of the world (I Peter 1:18-20).

> Known to God from eternity are all His works.
> (Acts 15:18 NKJ)

God's plan for humanity was accomplished in Christ; there was no need whatsoever for a new prophet or a new religion after Christ.

God in His wisdom chose Abraham, and through his son Isaac he raised the nation of Israel. He gave them the land of Canaan (now called Palestine) by a covenant (Genesis 15:18-21). He raised up prophets from among them, so there would be no mistake when the prophecies uttered by the Jewish prophets are fulfilled. The Apostle Paul said:

> What advantage then has the Jew, or what is the profit of circumcision? Much in every way! Chiefly because to them were committed the oracles of God.
> (Romans 3:1-2 NKJ)

Again he says:

> I tell the truth in Christ, I am not lying, my conscience also bearing me witness in the Holy Spirit, that I have great sorrow and continual grief in my heart. For I

62

could wish that I myself were accursed from Christ for my brethren, my kinsmen according to the flesh, who are Israelites, to whom pertain the adoption, the glory, the covenants, the giving of the law, the service of God, and the promises; of whom are the fathers and from whom, according to the flesh, Christ came, who is over all, the eternally blessed God.   (Romans 9:1-5 NKJ)

The Koran itself declares that the children of Israel were preferred over all other people:

O children of Israel! Remember My Favour which I bestowed upon you and that I preferred you to the Alalamin (mankind).   (Surat Al-Baqarah 2:47)

The same words are repeated in verse 122 and again in Surat Al-Jathiya:

And indeed We gave the children of Israel the scripture, and the understanding of the scripture and His laws, and the prophethood, and provided them with good things, and preferred them above the Alamin (all mankind).
(Surat Al-Jathiyah 45:16 HK)

Moreover, we read in the Koran that Allah assigned the Holy Land to the children of Israel:

And (remember) when Moses said to his people: 'O my people, remember the favour of Allah to you when He made prophets among you, made you kings and gave you what He had not given to any other among the mankind. O my people! Enter the Holy land (Palestine) which Allah has assigned to you...'
(Surat Al-Maida 5:20-21 HK)

Why all these privileges to the children of Israel? Because the plan of God for the salvation of mankind was focused in them. Jesus Christ said:

> ... for salvation is of the Jews. (John 4:22)

God gave the Jewish prophets the prophecies concerning his Son, Jesus Christ. They recorded these prophecies to declare that:

- Christ is the seed of the woman and will bruise the head of Satan (Genesis 3:15).
- He will be born of a virgin (Isaiah 7:14; Matthew 1:20-23).
- He will be crucified (Psalm 22:16).
- He will be buried in a rich man's tomb (Isaiah 53:9).
- He will arise from the dead (Psalm 16:10).

In the Old Testament, Christ was foreshadowed in types. A "type" is something in the present meant to resemble something in the future. Isaac, Joseph, Moses, David, and others were all types of Christ.

Christ was also foreshadowed in the offering mentioned in the book of Leviticus. He was the burnt offering, the grain offering, the peace offering, the sin offering, and the trespass offering (Leviticus -Chapters 1-7). When Christ died on the cross He fulfilled all these offerings.

> For by one offering He has perfected forever those who are being sanctified. (Hebrews 10:14 NKJ)

This is why we read in the book of John:

> Jesus, knowing that all things were now accomplished... He said, **'It is finished.'**
> (John 19:28,30 NKJ)

There was no need for Muhammad or Islam.

'It is finished,' Jesus said.   (John 19:30 NKJ)

Jesus' words indicate that He is the last prophet sent to all the world:

> God, who at various times and in different ways spoke in time past to the fathers by the prophets, has in these last days spoken to us by His Son. (Hebrews 1:1-2 NKJ)

Any prophet who comes to establish a new religion after the Son of God, Jesus Christ, is a false prophet and should be rejected.

Chapter Five

Muhammad in the Bible?

Ibn Taimiah, a Muslim Imam who lived during the lifetime of Muhammad, wrote many books. A number of these books criticized Christianity and tried to apply special prophecies from the Bible to Muhammad to authenticate his prophethood. Ibn Taimiah is considered the authority on this subject and many Muslim clerics have since followed his false interpretations. They say that a prophecy recorded in the book of Isaiah can be applied to Muhammad. It says:

> Behold! My Servant whom I uphold, My Elect One in whom My soul delights! I have put My Spirit upon Him; He will bring forth justice to the Gentiles. He will not cry out, nor raise His voice, nor cause His voice to be heard in the streets. A bruised reed He will not break, and smoking flax He will not quench; He will bring forth justice for truth. He will not fail nor be discouraged, till He has established justice in the earth; and the coastlands shall wait for His law.
>
> (Isaiah 42:1-4 NKJ)

However, when we read the Gospel of Matthew, we find out that that prophecy was fulfilled to the letter in Christ. On a Sabbath day Jesus went to a Jewish synagogue where he healed the withered hand of a man. The Pharisees took counsel against him to destroy him because He healed the man on a Sabbath day.

Then we read:

> But when Jesus knew it, He withdrew from there; and great multitudes followed Him, and He healed them all. And He warned them not to make Him known, that it might be fulfilled which was spoken by Isaiah the prophet, saying, 'Behold, My Servant whom I have chosen, My Beloved in whom My soul is well pleased; I will put My Spirit upon Him, and He will declare justice to the Gentiles. He will not quarrel nor cry out, nor will anyone hear His voice in the streets. A bruised reed He will not break, and smoking flax He will not quench, till He sends forth justice to victory. And in His name Gentiles will trust.'
>
> (Matthew 12:18-21 NKJ)

Matthew declares in clear words that Isaiah's prophecy was fulfilled in Jesus Christ. Matthew's words are final.

In their frustration to find a prophecy in the Bible concerning Muhammad, Muslim Imams also say the words of Psalm 84 apply to Muhammad:

> Blessed is the man whose strength is in thee; in whose heart are the ways of them, who passing through the valley of Baca make it a well.   (Psalm 84:5-6)

They say that the valley of Baca is Mecca, and Muhammad came from Mecca, so this is a prophecy about him. But those clerics do not know that these verses are not a prophecy. They speak about the believers whose strength is in God, who pass through the valley of weeping and suffering, and by the grace of God make it a well of blessings. The valley of Baca here is the valley of weeping, not Mecca.

Again, Muslim Imams say that the words of Christ concerning the Holy Spirit could be applied to Muhammad. Let us examine what Christ said to his disciples concerning the Holy Spirit:

> If ye love me, keep my commandments. And I will pray the Father, and he shall give you another Comforter, that he may abide with you for ever; even the Spirit of truth; whom the world cannot receive, because it seeth him not, neither knoweth him: but ye know him; for he dwelleth with you, and shall be in you. I will not leave you comfortless: I will come to you. (John 14:15-18)

> These things have I spoken unto you, being yet present with you. But the Comforter, which is the Holy Ghost, whom the Father will send in my name, he shall teach you all things, and bring all things to your remembrance, whatsoever I have said unto you. (John 14:25-26)

> Nevertheless I tell you the truth; it is expedient for you that I go away: for if I go not away, the Comforter will not come unto you; but if I depart, I will send him unto you. And when he is come, he will reprove the world of sin, and of righteousness, and of judgment: of sin, because they believe not on me; of righteousness, because I go to my Father, and ye see me no more; of judgment, because the prince of this world is judged. I have yet many things to say unto you, but ye cannot bear them now. Howbeit when he, the Spirit of truth, is come, he will guide you into all truth; for he shall not speak of himself; but whatsoever he shall hear, that shall he speak: and he will show you things to come. He shall glorify me; for he shall receive of mine, and shall show it unto you. (John 16:7-13)

69

And, being assembled together with them, commanded them that they should not depart from Jerusalem, but wait for the promise of the Father, which, saith he, ye have heard of me. For John truly baptized with water; but ye shall be baptized with the Holy Ghost not many days hence. But ye shall receive power, after that the Holy Ghost is come upon you; and ye shall be witnesses unto me both in Jerusalem, and in all Judea, and in Samaria, and unto the uttermost part of the earth.   (Acts 1:4-5, 8)

Muslim Imams say that the Greek word translated "Comforter" into English is "periklutos" which means "praised one," and that the praised one is Muhammad, because this is the meaning of his name. Furthermore, they say that Christians exchanged the word "periklutos" with the word "parakletos" to remove this prophecy concerning Muhammad from the New Testament.

Most certainly the word "parakletos," which means "comforter," is the original Greek word. More importantly, the attributes of the Comforter by all means cannot be applied to Muhammad.

1. The promised Holy Spirit is another Comforter; He is equal to Christ. Christ was the comforter of His disciples while he was in the flesh with them. The Holy Spirit is the other comforter, not Muhammad.
2. The Holy Spirit is to bring all things that Christ said and did to the disciples' remembrance, thus they were able to record all that He said in the gospels. Otherwise, how could it be possible for Matthew to record in his gospel the sermon Jesus delivered on the mount?
3. The Comforter Jesus promised is a spirit, not a human being. Muhammad was not a spirit.

4. The promised Holy Spirit is to come shortly after Jesus' ascension to heaven as He said to his disciples, "Not many days from now." Muhammad came after almost 600 years.

5. The promised Holy Spirit is to come upon the disciples of Christ in Jerusalem. The disciples died hundred of years before Muhammad. Muhammad came to Mecca, not to Jerusalem.

6. The promised Holy Spirit is to give power to the disciples of Christ that they might be His witnesses. That cannot be applied to Muhammad because he is not a spirit and he is not a witness for Christ.

7. The promised Holy Spirit was sent by Christ. Muhammad was not sent by Christ.

The Muslim clerics are deceitfully using Bible verses to win ignorant professed Christians to Islam.

The truth of the matter is there is not one single prophecy in the Bible concerning Muhammad. Why should anyone expect to find a prophecy concerning Muhammad while the plan of God for the salvation of mankind was fulfilled in the birth, crucifixion, burial, and resurrection of Christ? Christ declares:

> I am the way, the truth, and the life. No one comes to the Father except through Me. (John 14:6 NKJ)

The Apostle Peter declares:

> Nor is there salvation in any other, for there is no other name under heaven given among men by which we must be saved. (Acts 4:12 NKJ)

The door is once and for all shut for anyone coming after Christ claiming that he is a prophet and that he is going to establish a new religion. Muhammad was not a true prophet.

Chapter Six

The Wives

Polygamy, which means marrying more than one wife at the same time, was practiced by many of the Old Testament patriarchs such as Abraham, Jacob, Moses, David, Solomon. **But polygamy was never approved or commanded by God.** Polygamy was practiced in Arabia also, but not among Christians or Christian cults. Since Muhammad's marriage to Khadija was an Ebionite marriage, he could not marry any woman beside Khadija.

When it comes to the issue of polygamy, Christ set the record straight. Six hundred years before Muhammad Jesus established the absolute standard regarding this behavior when He said:

> Have you not read that He who made them at the beginning made them male and female, and said, 'For this reason a man shall leave his father and mother and be joined to his wife, and the two shall become one flesh?' So then, they are no longer two but one flesh. Therefore what God has joined together, let no man separate. (Matthew 19:4-6 NKJ)

Moreover, the Apostle Paul wrote:

> Nevertheless, to avoid fornication, let every man have his own wife, and let every woman have her own husband. (I Corinthians 7:2)

The plan of the true God for marriage is one woman for one man at one time. While the earth was void and needed to be populated God created one woman, Eve, for Adam. He created her not to be a sex object but to be "a helper comparable to him" (Genesis 2:20 NKJ).

Polygamy was never God's plan. Wherever polygamy was practiced, there was division in the family and jealousy and hatred between brothers. In fact, the Bible says that King Solomon ended his life shamefully because of his polygamous life (I Kings 11:1-10).

After the death of Khadija, his wife of almost twenty years, and after proclaiming himself the Messenger of Allah, Muhammad sanctified polygamy and permitted Muslims to have concubines. Here are the words of the Koran:

> Marry women of your choice, two, or three, or four; but if you fear that ye shall not be able to deal justly (with them), then only one, or that which your right hands possess (concubines or slaves); this will be more suitable, to prevent you from doing injustice.
>
> (Surat Al-Nisa 4:3)

Muhammad unleashed his sexual desires after Khadija died and in a span of ten years he married fourteen wives in addition to his many concubines. Not one of them was mentioned in the Koran by name, for Islam has no regard for women. They were, however, mentioned in Muhammad's biography written by Ibn Hesham.

Before we mention the wives of Muhammad we have to remember the words of the Koran concerning Muhammad himself:

> And surely thou hast sublime morals.(Surat Al-Qalam 68:4)

> Ye have indeed in the Messenger of Allah an excellent exemplar.   (Surat Al-Ahzab 33:21)

74

So if Muhammad married all these wives without any sense of guilt, a good Muslim man can also marry four women without any sense of guilt because Muhammad is his excellent example. A *Washington Post Parade Magazine* reporter printed a column entitled "Sex in Saudi Arabia." Here is that column:

This reporter rang up Dr. Seymour Gray in Brookline, Massachusetts, recently and asked the former Harvard Medical School professor if he really believed that the late King Ibn Saud, founder of modern-day Saudi Arabia, had married 300 women in his lifetime. Dr. Gray, 72, worked from 1975 to 1978 as physician in charge of the medical department at the King Faisal Specialist Hospital in Riyadh. He is the author of *Beyond the Veil - The Adventures of an American Doctor in Saudi Arabia*, a fascinating book published earlier in the year.

'I don't know if Ibn Saud was married to precisely 300 women,' Gray replied, 'but that approximate number, give or take a dozen or two, seems to be correct.'

We then asked if it is true that Moslems by law and tradition are permitted to have only four wives - admittedly a far cry from 300.

'Under Islamic law,' Gray explained, 'a man can have no more than four wives at any one time. What some royal Saudis do is to divorce their oldest wives when they reach 35 or 40 and take younger ones. Divorce in Saudi Arabia is quick and simple. All the husband has to do is to announce three times, 'I divorce you,' and that's it.'

Gray contends that many Saudi men are obsessed with sex because Islamic law segregates the sexes so strictly. Saudi women must wear veils and avoid the society of men.   Adultery is punishable by death. Premarital sex is so taboo that later, after a man marries, he often has a compulsion to engage in sexual relations as frequently as he can manage.   Gray writes in his book that many male Saudis consider themselves impotent if they cannot indulge in sexual intercourse more than two or three times a day.

One of Gray's most illustrious patients was Prince Ibrahim Mugrin el-Kabir, who had fought alongside Ibn Saud early in the century.   The prince complained of 'decreasing sexual prowess' and explained that he had fathered no offspring for five years.   He demanded improvement of his waning potency, but - at 90 - age was against him.   He soon died, leaving an estate valued at $32 billion, which was divided among his four wives, 23 sons and 11 daughters.(*Washington Post Parade Magazine*, November 13, 1983, p 9)

These people and many more are just following Muhammad's excellent example.

There is a story related to every wife of Muhammad, but space only allows us to mention the most interesting ones.

Muhammad Married Aisha When She Was A Six-Year-Old Child

Aisha, daughter of Abu-Bakr, one of Muhammad's intimate friends who became the first caliph, was a beautiful little girl. **Muhammad married her when he was fifty-three years old and she was only six years old.   He had intercourse with her when she was nine years old** (*Wives of the Prophet,* 57-61).

This is a gross case of child abuse by the prophet of Islam. When Muhammad married Aisha he set an example for the Muslims.   To this day older Muslim men marry much younger girls, following Muhammad's example.

The Egyptian weekly magazine *Almussawar* printed a letter sent to Ameenah Al-Saaeed, one of its editors, from a woman who was a teacher of languages in Egypt. The letter appeared in the September 6, 1991 issue. Here is a part of that letter:

> Dear mother Ameenah Al-Saaeed:
> My problem is . . my husband came home with a friend who is about his age. He requested that our daughter 'Marwa' who is nine years old bring tea to his friend. At night he told me with great joy that his friend agreed to marry 'Marwa.' His friend is fifty years old, 'Marwa' is nine years old. When I objected, he told me that he is following the prophet Muhammad's example when he engaged Aisha when she was six years old and had sex with her when she was nine years old as it is written in *Sahih Al-Bukhary*.

Muhammad Sobhi Alantabli, a high ranking police officer, sent a letter to the same editor, which was printed in *Almussawar* magazine in the December 20, 1991 issue. Here is a part of that letter:

> The chief of a tribe invited me to attend his wedding. He was eighty four years old and his bride was fourteen years old. 'Why do you marry a girl who is much younger than you?' I asked. 'Because my other three wives became old, and when the woman gets old she will be like a rusty car. I mean a car covered by rust,' he answered. The young bride's father was very happy because of that marriage.

Muhammad Married Zainab Bint Gahsh, his Daughter-In-Law

Dr. Aisha Abd-Alrahman cited in her book, *Wives of the Prophet*, on page 130, what Al-Tabari, the great Muslim expositor, wrote concerning Muhammad's marriage to Zainab:

> Muhammad asked his wife Khadija to give him one of her slaves. He asked her to give him 'Zaid.' When Zaid's father came to pay a ransom and take him back, Zaid chose Muhammad over his father and his family. Muhammad took Zaid to the chiefs of Quraysh and announced to them that he took Zaid to be his adopted son, and that Zaid was his heir, and that they were witnesses of that adoption. From that time on Zaid was called 'Zaid son of Muhammad.'

Zaid was one of the first persons who accepted Islam. When Zaid came of age to be married, Muhammad chose for him 'Zainab,' Muhammad's cousin. Zainab was a beautiful Hashemite woman of high rank, but Zaid was a slave freed by Muhammad. So Zainab rejected Muhammad's proposal to marry Zaid. In order to achieve his purpose, and to convince Zainab to marry Zaid, a revelation was given to Muhammad from Allah.

It is not fitting for a believer, man or woman, when a matter has been decided by Allah and his Messenger [Muhammad], to have any option about their decision: If anyone disobeys Allah and his Messenger, he is indeed in a clearly wrong path. (Surat Al-Ahzab 33:36)

Facing that so-called divine revelation, Zainab submitted to Muhammad's decision and married Zaid.

One day Muhammad went to visit Zaid, his adopted son. Zainab was in her room wearing her nightgown, the wind moving the drape hanging at the door. Muhammad saw his daughter-in-law and his heart was moved by her beauty. She asked him to come in. He refused and went talking to himself in a loud voice saying, 'Praise be Allah who changes the hearts.' When Zaid came home Zainab told him about Muhammad's visit and what he said. Zaid went to Muhammad and asked him 'Shall I divorce Zainab?' 'Retain her as your wife,' Muhammad answered. After that day Zainab treated her husband, Zaid, harshly and with no respect. He could not take it any more, so he divorced her.

It was a very difficult situation for Muhammad. He had a great desire for Zainab, and he wanted to marry her, but she was his daughter-in-law. Muhammad needed help and that help must come from his Allah. At last the help came in a revelation brought by the spirit who appeared to him at the cave of Hira in the following verses recorded in the Koran:

'Behold! Thou didst say to one who had received the grace of Allah and thy favour: "Retain thou [in wedlock] thy wife, and fear Allah." But thou didst hide in thy heart that which Allah was about to make manifest: Thou didst fear people, but it is more fitting that thou shouldst fear Allah.' Then when Zaid had dissolved [his marriage] with her we joined her in marriage to thee: In order that [in future] there may be no difficulty to the believers in [the matter of] marriage with the wives of their adopted sons, when the latter have dissolved [their marriage]' (Surat Al-Ahzab 33:37). (The whole story is written in the book, *Wives of the Prophet*, 127-140.)

Muslim commentators tried very hard to justify that marriage but in vain. For Muhammad to marry his daughter-in-law was a disgrace.

Since the marriage of Zainab to Zaid was planned according to the Koran by Allah and his messenger Muhammad, we would rightly expect that the married couple would live happily ever after. Instead, that marriage turned out to be a very miserable marriage.

Furthermore, Muhammad claimed that he counseled with Allah before they (he and Allah) made the decision that Zainab should marry Zaid. But we read in the pure word of God:

> . . . who has known the mind of the Lord? or who has become His counselor? (Romans 11:34 NKJ)

When Muhammad claimed that he counseled with Allah he made himself equal to Allah, but no human can counsel with the True God.

In addition, when Muhammad made the decision that Zainab should marry Zaid so he could demonstrate that in Islam there is no difference between the rich and the poor, the slave and the free, he did not care about Zainab's happiness and satisfaction. Muhammad's decision regarding that marriage was a political decision to demonstrate his own authority.

In light of the words of the Holy Bible, Muhammad committed many sins by his marriage to Zainab:

First: He lusted after his daughter-in-law.

The Bible says "You shall not covet your neighbor's wife"(Exodus 20:17 NKJ) - let alone your daughter-in-law.

Second: In light of Jesus' words, Muhammad is considered an adulterer because he married a divorced woman.

Jesus Christ said, "Whosoever shall marry her that is divorced committeth adultery" (Matthew 5:32).

Third: He opened the door for Muslim men to covet their neighbor's wives and lure them to divorce their husbands so they can marry them.

Fourth: He eliminated adoption in Islam.

After he married his adopted son's wife, Muhammad declared, "Muhammad is not the father of any of your men, but he is the messenger of Allah" (Surat Al-Ahzab 33:40 HK). Since that time adoption has been illegal in Islam.

Fifth: He used Allah to fulfill his sinful desire. Allah says to Muhammad in the Koran:

> Then when Zaid had dissolved (his marriage) with her We joined her (Zainab) in marriage to thee (Muhammad): in order that (in future) there may be no difficulty to the Believers in (the matter of) marriage with the wives of their adopted sons, when the latter have dissolved (their marriage) with them. And Allah's command must be fulfilled. (Surat Al-Ahzab 33:37)

By claiming that Allah gave him Zainab for marriage, Muhammad profaned the Holy name of God. God would never command anything contrary to what he revealed in the Bible.

Zainab used to boast and say to her rivals that everyone of them was married to Muhammad by their fathers or by their own consent, but that she was married to him by Allah's command.

No wonder that Muhammad's wife Aisha said to him when she knew that he married Zainab, "I see that your Allah is quick in granting you what you desire" (Abd-AlRahman, 76).

In the name of Allah Muhammad committed all these gross sins. For Muhammad to claim that Allah joined him in marriage to Zainab is an insult to the word and holiness of God. Most assuredly, the Allah of Muhammad and Islam is not the True God of the Bible.

Let us list the names of Muhammad's wives after Khadija:

1. Suda, daughter of Zamma
2. Aisha, was six years old when Muhammad married her
3. Hafsa, daughter of Omar
4. Zainab, daughter of Ghash
5. Zainab, daughter of Khuzima
6. Om Salma, her name was Hind
7. Gawariah, daughter of Al-Harith
8. **Muhammad married Safiya Bint Huyay, a Jewess, after he killed her husband. She was seventeen years old.** Paul Fregosi recorded in his book *Jihad* the story of that marriage in the following words:

Muhammad was pitiless with those who fought him, stole from him, who acted against his interests, or whose wealth he hankered to acquire. Kinana, the chief of a Jewish settlement at Kheibar, automatically became Muhammad's foe when the Prophet learned that Kinana had a fortune in gold vessels hidden away somewhere, and Muhammad ordered him to be tortured until he revealed its hiding place. His executioners tied him down to the ground and lit a fire on his chest 'till his breath had almost departed.' When Kinana finally died under torture, Muhammad ordered his head to be cut off, and that night went to bed with the victim's widow, Safiya, aged 17, who later became one of his wives.

(Jihad, 46)

Al-Serra Anabawia recorded that Muhammad ordered that Safiya should follow him. Then he spread his robe over her so people would know he chose her for himself (*Wives of the Prophet,* 149).

Let us read the rest of the names of Muhammad's wives:

9. Om Habiba

There are five other wives who are not mentioned by Ibn Hesham:

10. Sharaaf, daughter of Khalifa
11. Al-Alia, daughter of Zabian
12. Wasna, daughter of Al-Naaman
13. Maria, the Egyptian Coptic Christian who was given to Muhammad by Al-Mockawkas, the ruler of the Coptics in Egypt. She bore Muhammad's son Ibrahim who died before he was two years old. Maria did not convert to Islam.
14. Maimona, daughter of Harith

Added to these fifteen wives were many concubines and many women who were taken captive during his battles.

Muhammad violated the law of God and married all those women, claiming falsely that he married them by Allah's command. Even though he declares in his Koran that a Muslim can marry only four women at one time, he gave himself the privilege of marrying fifteen women demonstrating that he is above the law of Allah. Moreover, Muhammad says in his Koran that he can marry any woman who offers herself to him, and this privilege is reserved for him only.

Here are the words of the Koran:

> O Prophet (Muhammad)! Verily, We have made lawful to you your wives, to whom you have paid their Mahr (bridal money given by the husband to his wife at the time of marriage), and those (slaves) whom your right hand possesses - whom Allah has given to you, and the daughters of your Amm (paternal uncles) and the daughters of your Ammat (paternal aunts) and the daughters of your Khal (maternal uncles) and the daughters of your Khalat (maternal aunts) who migrated (from Mecca) with you, and a believing woman if she offers herself to the Prophet, and the Prophet wishes to marry her - a privilege for you only, not for the (rest of) the believers. Indeed We know what We have enjoined upon them about their wives and those (slaves) whom their right hands possess, in order that there should be no difficulty on you. And Allah is Ever Oft-Forgiving, Most merciful.   (Surat Al-Ahzab 33:50)

According to the Koran, marrying many women was a privilege for the prophet of Islam.

What a prophet!

Chapter Seven

The Hijra

Al-Madina was a city located 200 kilometers from Mecca which was called Yathib. Muhammad migrated with many of his followers to Al-Madina in the year 622 A.D. This migration, called *hijra* in arabic, is regarded by Muslims as the key date in the history of Islam, and the Muslim calendar begins with that year. Today in Muslim countries documents, letters, and newspapers are dated from the *Hijra*.

Islamic history does not begin with the birth of Muhammad or the year of his alleged call to be a prophet, but by the *Hijra*. This is because it was at Al-Madina that Muhammad established a government, organized an army, and Islam first became a state religion. It is of great importance to notice that without the power and authority of the state, Islam cannot survive.

Muhammad migrated to Al-Madina because when he began calling the people of Mecca to Islam the majority of the Meccans rejected his call. They mocked him and called him *mad* (Surat Al-Hijr 15:6, Surat Al-Qalam 68:51), a *possessed poet* (Surat Al-Saffat 37:36), a *forgerer* (Surat Al-Nahal 16:101) and *bewitched* (Surat Al-Furqan 25:7, 8). They persecuted his followers.

In the beginning of his call to Islam Muhammad spoke highly concerning the Jews and declared that Allah assigned the Holy Land to them. The Koran says:

And verily we gave the children of Israel the Scripture and the command and the Prophethood, and provided

85

them with good things and favored them above [all] peoples. (Surat Al-Jathiya 45:16 MPT)

And [remember] when Moses said unto his people: O my people! Remember Allah's favour unto you, how he placed among you prophets, and he made you kings, and gave you that [which] He gave not to any [other] of [His] creatures. O my people! Go into the Holy Land which Allah hath ordained for you.
(Surat Al-Maidah 5:20-21 MPT)

These verses in the Koran clearly show that prophethood is exclusively for Israel, not for the Arabs. Moreover, it declares that the Holy Land was ordained for Israel. The Holy Land was given to Israel by God's decree. The God of the Bible does not abrogate His promises. Muslims have no right to object to Jerusalem being the capital of Israel if they believe the Koran.

Muhammad tried to win the Jews to his side. He also tried to win the people of other religions. He declared in the Koran:

Lo! Those who believe [in that which is revealed unto thee Muhammad], and those who are Jews, and Christians, and Sabaeans - whoever believeth in Allah and the Last Day and doeth right - surely their reward is with their Lord, and there shall no fear come upon them neither shall they grieve. (Surat Al-Baqarah 2:62 MPT)

Muhammad was very kind to the above mentioned people while he was in Mecca. But they rejected him as did his own tribesmen.

Because of this rejection, Muhammad asked his followers to make their way in small numbers to Al-Madina, a journey of several weeks by camel, in the year 622 A.D. Learning that the Quraysh were planning to prevent him from leaving Mecca, he and Abu-Bakr escaped from the city, hid for several days in a cave, and then took a safe route to Al-Madina.

In Al-Madina Muhammad established a kingdom for himself. **He tried to win the Jews of Al-Madina to his side, so he commanded the Muslims to pray toward the destroyed Jewish temple in Jerusalem, which he called the Al-Aqsa mosque.** But the Jewish clans rejected his claim that he was a true prophet; first, because he was an Arab, not a Jew, and also because they saw that he lacked all the qualifications of a true prophet.

They realized that Muhammad performed no miracles. He uttered no prophecies. He contradicted the clear teachings of the Torah by his revelations. And He used the revelations that he claimed to receive from Allah to satisfy his own desires and achieve his purposes.

They rejected him and rightly so.

At Al-Madina, there were two groups: those who migrated with Muhammad from Mecca, who were called "Al-Muhajeroun" and those who embraced Islam from Al-Madina, who were called "Al-Ansaar." Muhammad united both groups by Islam and established the first religious state.

Thus, we can say that Islam is a state religion. It does not believe in the separation of church and state.

Chapter Eight

The Sword of Islam

Christianity conquered the world by the power of the Holy Spirit and the gospel of the crucified Christ without a sword or a fight. Before His ascension to heaven, Christ said to His apostles:

> You shall receive power when the Holy Spirit has come upon you; and you shall be witnesses to Me in Jerusalem, and in all Judea and Samaria, and to the end of the earth. (Acts 1:8 NKJ)

The Apostle Paul wrote to the Christians in Rome:

> For I am not ashamed of the gospel of Christ, for it is the power of God to salvation for everyone who believes, for the Jew first and also for the Greek.
> (Romans 1:16 NKJ)

It is a historical fact that Islam subdued the Arabs in the Arabian Peninsula as well as peoples of other countries by the sword. When the Meccans, the Jews, and the true Christians rejected Muhammad and his Islam, Muhammad claimed that he received a revelation from Allah to fight.

In Al-Madina, Muhammad organized a Muslim army to fight the Meccans and annihilate the Jews and Christians who rejected Islam. He became the commander in chief of that army.

Muhammad had decided that he could achieve with the sword the results his new religion had failed to produce.

Using force is a sign of weakness. When a head of state resorts to force against his own people, it shows that he is unable to solve his problems by peaceful means. It is a clear indication of his weakness: fear of losing authority and a troubled mind.

Muhammad was a genius commander and to convince his followers to fight, he used a brilliant strategy.

First: He convinced Muslims that they were superior to all mankind:

> You (Muslims) are the best of people ever raised for mankind. (Surat Al-Imran 3:110)

Second: He convinced Muslims that those who rejected him and his Islam were infidels; consequently they were subhuman and deserved to be killed.

He declares in the Koran that Jews and Christians are polytheists, and as such they are infidels who must be killed:

> The Jews call Uzair a son of Allah, and the Christians call Christ the Son of Allah. That is a saying from their mouth; (in this) they but imitate what the infidels [Author's literal translation] of old used to say. Allah's curse be on them: how they are deluded away from the truth. (Surat At-Tawbah 9:30)

Third: He desensitized the Muslims' conscience, so that they would kill non-Muslims, even their relatives, without feeling any sense of guilt:

You killed them not, but Allah killed them. And you (Muhammad) threw not when you did throw, but Allah threw, that He might test the believers by a fair trial from Him. Verily, Allah is All-Hearer, All-Knower.

(Surat Al-Anfal 8:17)

This is why, when they kill Jews or Christians, Muslims shout with jubilation, *Allahu Akbar* (Allah is great).

Hitler used the same strategy to motivate the Germans to fight so he could establish the Third Reich. He told the Germans they had pure Aryan blood, and that Jews were sub-human.

To achieve his goal, Muhammad convinced Muslims with revelations that he claimed he received from Allah. Here are the verses of the Koran calling Muslims to fight Jews, Christians, and non-Muslims:

O Apostle [Muhammad] incite (Author's literal translation) the believers [Muslims] to fight.

(Surat Al-Anfal 8:65)

Allah hath purchased of the believers [Muslims] their persons and their goods; for theirs [in return] is the garden [of Paradise]. They fight in His cause, and slay and are slain a promise binding him.

(Surat At-Tawbah 9:111)

Warfare is ordained for you, though it is hateful unto you; but it may happen that ye hate a thing that is good for you and it may happen that ye love a thing that is bad for you. Allah knoweth, ye know not.

(Surat Al-Baqarah 2:216 MPT)

More revelations were given to Muhammad to convince the Muslims to fight:

[Remember] when your Lord revealed to the Angels (verily), I am with you so keep firm those who have believed. I will cast terror into the hearts of those who have disbelief, so strike them over the necks, and smite over all their fingers and toes.(Surat Al-Anfal 8:12 MPT)

These verses demonstrate how brutal the Muslim army was, and how they were ready to die for the cause of Allah.

Abu Torab Al-Zahry, in his Arabic book of 549 pages entitled *The Battles of the Messenger of Allah,* recorded Muhammad's sixty-eight battles which included the assassinations he ordered. Al-Zahry recorded that the command of Muhammad to anyone he installed as captain to lead a battle was:

When you meet your enemies of the polytheists, call them to convert to Islam. If they accept Islam, leave them safely. If they reject Islam then demand that they pay jezia (high tax paid by those who do not want to renounce Judaism or Christianity). If they reject that, then kill them. (pg 13)

Muhammad commanded the assassination of Asma Bint Marawani, a Jewess, because she criticized those who followed Muhammad, and ridiculed him in her poetry. Omai Ibn Adi, a blind man, went to her home by night. She was in bed with some of her children who were asleep, and she was nursing her baby.

Omair snatched the baby from her and put a sword in her breast until it came out of her back. Then he prayed the morning prayer with Muhammad in Al-Madina. "Did you kill the daughter of Marawani?" Muhammad asked Omair. "Yes," Omair answered. Then Muhammad said, "She took what she deserved" (Pg 46).

Muhammad also ordered the assassination of Abu Afak, another Jew, who also ridiculed Muhammad in his poetry. "Who would kill that man Abu Afak?" Muhammad said. Salim Ibn Omair vowed to kill him.

Abu Afak was 120 years old. Salim watched Abu Afak one summer night as he slept in his yard. Salim went to him and struck his liver with his sword until it came out of his back. Abu Afak died and was buried in his house (pg 52).

Muhammad also commanded the assassination of a rich Jewish man named Kaab Ibn Al-Ashraf, and another Jewish man, Abu Raffe Salaam (pg 55, 245).

Muhammad's first raid which led to the battle of Badr, was not to promote Islam, but rather to attack and loot the caravan of Abu-Sufian which carried a significant amount of wealth and precious goods (*Prophets of Allah, 438*). Muhammad planned that raid to ease the economic troubles at Al-Madina.

Aubu-Sufian knew of Muhammad's scheme, however, and escaped by taking another route. He also incited the Meccans to fight Muhammad, so they fought him at the battle of Badr but were defeated.

As he began to win battles and his power increased, Muhammad dreamed of establishing a united Islamic Kingdom in the Arabian Peninsula. It would be a kingdom where the Jews and the Christians would live as second class citizens, despised, deprived of all privileges, and forced to pay high taxes or be killed.

This is what Muhammad said to the Muslims concerning the Jews and Christians:

> Fight against such of those who have been given the Scriptures [Jews and Christians] and believe not in Allah nor the Last Day, and forbid not that which Allah hath forbidden by His Messenger [Muhammad] and follow not the religion of truth [Islam], until they pay tribute (taxes paid by Jews and Christians who do not want to renounce their religion), being brought low.
>
> (Surat Al-Tawbah 9:29 MPT)

The above mentioned verse clearly shows that Islam was promoted by the sword, and that Jews and Christians living in an

Islamic country are to be treated as second class citizens and are obliged to pay high taxes to retain their religion. The following verses demonstrate the intention of Islam to build an Islamic empire by force and terrorism:

> Say to the infidels (Author's literal translation), if [now] they desist from unbelief their past would be forgiven them: but if they persist, the punishment of those before them is already [a matter warning for them]. And fight them until there is no more sedition (Author's literal translation) and religion [Islam] becomes Allah's in its entirety. (Surat Al-Anfal 8:38-39)

> The only reward of those who make war upon Allah and His messenger and strive after corruption in the land will be that they will be killed or crucified, or have their hands and feet on alternate sides cut off, or will be expelled out of the land. Such will be their degradation in the world, and in the Hereafter theirs will be an awful doom. (Surat Al-Maidah 5:33 MPT)

For the Muslims to kill, crucify, or cut off the hands and feet of those who do not believe in Islam was clear sadistic behavior. These Koranic verses are still used as commandments and rules in Islamic countries. The Muslims think they are the agents of Allah on earth, and that their duty is to promote Islam by force and terrorism.

To ensure that Muslims would fight even until death, Muhammad promised every Muslim who dies in battle total forgiveness of all his sins and eternal life in Paradise where he will be wedded to women of wide lovely eyes and where he will enjoy rivers of wine (Surat Al-Tur 52:17-24). Martyrdom is therefore the only way for a Muslim to obtain forgiveness of sins.

Allah hath purchased of the believers [Muslims] their persons and their goods; for theirs [in return] is the garden [of Paradise]. They fight in His cause, and slay and are slain a promise binding him.

(Surat Al-Tawbah 9:111)

Allah is bound by his promise to those who kill and are killed that they will go to paradise. Here is the description of the Islamic paradise as mentioned in the Koran:

The description of Paradise which the Muttaqun (the pious Muslims) have been promised (is that) in it are rivers of water the taste and smell of which are not changed, rivers of milk of which the taste never changes, rivers of wine delicious to those who drink, and rivers of clarified honey (clear and pure) therein for them is every kind of fruit, and forgiveness from their Lord. (Surat Muhammad 47:15 HK)

It is of great interest to notice that while the Koran totally forbids Muslims to drink wine while they are on earth, in paradise Muslims will have rivers of wine. That demonstrates that Allah has double standards - one for earth and one for paradise.

...will be in Gardens (Paradise) and Delight. Enjoying in that which their Lord has bestowed on them, and (the fact that) their Lord saved them from the torment of the blazing Fire. 'Eat and drink with happiness because of what you used to do.' They will recline (with ease) on thrones arranged in ranks. And We shall marry them to Hur (fair female)with wide lovely eyes.

(Surat Al-Tur 52:17-20)

Sex occupies the Muslim's mind while on earth and in paradise.

95

With this kind of ammunition, the followers of Muhammad were ready to fight until death. Muhammad continued his raids against the Meccans. Meanwhile he decided to exterminate the Jewish clans from Al-Madina. He expelled the Jewish clan of Banu Qainuqa, attacked another Jewish clan, Banu Alnadir, and drove them out of Al-Madina.

Banu Quraiza, who had sympathized with the Meccans during the battle of Ditch, suffered a worse fate from Muhammad's army. Their women and children were enslaved and their men were slaughtered. In 628 A.D. the Jews of Khaybar were dispossessed of their lands. Therefore it was not long before Al-Madina had no more Jews.

Muhammad decided to use force in order to subdue the Meccans and all who opposed him. He led several raids: the raid of Uhud, the greater raid of Badr, the raid of Hunain, and the raid of Tabuk. These raids resulted in several small Jewish and Christian clans submitting to Muhammad.

Finally, Muhammad led his last conquest of Mecca in the year 632. This time the Meccans received him. He was from the Quraysh tribe and from now on his tribe would reign over a united Arabian Peninsula.

Thus, by the sword Muhammad eliminated Judaism and Christianity from the Arabian Peninsula. He declared that the Jews and Christians were polytheists, and as such they were unclean and should not be allowed to approach the sacred mosque, the Kaabah in Mecca.

Muhammad commanded the Muslims to prohibit Jews and Christians from approaching the Kaaba:

> O ye who believe! Truly the polytheists (Author's literal translation) are unclean, so let them not, after this

year of theirs, approach the sacred mosque [Al-Kaabah in Mecca].   (Surat Al-Tawbah 9:28)

This is plain racism, and it is in contrast to what was recorded in the Bible concerning God's Holy Temple. King Solomon, in the day of dedication of the temple in Jerusalem, prayed:

> Moreover, concerning a foreigner, who is not of Your people Israel, but has come from a far country for Your name's sake, (for they will hear of Your great name and Your strong hand and Your outstretched arm), when he comes and prays toward this temple, hear in heaven Your dwelling place, and do according to all for which the foreigner calls to You, that all peoples of the earth may know Your name and fear You, as do Your people Israel, and that they may know that this temple which I have built is called by Your name.(1 Kings 8:41-43 NKJ)

It is clear from the history of Islam that it is not a religion of peace. What would anyone expect from the Muslims after they read all these violent verses in the Koran inciting them to fight? It is not surprising to see them fighting until death and sacrificing their lives in suicidal attacks against Jews and Christians whom the Koran stigmatizes as infidels.

It is clear that the Koran condones racism, violence, terrorism, and killing of Jews and Christians in the name of Allah. When there is a command in the Koran, the Muslims must obey it. In that case, all Muslims are technically fundamentalists.

The question then arises as to why there is such animosity from Islam toward Judaism and Christianity. Why don't we read in the Koran verses against Buddhism and Hinduism and other pagan religions which were in existence before Islam? The answer is that the Bible, the Holy Book of Jews and Christians, contradicts and exposes the teachings, atrocities and brutality of Islam.

97

It is said concerning Christ in the Bible that His name will be called "Prince of Peace" (Isaiah 9:6) and rightly so, for by his shed blood on the cross he made peace between God and those who believe in Him. He also blessed the peacemakers, saying:

> Blessed are the peacemakers, for they shall be called Sons of God.   (Matthew 5:9 NKJ)

But in light of Muhammad's bloody battles and the multitude of assassinations he ordered, we can only call him "Prince of Terror."

Chapter Nine

Muhammad's Death

The final days of Muhammad arrived. He had gained total control of the Arabian Peninsula and made the Kaabah in Mecca the only holy shrine to be acknowledged although there were many other Kaabas in Arabia.

In the tenth year after the *Hijra*, Muhammad made his farewell pilgrimage to Mecca. Soon after his return to Al-Madina he fell ill. Two verses in the Koran refer to his death:

> Muhammad is no more than a Messenger: many were the messengers that passed away before him. If he died or were slain, will ye then turn back on your heels?
> (Surat Al-Imran 3:144).

> Say: I have no power over any good or harm to myself except as Allah willeth. If I had knowledge of the unseen, I should have multiplied all good, and no evil should have touched me: I am but a warner . . . .
> (Surat Al-Araf 7:188)

Abdallah Abd al-Fadi gave a detailed accounting of Muhammad's death in his book *Is the Koran Infallible*

> Writing about Muhammad's death, Al-Baidawi the great expositor of the Koran, said: 'If he should die or be slain, will you then turn back on your heels?' [refers to the incident in which] Abdallah Ibn Qami'a al-

Harithi threw a rock at Allah's Messenger that broke four of his front teeth and gashed his face. Mus'ab Ibn Umair, who was the standard-bearer defended [Muhammad]. So Ibn Qami'a killed [Mus'ab], assuming that he killed the Prophet. Then, as it is reported, he said 'I killed Muhammad.' Someone cried out, 'Behold, Muhammad has been killed,' and the people turned on their heels. Then the Messenger cried out, 'Come to me, servants of Allah.' Thirty of his followers joined him and protected him until they scattered the unbelievers. Some hypocrites said, 'Had he been a prophet, he would not have been killed. Go back to your brothers and your religion.' Anas Ibn Nadr, the uncle of Anas Ibn Malik, said, 'O people, if Muhammad is slain, Muhammad's Lord is alive, and dies not; what shall you do if you live after him? So fight for what he fought for,' and added, 'O Allah, I acquit myself of what they say and exonerate myself from it.' He then clasped his sword firmly and fought till he was killed, and the verse was revealed.

When Khaybar was conquered, and the people felt secure, Zainab Bint al-Harith, Salam Ibn Mishkam's wife, went about asking which part of the lamb was Muhammad's favorite to eat. People told her, 'It is the front leg, for it is the best part and the farthest from harm.' So she took a lamb, slaughtered it, and cut it up. Then she took a deadly poison that kills instantly and poisoned the lamb, putting more poison in the leg and shoulder. When the sun set, Muhammad led the people in the evening prayer. When he finished, he wanted to go, but she was sitting at his feet. He asked about her, and she said, 'O Abu al-Qasim, here is a gift I have for you.' Muhammad ordered some of his friends to take it from her, and it was put before him in the presence of his friends, among whom was Bishr Ibn al-Bara' Ibn Ma'rur. Muhammad said, 'Come near and be seated.' Muhammad took the leg and ate, too. When Muhammad had swallowed his bite, Bishr swallowed his, and the rest of the people ate of it. Muhammad said, 'Raise your hands; this leg and this shoulder tell me they are poisoned.' Bishr said, 'By the One who honored you, I found the same in my morsel, but nothing kept me from spitting it out except that I would spoil the pleasure of your food. When you ate that which was in your mouth, I did not desire my own soul more than yours, and wished that you had not swallowed it.' [One opinion has it that] Bishr died then and there. A part of the lamb was thrown to a dog, and the dog died. Another opinion says that [Bishr's] color turned black and his pain lasted two years, after which he died. It was also said that Muhammad took a bite of the lamb, chewed it, and spit it out, whereas Bishr swallowed his morsel. Then Muhammad sent for this Jewess and asked her, 'Have you poisoned this lamb?' She said 'yes.' He asked, 'What prompted you to do that?' She said, 'You have acquired certain powers with which you judge those who are not loyal to you. You killed my father, my uncle and my brother. . . . So I said, 'If he is a king, then I would be relieving us of him, and if he is a prophet, he will be able to perceive.'" It was said that he pardoned her, while others say he commanded her to be put to death and crucified. When Muhammad fell ill just before his death, he said to Aisha, 'Aisha, I still feel the effect of the poisoned food I ate; this is the time of my demise by that poison.' When Bishr's sister entered his room during the time of his last sickness, he said to her, 'This is the time of my demise by the meal I ate with your brother in Khaybar.'

(al-Fadi, pp 378-381)

101

Finally, in June 632 A.D., death came to Muhammad, and that was the end of the man who claimed to be the prophet of Allah. Muhammad had totally contradicted the plan of God for the salvation of mankind through the shed blood of His beloved Son, Jesus Christ.

The prophet of Islam had shed much innocent blood of Jews and Christians in the Arabian peninsula during his lifetime, and because of his example Muslims are still killing Jews and Christians in many parts of the world today.

PART TWO

THE KORAN

The Holy Book of Islam

Chapter Ten

The History Of The Koran

The Koran is the Muslims' Holy Book - they call it "The Glorious Koran," or *Al-Mushaf Al-Shareef* or *Al-Koran Al-Kareem*. It contains 114 surahs (a surah is a chapter). The surahs are not arranged chronologically but by length, because those who arranged the Koran put the longest surahs first and the shortest at the end. However, scholars recognize that the shortest surahs were given to Muhammad first, in the Meccan period, and the longest came to him in Al-Madina, where he became a military and political leader.

Strange Names

Many surahs in the Koran are named after animals or small creatures or other objects. One surah is named after the *jinn* (demons or evil spirits).

Surat Al- Baqarah - The Cow (Number 2)
Surat Al-An'am - The Cattle (Number 6)
Surat Al-Ra'd - The Thunder (Number 13)
Surat Al-Nahl - The Bee (Number 16)
Surat Al-Kahf - The Cave (Number 18)
Surat Al-Naml - The Ants (Number 27)
Surat Al-Ankabut - The Spider (Number 29)
Surat Al-Dukhan - The Smoke (Number 44)
Surat Al-Tur - The Mount (Number 52)
Surat Al-Najm - The Star (Number 53)

Surat Al-Qamar - The Moon (Number 54)
Surat Al-Hadid - The Iron (Number 57)
Surat Al-Qalam - The Pen (Number 68)
Surat Al-Jinn - The Jinn (Number 72)
Surat Al-Buruj - The Mansions of the Stars (Number 85)
Surat Al-Fajr - The Dawn (Number 89)
Surat Al-Shams - The Sun (Number 91)
Surat Al-Layl - The Night (Number 92)
Surat Al-Duha - The Morning Hours (Number 93)
Surat Al-Tin - The Fig (Number 95)
Surat Al-Alaq - The Clot (Number 96)
Surat Al-Asr - The Late Afternoon (Number 103)
Surat Al-Fil - The Elephant (Number 105)
Surat Al-Falaq - The Day Break (Number 113)

These are strange names for sections of a book which Muhammad claimed was the book of Allah. It is difficult to understand why Allah would title the chapters of his book with such vague and insignificant titles as: The Cow, The Bee, The Ant, The Spider, The Star, The Sun, The Night, The Fig, The Elephant and even The Jinn.

How the Koran was Written

Sheikh Abd El-Fatah El-Kady wrote in his book *Al Mushaf Al-Shareef* (*The Koran - Its History and Tests*), pages 14 and 55:

The Koran was not delivered to Muhammad all at once. It came piecemeal according to the events and occasions, as we read in the Koran. '[It is] a Quran which we have divided (into parts from time to time), in order that thou mightest recite it to men at intervals: We have revealed it by stages' (Surat Al-Isra 17:106).

He continues:

> The Koran was written during Muhammad's life, on the branches of palm trees, on thin stones, on paper, on skin, on shoulders and side bones of animals.
>
> All of the Koran was written during Muhammad's life, but was not collected in one volume, its surahs were not organized. It was scattered on the branches of palm trees, skin and in the memories or breasts of Muhammad's 'close friends' (*Al-Sahaba* in Arabic).

Not only were the Koranic writings disorganized, but there were seven different versions of them. The reason for these different versions of the Koran is that the Koran was revealed to Muhammad in seven different dialects (*Al-Mushaf Al-Shareef*, p 64). Muhammad said in the Hadith:

> The Koran has been revealed to be recited in seven different dialects, so recite of it that which is easier for you. (*Sahih-al-Bukhari*, Vol. 6, p 510)

Tabari, the great expositor of the Koran, said that the difference between the seven versions of the Koran (*Al-Ahruf Al-Sabaa*) was not in the meaning but in the words. To illustrate: a person can use the word grace, gracefulness or elegance, or the word goods, possessions or property. But the fact is that the differences in those seven versions were not purely of words but at times related to the basic content of the Koran's text itself.

After Muhammad's death, at the time of Caliph Abu-Bakr, many of those who had memorized the Koran died while fighting the apostates in the battle of "Alyamama." Omar feared that the death of those men would result in the loss of a great portion of the Koran and suggested to Abu-Bakr that the Koran should be collected in one volume. Abu-Bakr was reluctant to do that because Muhammad did not collect the Koran in one volume during his life. After much discussion Omar persuaded him to call for the collection of the Koran. Abu-Bakr ordered Zaid Ibn Sabit to do the job (*Al-Mushaf Al-Shareef*, p 59-60).

> 'By Allah! If they had ordered me to shift one of the mountains, it would not have been heavier for me than this ordering me to collect the Koran,' Zaid Ibn Sabit said. Then I said to Abu-Bakr, 'How will you do something which Allah's Apostle did not do?' Abu-Bakr said 'By Allah, it is a good thing.'
>
> *(Sahih-al-Bukhari*, Part 6, p 477)

It is quite clear that the collection of the Koran is something which Muhammad did not do or decree. It is also clear that the Koran was not completely written in one volume during his life which is why Omar and Abu-Bakr feared the loss of great portions of the Koran if the men who had memorized it should die.

Therefore, Zaid Ibn Sabit agreed to collect the various pieces of the Koran. However, when Islam became the religion of many countries, every country used the version of the Koran which was known among them: the Syrians read Abi Kaab's version, the people of Kofa read Abdallah Ibn Massoud's version, others read Abu Moussa Alashaby's version and so on.

When Caliph Uthman took the caliphate, he was confronted by such confusion and sedition concerning the readings of the Koran in the different Islamic countries, so he ordered it to be rewritten.

> Uthman ordered Zaid Ibn Sabit and three other men from Quraysh, Abdullah Ibn Al-Zubeer, Saeed Ibn El-Uss, and Abdelrahman Ibn Al-Harith Ibn Hesham, to rewrite the Koran. It was Uthman's order to the scribes 'If you disagree with Zaid Ibn Sabit in anything of the

Koran, write it in the language of Quraysh, because the Koran was revealed in the language of Quraysh.' They did. (*Al-Mushaf Al-Shareef*, pp 66, 70)

For Caliph Uthman to order the scribes, "If you disagree with Zaid Ibn Sabit in anything of the Koran, write it in the language of Quraysh, because the Koran was revealed in the language of Quraysh," shows that the Koran was not completely Allah's words. The Koran was rewritten by the scribes whom Uthman appointed and it contained words written in the language of Quraysh, the tribe from which Muhammad came. **After Uthman completed his Koran, he forced all the Islamic countries to have one Koran - his Koran. He finished the matter by banning all other codices and burning them.**

Dr. Taha Hussein, a well known author, college professor, and minister of education in Egypt, wrote in his book *Al-Fitnato Al-Kobra* (*The Great Sedition*):

The prophet Muhammad said: 'The Koran was revealed in seven dialects, all of them are right and perfect.' When Uthman banned whichever he banned from the Koran, and burned whichever he burned of it, he banned passages Allah has revealed and burned parts of the Koran which were given to the Muslims by the messenger of Allah. He appointed a small group of the Sahaba (close friends of Muhammad) to rewrite the Koran and left out those who heard the prophet and memorized what he said. This is why Ibn Massoud was angry, because he was one of the best men who memorized the Koran. He said that he took from the mouth of the prophet seventy surahs of the Koran while Zaid Ibn Sabit was yet a young lad. When Ibn Massoud objected to the burning of the other codices of the Koran, Uthman took him out of the mosque with violence, and struck him to the ground, and broke one of his ribs.

(The Great Sedition, pp 160-161, 181-182)

It is clear that much of the original Koran was burned, while other parts were rewritten. How can we reconcile these historical facts with the following words of the Koran?

Nay, this is a Glorious Koran [inscribed] in a Tablet preserved. (Surat Al-Buruj 85:21-22)

That this is indeed a Koran most honorable in a book well guarded. (Surat Al-Waqiah 56:77-78)

If the Koran was inscribed in "a tablet preserved," and in "a book well-guarded," why was it necessary for Uthman to rewrite the Koran? How could he burn the other versions? Why were there other versions in the first place? Why didn't he keep the other codices so that Muslims could turn to them and compare? These are very serious questions regarding a book said to be Allah's word. They create doubt concerning the source of the Koran.

There are many English versions of the Koran: here are their names (the word "Koran" can be spelled in three different ways in English; Quran, Qur'an and Koran.):

1. *The Noble Qur'an,* translated by Dr. Muhammad Taqi-ud-Din Al-Hillali and Dr. Muhammad Muhsin Khan.

2. *The Glorious Qur'an,* translated by Muhammad Marmaduke Pickthall.

3. *The Holy Qur-an, English Translation of the Meaning and Commentary*; Revised and edited by The Presidency of Islamic

110

Researchers, Ifta, Call and Guidance; Known as Mushaf Al-Madinah An-Nabawiyah.

4. *Quran, The Final Testament, Authorized English Version*, translated by Rashad Khalifa, Ph.D.

5. *The Koran*, published in the United States by Ballantine Books.

6. *The Koran*, translated with notes by N. J. Dawood.

7. *The Qur'an*, the *First American Version*, translation and commentary by T. B. Irving (Al-Hajj Talim Ali).

I have to mention, as one who has mastered the Arabic language as my first language and who has read the different versions of the Koran, that some of those who translated the Koran into English were not honest; they tried to deceive the English speaking reader. Here are a few examples of their deception.

(1) In Surat Al-Zukhruf we read the Arabic original verse:

> *Qul in Kana Lilrahmani waladon, Fa-Ana Awalo Al-Abedeen.* (Surat Al-Zukhruf 43:81)

The literal translation of this verse is:

> Say (O Muhammad) if the Most gracious had a son, I would be the first to worship.

Muhammad Marmaduke Pickthall translated this verse in the following words:

> Say (O Muhammad); The Beneficent One hath no son. I am the first among the worshippers.

Pickthall was afraid to write the correct translation because it means that if we can prove that Christ is the Son of God, the Muslims would be obliged to worship Him.

(2) The word "disbelievers," which is repeated again and again in the English versions of the Koran, should be translated "infidels." There is a great difference between the meaning of these two words.

(3) In Surat Al-Imran Allah is described as the Best Cunning. Here is the original Arabic verse in the Koran:

> *Wa Makaru, Wa Makara Allaho Wallaho Khairo Al-Makereen.*   (Surat Al-Imran 3:54)

This should be literally translated:

> They were cunning, Allah was cunning, and Allah is the Best of Cunnings.

"Cunning" is not and can not be one of the attributes of the Holy God. But the words "Best of Cunnings" is the literal translation of the words of the Koran.

In the English translation by Dr. Al-Hillali and Dr. Khan, this verse is translated:

> And they plotted, and Allah planned too, and Allah is the Best of the planners.

(4) In Surat Al-Isra we read this Arabic verse in the Koran, where Allah is saying:

Wa eza aradna an nohlika kariatan amarna motrifiha fafasako feha fahaqa Alliah alkowl fadamarnaha tadmira. (Surat Al-Isra 17:16)

The correct translation of this verse should be:

And when we (Allah) decide to destroy a village, we send a definite command to those who lead a life of luxury in it to commit lewdness, and thus the word of torment is justified against them. Then we destroy it with complete destruction.

This means that when Allah wants to destroy a village that he will command the elite of that town to commit gross sins. Then after that he will punish them because they obeyed his commands. But this verse is translated in Drs. Al-Hillali and Khan translation in the following deceptive way:

And when we decide to destroy a town we (first) send a definite order (to obey Allah and be righteous) to those among them who lead a life of luxury. Then they transgress therein, and thus the word (of torment) is justified against (them). Then we destroy it with complete destruction. (Surat Al-Isra17:16)

The Hillali translation reverses the meaning so that it reads as though Allah is commanding the elite to do good.

The English reader should be aware of these and other mistranslations and erroneous interpretations of verses in the Koran.

113

Chapter Eleven

The Koran Is Not A Miracle

When a Muslim is asked to tell even one miracle performed by the prophet Muhammad to authenticate his prophethood, the Muslim's answer is "the Koran is the miracle of miracles." Is the Koran really a miracle?

Definition of a Miracle

The definition of the word miracle according to the *Reader's Digest Illustrated Encyclopedic Dictionary* (p 1083), is:

(1) An event that appears unexplainable by the laws of nature and so is held to be supernatural in origin or an act of God.

(2) Broadly, any event that seems exceptionally fortunate: It was a miracle she escaped unhurt.

(3) A person, thing, or event that excites admiring awe.

Is the Koran a miracle by any of these definitions?

Testimony of Muhammad's Contemporaries

Muhammad's contemporaries did not believe that the Koran was a miracle, rather they called Muhammad a mad poet (Surat Al-Saffat 37:36). They called the Koran tales of the ancients dictated to Muhammad (Surat Al-Furqan 25:5) and they called it magic derived from old and nothing but a word of a human being (Surat Al-Mudathir 74:24-25).

What the Caliphs Said

Caliph Alwaleed Ibn Yazid, who ruled the Muslims in the year 743 A.D., said about Muhammad and his Koran these arabic words: *Talaaba be-inoboati Hashimeon bela wahion attaho wala kitabo.* This translates to: **Muhammad the Hashemite manipulated people by his claim that he was a prophet, without true inspiration or an inspired book.** Abd-Allah Ibn Al-Zaabari also denied the prophethood of Muhammad (*The Islamic Caliphate*, p 59).

Caliph Abd-Almalik Ibn Marawan who was a Muslim cleric and a scholar of the Koran and held the Koran on his lap when he was appointed Caliph. After he became a Caliph he folded the Koran and said' **"this is the last time I will ever use you"** (*Islamic Caliphate*, p 173).

Caliph Alwaleed Ibn Yazeed used to shoot the Koran with arrows until holes covered it. Then he wrote a poem in which he spoke to the Koran saying:

In the day of judgment, when Allah asked you: Who made all these holes in you? say: Alwaleed did that.
(The Hidden Truth, pp 86-87)

Certainly the Koran is not a miracle because it contains a lot of errors.

Scientific Errors

(1) In the very first revelation given to Muhammad by the spirit who squeezed him at the cave of Hira, we find a very clear scientific error. That first revelation given to Muhammad says:

Read! In the name of your Lord who has created. He has created man from a clot.   (Surat Al-Alaq 96:1-2)

The word "clot" means frozen blood, or a piece of thick coagulated blood. In a book entitled *A Brief Illustrated Guide to Understanding Islam*, written by I. A. Ibrahim and published by Darussalam, Houston, under the sub-title, *The Qur'an on Human Embroynic Development*, we read:

> In the Holy Quran Allah speaks about the states of man's embryonic development: 'We created man from an extract of clay. Then We made him as a drop in a place of settlement, firmly fixed. Then We made the drop into an *alaqah*. Then We made the *alaqah* into a *mudghah*' (chewed-like substance).'
> (Surat Al-Muminun 23:12-14)

Science editors of the above mentioned book claim that the Koran explains human embryology and development. The fact is that the Koran does not contain any evidence or hints concerning the development of the human fetus.

Science tells us that the human embryo begins at conception by two cells, one called a sperm which comes from the man, and one called an egg, which comes from the woman. When these two cells unite in the process of conception they form one cell that begins to divide until it reaches the sixteen cell phase (morula stage). From this unit the embryo is developed. The Koran does not tell us anything about a cell. It does not even tell us about the very basic scientific fact that both the man and the woman contribute in the formation of the human embryo.

When the Koran says in its first revelation to Muhammad that Allah created man from a clot, that was a clear scientific error. Dr. William Campbell, a physician who dedicated five years of his life

117

to studying the Arabic language, wrote in his book, *The Qur'an and the Bible*:

> As every reader who has studied human reproduction will realize, there is no state as a clot (frozen blood) during the formation of a fetus, so this is a very major scientific problem. (p 185)

He added:

> I personally find it difficult to believe that God's first words to Muhammad would be 'Read the genetic code.' (p 187)

(2) Another major scientific error in the Koran is seen in its declaration that the world is flat. Four times the Koran declares that the world is flat:

> Do they not consider...How the earth has been flattened out? (Surat Al-Ghashiyah 88:20,T.B. Irving - *The First American Version of the Koran*)

> Have We not made the earth as a wide expanse, and the mountains as pegs? (Surat AL-Nabaa 78:7)

> By the earth and Him who spread it. (Surat Al-Shams 91:6)

> And the earth have we spread out. (Surat Al-Hijr 15:19)

Hundreds of years before Copernicus and Galileo, the prophet Isaiah declared that the earth is a sphere. He wrote:

It is He who sits above the circle of the earth.

(Isaiah 40:22 NKJ)

This is clear evidence that the Bible was inspired by God, while the Koran was not. If the Koran was inspired by God, the spirit who spoke to Muhammad would have told him that the earth is a sphere.

Moreover, the Bible declared thousands of years before any scientific discoveries that the earth is suspended in space:

He hangs the earth on nothing.   (Job 26:7 NKJ)

The Bible is accurate and precise.

(3) A third major scientific error is the declaration of the Koran that the sun sets in black muddy water. Here are the words of the Koran:

... when he reached the setting place of the sun, he found it setting in a spring of black muddy water....

(Surat Al-Kahf 18:86 HK)

We know scientifically that the sun remains at a fixed point in our galaxy while all nine planets revolve around it.

Historical Errors

Many historical errors exist in the Koran, but I will just mention one. The Koran confuses the identity of Mary, the mother of Jesus, and Miriam, the sister of Aaron and Moses.

In the Arabic Bible both Miriam, the sister of Aaron, and Mary, the mother of Jesus, are named "Maryam." But in the Koran we read that Mary, the mother of Jesus, is also the sister of Aaron (i.e, the daughter of Imran).

And Mary, the daughter of Imran, who guarded her virginity [Author's translation], and we breathed into (her body) of our spirit.   (Surat Al-Tahrim 66:12)

O Sister of Aaron!   (Surat Maryam 19:28)

Read also verses 29-34 of the same surah.

The fact is that Mary, the mother of Jesus, is <u>not</u> the daughter of Imran or the sister of Aaron. The difference in time between the two Marys is more than 1300 years! Besides, Mary, the mother of Jesus, was from the tribe of Judah, Miriam the sister of Aaron was from the tribe of Levi.

Grammatical Errors

The Koran was revealed to Muhammad in clear Arabic:

Verily, We have sent it down as an Arabic Qur'an in order that you may understand.   (Surat Yusuf 12:2 HK)

That was repeated again and again in the Koran. Therefore, we would expect the Koran to not include grammatical errors, but there are many.

Chief Judge Muhammad Saeed El-Eshmawe of Egypt wrote:

Al-Hagaag Ibn Yousof Al-Thakafi, who lived in the years 660-714 A.D. was a teacher of Arabic language in the city of Taif. Then he joined the military and became the most powerful person during the reign of Caliph Abd-Elmalik Ibn Marawan and after him his son Al-Waleed Ibn Abd-Elmalik. Because Al-Haagag taught Arabic, he gave himself the liberty to change several words of Caliph Uthman's Koran, which is an indication that he did not believe that the Koran was

120

verbally inspired or was inscribed in a 'tablet preserved.'

(Al-Khalipha Al-Islamiah pages 195-196)

We will mention but a few of the words Al-Haagag Ibn Yousof Al-Thakafi changed:

(1) In Surat Yunus 10:22, he changed the word *yanshorokom*, which means "spread you," to *yousayerokom*, which means "makes you to go on."
(2) In Surat Ash-Shuara 26:116, he changed the *word Al-Mukhrageen*, meaning "the cast out," to *Al-Margoomeen*, which means "those who are to be stoned [to death]."
(3) In Surat Ash-Shuara 26:167, he changed the word *Min Al-Margoomeen*, which means "those who are to be stoned to death," to *Al-Mukhrageen*, which means "those who will assuredly be cast out."
(4) In Surat Muhammad 47:15, he changed the word *yasen*, which is poor Arabic to *Asen*, meaning "unpolluted."
(5) In Surat Al-Hadid 57:7, he changed the word *wataqu*, which means "feared Allah," to *Wa-anfaqu*, which means "spend in charity."

With all the changes Al-Haggag made, there are still grammatical errors in the Koran. To our Arabic readers these errors will be dramatic:

1) In Surat Ta Ha 20:63, the Arabic word *Hazani Lasaherani* should be *Hazaini Lasahirieni*.
2) In Surat Al Maidah 5:69, the Arabic word *Alsabeoun* should be *Alsabieen*.
3) In Surat Al-Maidah 5:38, the Arabic word *Aidyahoma* should be *Yadihoma*.

121

4) In Surat Al-Nisa 4:162, the Arabic word *Almukemeen* should be *Almukemoon*.

5) In Surat Al-Munafiqun 63:10, the Arabic word *Akon* should be *Akoon*.

Muhammad claimed that the Quran was given to him in pure Arabic (Surat Al-Nahl 16:103), but with all these grammatical errors, how could this be?

Can the Koran, which is full of scientific, historical, and grammatical errors, be considered a miracle?

Chapter Twelve

The Doctrine Of Abrogation

It is extremely important for the student of the Koran to know the doctrine of abrogation. The word "abrogate" means to abolish, cancel or terminate. The Koran declares Allah abrogated verses of the Koran and gave Muhammad other verses to replace them:

> Whatever verse do We abrogate or cause to be forgotten, We bring a better one or similar to it. Know you not that Allah is able to do all things?
>
> (Surat Al-Baqarah 2:106 HK)

Professor Khalil Abd-Alkareem wrote in his Arabic book *An-Nuss Al-Mouassas Wa-Mujtamaoh (The Original Language of the Koran and its Society)*:

> The first verses abrogated in the Koran were those concerning the 'Kibla' (the direction Muslims should take when they pray). When Muhammad migrated to Al-Madina, Allah commanded him to direct his prayer toward Beit-Al-Makdes (Jerusalem). Muhammad knew that the Jews have great influence there, so he commanded Muslims to pray toward the destroyed Jewish temple in Jerusalem. After eighteen months, he realized that the Jews rejected his Islam, so Allah abrogated his first command and revealed to

Muhammad that he should direct Muslims to pray toward the Kaaba. (Volume One, p 52)

Verily, We have seen the turning of your face (Muhammad) toward the heaven. Surely we shall turn you to a Qiblah (prayer direction) that shall please you, so turn your face in the direction of Al-Masjid-Al-Haram (The Kaabah at Mecca). And wherever your people are, turn your faces (in prayer) in that direction...
(Surat Al-Baqarah 2:144)

Allah gave Muhammad what pleased him even though the Kaabah at that time was a place of 360 idols. It was a political move to please the Arabs, so he needed a revelation to do it, and he got it. Would a Holy God direct his people to pray toward a shrine filled with idols?

Professor Abd-Al-Kareem says in the same volume:

In the one hundred fourteen surahs of the Koran, seventy-one of them have abrogated verses, that means two-thirds of the Koran. [Author's Emphasis] Twenty-five surahs have the abrogated and abrogating verses, six of them have the abrogating, and the remaining forty have the abrogated only.
(Volume One, p 38)

Abdullah Ibn Massud states that the Prophet one day recited a verse, which he immediately wrote down. The next morning he found it had vanished from the material on which it had been written. Astonished at this, he acquainted Muhammad with the fact, and was informed that the verse in question had been revoked. There are, however, many verses still in the Koran which have been abrogated. It was an exceedingly convenient doctrine, and one needed to explain the

124

change of front which Muhammad made at different periods of his career.

(The Faith of Islam, p 73)

This doctrine of abrogation also convinces Muslims that the Koran abrogated the Bible, so the Bible is not needed. Ibn Warraq, in his book, *Why I Am not a Muslim*, wrote:

The doctrine of abrogation makes a mockery of the Muslim dogma that the Koran is a faithful and unalterable reproduction of the original scriptures that are preserved in heaven. If God's words are eternal, uncreated, and of universal significance, then how can we talk of God's words being superseded or becoming obsolete? Are some words of God to be preferred to other words of God? Apparently yes. According to Muir, some 200 verses have been canceled by later ones. Thus we have the strange situation where the entire Koran is recited as the word of God, and yet there are passages that can be considered not 'true,' in other words, they are acknowledged as falsehood. (p 115)

Abdallah Abd Al-Fadi said:

Abrogation in God's words goes against His wisdom, truthfulness and foreknowledge. It is the short-sighted man that issues laws and replaces them according to situations and circumstances. The omniscient God, however, knows about all things before they come to pass. How then could it possibly be said about God that He changes, exchanges, abrogates and blots out? [Author's Emphasis]

(Is the Koran Infallible? p 331)

The question concerning the doctrine of abrogation is, "How could anyone trust a God who cancels his word and causes people to forget it?" Muslim clerics use the abrogated verses of the Koran to prove that Islam is a religion of peace, while they know that these verses are abrogated.

What a deception!

On the other hand, the true God revealed in the Bible says:

> My covenant I will not break, nor alter the word that has gone out of my lips.   (Psalm 89:34 NKJ)

This is the only God the Believer can trust.

Chapter Thirteen

The Koran Is not Divinely Inspired

God was not the source of inspiration for the Koran. Dr. Caesar E. Farah wrote in his book, *Islam*, concerning the Koran:

> The style of expression underlying the Koran is a curious blend of poetic rhymed prose and a lyrical flow, familiar modes of expression to the pre-Islamic Arab. Whether owing to accident or design, the sacred text was particularly adaptable for oral recitation, a carry-over from the Jahiliyah when this method of expression was most popular in Arabia. Stylistically, the Koran shows the strong predominance of saj (rhymed prose), a form of rhyme which adheres to no meter, but was popularly utilized by the soothsayers of pagan Arabia.
>
> (p 82)

The Koran is not divinely inspired in its style nor in its contents. The Bible is the absolute standard in this area.

When God called Moses to be the founder of Judaism he spoke to him directly. The Bible tells the whole story in Exodus 3:1-10. There are many such instances mentioned in the Torah - thirty-five times in the book of Leviticus alone - where it is said "The Lord spoke to Moses." Even the Koran attests to this:

> And to Moses Allah spoke direct.
>
> (Surat Al-Nisa 4:164)

The line of communication never stopped between God and Moses, since he was called to be a prophet, and Moses followed God's direction.

God confirmed His call to Moses with miracles. When Moses erected the Tabernacle of Meeting, and the first offerings were given, God demonstrated His glory to authenticate Moses' prophethood:

> And Moses and Aaron went into the tabernacle of meeting, and came out and blessed the people. Then the glory of the Lord appeared to all the people, *and fire came out from before the Lord and consumed the burnt offering and the fat on the altar.* When all the people saw it, they shouted and fell on their faces.
> (Leviticus 9:23, 24 NKJ-Author's emphasis)

Now we come to Muhammad. His call came by the spirit who met him at the cave of Mount Hira, squeezed him so tightly that he thought he would die, and left him in great distress of mind. The spirit then left him with no revelations for a period of time. Muhammad suffered greatly every time he received a revelation from that spirit.

Al-Imam (cleric) Al-Bukhary quoted Aisha, Muhammad's wife, when she said:

> Harith Ibn Hesham asked the messenger of Allah: 'Messenger of Allah, how do you receive the revelation?' 'Sometimes it comes to me like a ringing bell, and this is the hardest. When he leaves me I remember what he said,' Muhammad answered. Then he continued, 'Sometimes the angel appears to me as a man, he speaks to me and I remember what he said.' Aisha said, 'I saw him when revelation comes down to him, sweat covers his forehead in the very cold day.'

128

Imam Ahmad cited Abdallah Ibn Omar, who asked Muhammad, "Do you feel the revelation?" "I hear ringings, then I stay silent. Every time the spirit came with revelation I thought I would die," Muhammad answered.

Ibn Saad quoted Aisha when she said:

> When revelation comes down to Muhammad, he submerged his head in water, his face turns pale, he feels that he is very cold and he sweats with large drops of sweating.
>
> (*Al-Helal Magazine*, December 1970, p 73)

Allah did not speak to Muhammad directly, only the spirit of unknown origin did.

Moreover, when Muhammad entered Mecca victoriously and cast out all of the idols from the Kaaba, God did not reveal His glory there as he revealed it in the Tabernacle of Meeting. No sign of God's presence was felt in the Kaaba.

Ibn Hesham recorded that the prophet stood there to display the Muslims' armies with all their banners. Abu-Sufian the Amowite and Al-Abaas, the Prophet's uncle, stood to watch the parade.

> 'The Kingdom of your nephew Muhammad became so great today' Abu-Sufian said to Al-Abaas. 'It is the prophethood, not the Kingship, Abu-Sufian,' Al-Abaas answered. 'As to prophethood, I still have my reservations concerning it,' Abu-Sufian answered.
>
> (*Islamic Caliphate*, p 103)

There were great doubts in the hearts of many in Arabia concerning Muhammad's prophethood.

Now, as we turn to the Koran itself, we will find that

some of the contents of the Koran cause us to question whether it was inspired by God. For example, the Koran actually refers to a pagan god as a prophet:

> Also mention in the book Idris: He was a man of truth [and sincerity], and a prophet. And we raised him to lofty station. (Surat Maryam 19:56-57)

Ahmad Bahgat recorded on page 164 of his book, *The Prophets of Allah*:

> Legends say that Idris is Osiris the hero of the ancient Egyptian legend.

Idris is the Arabic pronunciation of Osiris. *The Reader's Digest Illustrated Encyclopedic Dictionary* defines "Osiris" as:

> The ancient Egyptian god of the underworld. In Egyptian mythology the god who was ruler and judge in the underworld and the brother and consort of Isis. He is identified with the Nile, and his annual death and resurrection symbolized the self-renewing vitality and fertility of nature. (p 1203)

The Koran declares that Idris, or Osiris, who was the ancient Egyptian god of the underworld, is:

> . . . a man of truth [and sincerity], and a prophet. And We [Allah] raised him to lofty station.
> (Surat Maryam 19:56-57)

Amazing!! Is Osiris the god of the underworld, or a prophet? With such an error, could the Koran be the inspired word of the true God?

Another person was mentioned in the Koran and commentators have no idea who he was. His name is Zul-Kifl and he is mentioned in Surat Al-Anbiyaa 21:85, 86:

> And remember Ismail, Idris, and Zul-Kifl, all [men] of constancy and patience.

Who is Zul-Kifl? Nobody knows - even the best of expositors! That is contrary to what is written in the Bible:

> For whatever things were written before were written for our learning, that we through the patience and comfort of the Scriptures might have hope.
>
> (Romans 15:4 NKJ)

But the Koran has recorded things of no benefit to its readers. Professor Abd-Al-Kareem wrote:

> The books of the two former religions, Judaism and Christianity, recorded the stories and miracles of the great prophets and patriarchs, Abraham, Moses, and Isa (Jesus), but they did not indulge in their private lives, while the Koran is full of details of Muhammad's private life.
>
> (*An-Nuss Al-Mouassas Wa-Mujtamaoh, Vol. I* p 36)

As I mentioned before, the Koran came to Muhammad piecemeal according to different events and occasions. Why did the Koran come piecemeal like this? **The reason is that Muhammad used the Koran to satisfy his own lusts and solve his problems and this** is clear from the following examples:

131

Example One

Muhammad lusted after Zainab, his daughter-in-law, and he desired to marry her, so a revelation came to him from his Allah, saying:

> So when Zaid had accomplished his desire from her, We gave her to you in marriage.
>
> (Surat Al-Ahzab 33:37 HK)

It is unacceptable that the God who said, "Whoever marries a woman who is divorced commits adultery" (Matthew 5:32) would permit Muhammad to marry his divorced daughter-in-law!

Example Two

When Mary, the Egyptian Coptic slave, became pregnant by Muhammad, Aisha became very jealous. One day, Mary came to meet Muhammad. He slept with her in the private room of his wife Hafsa, the daughter of Omar. Hafsa came suddenly and found the veil of her room closed, and she knew that Mary was inside with Muhammad. She waited until Mary came out and she entered her room to confront Muhammad, crying and sad because he violated her bed.

She continued to cry until Muhammad promised her to shun having sex with Mary again. He told Hafsa not to tell his other wives, but Hafsa told Aisha. Aisha became angry and convinced her rivals not to have sex with Muhammad to punish him. One month passed by. Rumors spread that Muhammad would divorce his wives.

Muhammad needed a revelation to threaten them and subdue them. Then the following revelation came:

When the Prophet disclosed a matter in confidence to one of his consorts, and she then divulged it [to another], and Allah made it known to him, he confirmed part thereof and passed over a part. Then when he told her thereof, she said, 'Who told thee this?' He said, 'He told me Who is the Knower, the Aware.' If ye two turn in repentance to Allah, your hearts are indeed so inclined; but if ye back up each other against him, truly Allah is his Protector, and Gabriel, and [every] Righteous one among those who believe and furthermore, the angels will back [him] up.

It may be, if he divorced you [all], that Allah will give him in exchange consorts better than you - who submit [their wills], who believe, who are devout; who turn to Allah in repentance, who worship [in humility], who fast - previously married or virgins.

(Surat Al-Tahrim 66:3-5)

Muhammad's wives were scared to be divorced so they repented with total submission to him. The revelation did what, Muhammad wanted, and he came back to them. The full story is in the book, *The Wives of the Prophet*, pp 100-104. (Obviously, the angels mentioned in these verses are not the holy angels of heaven.)

Example Three

Muhammad's wives asked him to raise their allowances and permit them to adorn themselves. To solve this problem, without raising his wives allowances, a threatening revelation was delivered to him:

O Prophet! say to thy consorts: 'If it be that ye desire the life of this world, and its glitter - then come! I will

133

provide for your enjoyment and set you free in a
handsome manner.' (Surat Al-Ahzab 33:28)

This meant that he would give them financial gifts and divorce
them. The sword of divorce was always ready to threaten
Muhammad's wives and subdue them in the name of Allah. And in
that case it worked.

Example Four

When Muhammad grew old, his wives were young and
beautiful. so he was afraid that they would be seduced by younger
men. He needed a revelation to order them to cover their beauty
and of course that would be applied to all Muslim women. The
revelation came in the following words:

> O Prophet! Tell thy wives and daughters, and the
> believing women, that they should cast their outer
> garments over their persons [when out of doors]: That is
> most convenient, that they should be known [as such]
> and not molested. And Allah is Oft-Forgiving, Most
> Merciful. (Surat Al-Ahzab 33:59)

Another verse was given to Muhammad's wives:

> O ye wives of the Prophet! Ye are not like any other
> women. If ye keep your duty [to Allah], then be not
> soft of speech, lest he in whose heart is a disease aspire
> [to you], but utter customary speech.
> (Surat Al-Ahzab 33:32)

He is telling his wives that they should not use their voice in
order to intice men but rather they should cover themselves. This
is why the Koran commands Muslim women to wear the *hejab*, an

134

outfit with which Muslim women cover themselves from head to toe.

This rule is imposed on the women of Saudi Arabia. One Saudi princess wrote about her sister, when she was ordered by her father to wear the hejab:

> Sara had been veiling since her menses. *The veil stamped her as a nonperson* [Author's Emphasis], and she soon ceased to speak of her childhood dreams of great accomplishment. She became distant from me, her younger sister, who was as yet unconcerned with the institution of veiling. The sharpening of Sara's distance left me longing for the remembered happiness of our shared childhood. It suddenly became apparent to me that happiness is realized only in the face of unhappiness, for I never knew we were so happy until Sara's unhappiness stared me in the face.
>
> (*Princess*, by Jean P. Sasson, p 27)

The *hejab* is a way to eliminate the existence of women. The woman who wears the *hejab* does not exist. She has no face, no personality.

This is tragic!

Martha McSally, an American Air Force fighter pilot, was ordered by the Department of Defense to wear the Muslim-style head-to-toe robes called "abaya" in Saudi Arabia. Martha saw it was outrageous to comply with this order. She instituted a lawsuit challenging the military policy, saying it violated her constitutional rights to freedom of speech and religion.

The Washington Post reported on June 29, 2002, that the Senate had voted unanimously to prevent the Department of Defense from requiring US service women in Saudi Arabia to wear Muslim-style head-to-toe robes.

The Post said, "the Senate vote is a great victory for freedom and the democratic process, and the rights of women in the armed services." The American Army is in Saudi Arabia to protect the Saudi kingdom. The Saudis want to impose Islam and Islamic traditions on the women serving there! What a shame.

Example Five

Muhammad was constantly worried that his wives might commit adultery behind his back, especially since they were much younger than him, so the following revelation came to threaten them and instill terror in their hearts:

> O ye, wives of the Prophet! Whoever of you committeth an open illegal sexual intercourse, the torment for her will be doubled, and that is ever easy for Allah. (Surat Al-Ahzab 33:30 HK)

The question is: If Muhammad's godly example and the teachings of the Koran had an influence on his wives, to keep them honest and pure, why would such a threat be needed?

Example Six

Muhammad did not want his wives to marry after his death, so he needed a revelation to convince Muslims not to marry them. The revelation came:

> ... And it is not right for you that you should annoy Allah's messenger, nor that you should ever marry his wives after him (his death). Verily, with Allah that shall be an enormity. (Surat Al-Ahzab 33:53 HK)

Muhammad had the privilege to marry any number of women, but his young wives could not marry after his death.

Example Seven

A Muslim woman offered herself to Muhammad. He wanted to marry her and he needed a revelation to justify his behavior. The revelation came as follows:

... and a believing woman if she offers herself to the prophet and the prophet wishes to marry her - a privilege for you only, not for the (rest of) the believers (Muslims). (Surat Al-Ahzab 33:50 HK)

Do you see how the revelations of the Koran were very much concerning Muhammad's marriages and sex life, and how it was a privilege for him and for him only to marry any woman who offered herself to him? Does this indicate that the Koran was inspired by God?
Think it over!

Example Eight

Muhammad was annoyed by those who used to enter his houses without permission and was afraid that they might seduce his wives, so the following revelation came to him:

O ye who believe! Enter not the Prophet's houses, until leave is given you, for a meal, [and then] not [so early as] to wait for its preparation: but when ye are invited, enter; and when ye have taken your meal, disperse, without seeking familiar talk. Such [behavior] annoys the Prophet he is shy to dismiss you, but Allah is not shy [to tell you] the truth.
And when ye ask [his ladies] for anything ye want, ask them from before a screen: that makes for greater purity for your hearts and for theirs.
(Surat Al-Ahzab 33:53)

Example Nine

Muhammad was annoyed by those who called him from behind his apartment, so he needed a revelation to stop them from doing so.

> Those who shout out to thee from without the inner apartments - most of them lack understanding. If only they had patience until thou couldst come out to them, it would be best for them: but Allah is Oft-Forgiving, Most Merciful. (Surat Al-Hujurat 49:4-5)

Example Ten

Muhammad wanted his followers to pay him alms for counsel and prayer. So he needed a revelation. The revelation came in the following words:

> O ye who believe! When ye hold conference with the messenger, offer an alms before your conference. That is better and purer for you. But if ye cannot find [the wherewithal] then lo! Allah is Forgiving, Merciful.
> (Surat Al-Mujadilah 58:12 MPT)

> Of their wealth take alms, that so thou mightest purify and sanctify them; and pray on their behalf. Verily thy prayers are a source of security for them: And Allah is One Who heareth and knoweth.
> (Surat At-Tawbah 9:103)

Incidentally, the reader may ask how Muhammad, who is himself a sinner, can purify and sanctify his followers, something only God can do!

Example Eleven

Muhammad wanted a large amount of the spoils of war to be given to him. He needed a revelation, and it came as follows:

> They ask you (O Muhammad) about the spoils of war. Say: 'The spoils are for Allah and His Messenger Muhammad.' So fear Allah and adjust all matters of differences among you, and obey Allah and His Messenger (Muhammad). (Surat Al-Anfal 8:1 HK)

Again, the Koran says:

> And know that whatever of war-booty that you may gain, verily, one-fifth of it is assigned to Allah, and to the Messenger, and to the near relatives (of the Messenger Muhammad) (and also) the orphans, Al-Masakin (the poor) and the wayfarer, if you have believed in Allah and in that which We sent down to Our slave Muhammad. (Surat Al-Anfal 8:41 HK)

Of course, if the spoils of war are for Allah and Muhammad, they will end up to be all for Muhammad.

Example Twelve

According to the Koran, Allah had commanded that a Muslim could marry up to four women at any one time:

> Marry women of your choice, two, or three, or four. (Surat Al-Nisa 4:3)

Four women were not enough for Muhammad, so he needed special permission from Allah to marry any number of women he wished. The revelation came as follows:

O Prophet! We have made lawful to thee thy wives to whom thou has paid their dowers; and those whom thy right hand possesses out of the captives of war whom Allah has assigned to thee; and daughters of thy paternal uncles and aunts, and daughters of thy maternal uncles and aunts, who migrated with thee; and any believing woman who gives herself to the Prophet if the Prophet wishes to wed her - this only for thee, and not for the believers [at large]; we know what we have appointed for them as to their wives and the captives whom their right hands possess - in order that there should be no difficulty for thee. And Allah is Oft Forgiving, Most Merciful. (Surat Al-Ahzab 33:50)

Now it is clear that the Koran dealt to a great extent with Muhammad's desires, affairs and problems. Jesus rejected Satan's suggestion to turn stones into bread to satisfy his hunger. He never used any event for his own advantage or to satisfy his desires.

Certainly, the Koran is not divinely inspired.

Chapter Fourteen

Contribution of the *Jinn*

The Koran challenged mankind and *jinn* to produce the like of it. This challenge is recorded in the Koran in the following verse:

> Say: 'If the whole of mankind and Jinn were to gather together to produce the like of this Koran they could not produce the like thereof, even if they backed up each other with help and support.'   (Surat Al-Isra 17:88)

This challenge was met. In the age of Jahilia before Muhammad there were men who produced the like of the Koran.

Before he became a prophet, Muhammad heard Qus Ibn Saedah Al-Ayadi, who died in the year 600 A.D., speaking in the Okaz Market and admired him greatly. Abu-Bakr memorized what Qus Ibn Saedah said and used to repeat his speeches to Muhammad. His Arabic speech was similar to the Koran and many of his words were repeated in the Koran.

The poet Omaia Ibn Abi Alsalat, who died in the year 624 A.D., mentioned in his poetry Gabriel and Michael, whom Muhammad mentioned in his Koran. The poet Al-Haseen Ibn Hamam, who died in the year 611 A.D., mentioned in his poetry the scales by which the deeds of men will be weighed in the day of judgment. The same wording is used in the Koran in Surat Al-Araf 7:8, 9.

The poets Waraka Ibn Nofal (who died in 592 A.D.), Antara Al-Abasi (who died in 610 A.D.) and Lubaid (who died in 671 A.D.) all wrote poetry in a style that is quite similar to the Koran.

141

The poet Roba Ibn Al-Ajaj wrote something comparable to Surat Al-Fil (*Islamic Caliphate*, pp 60-71).

Now, how about the *jinn*? Were these evil spirits also able to produce the like of the Koran? The answer is: certainly. The *jinn* contributed mostly a whole surah in the Koran. It is surah number 72 and it is called Surat Al-Jinn. Here are the words of that surah:

Say (O Muhammad): It has been revealed to me that a group (from three to ten in number) of jinn listened (to this Koran). They said: 'Verily, we have heard a wonderful Recitation (this Koran)!

It guides to the Right Path, and we have believed therein, and we shall never join (in worship) anything with our Lord (Allah).

And He, exalted is the Majesty of our Lord, has taken neither a wife nor a son (or offspring or children).

And that the foolish among us [i.e. Iblis (Satan) or the polytheists amongst the jinn] used to utter against Allah that which was an enormity in falsehood.

And verily, we thought that men and jinn would not utter a lie against Allah.

And verily, there were men among mankind who took shelter with the males among the jinn, but they (jinn) increased them (mankind) in sin and transgression.

And they thought as you thought, that Allah will not send any Messenger (to mankind or jinn).

And we have sought to reach the heaven; but found it filled with stern guards and flaming fires.

And verily, we used to sit there in stations, to (steal) a hearing, but any who listens now will find a flaming fire watching him in ambush.

And we know not whether evil is intended for those on earth, or whether their Lord intends for them a Right Path.

There are among us some that are righteous, and some the contrary; we are groups having different ways (religious sects).

And we think that we cannot escape (the punishment of) Allah in the earth, nor can we escape Him by flight.

And indeed when we heard the Guidance (this Koran), we believed therein (Islamic Monotheism), and whosoever believes in his Lord shall have no fear, either of a decrease in the reward of his good deeds or an increase in the punishment for his sins.

And of us some are Muslims (who have submitted to Allah, after listening to this Koran), and of us some are Al-Qasitun (disbelievers - those who have deviated from the Right Path). And whosoever has embraced Islam (i.e. has become a Muslim by submitting to Allah), then such have sought the Right Path.

And as for the Qasitun (disbelievers who deviated from the Right Path), they shall be firewood for Hell.

If they (non-Muslims) had believed in Allah, and went on the Right Way (i.e. Islam) We would surely have bestowed on them water (rain) in abundance.

That we might try them thereby. And whosoever turns away from the Reminder of his Lord (i.e. this Koran, - and practice not its laws and orders), He will cause him to enter in a severe torment (i.e. Hell).

And the mosques are for Allah (Alone): so invoke not anyone along with Allah.

And when the slave of Allah (Muhammad) stood up invoking Him (his Lord - Allah) in prayer they (the jinn) just made round him a dense crowd as if sticking one over the other (in order to listen to the Prophet's recitation). (Surat Al-Jinn 72:1-19 HK)

143

Do you notice what the *jinn* say in this surah, how they used to sit in heaven to steal a hearing, and how they cannot do it anymore for fear of flaming fire and how some of them are Muslims.

The most important thing is that all the verses mentioned here were the words of the *jinn* but written in the Koran as if they were the inspired words of Allah. It is clear that the style of the *jinn* is very similar to the style of the Koran.

The Koran declares that the *jinn* are evil creatures associated with Satan:

> Iblis [Satan] he was one of the jinn, and he broke the command of his lord.   (Surat Al-Kahf 18:50)

The *jinn* were able to produce the like of the Koran and in fact, they produced one whole chapter of the Koran and this is why it is called "Surat Al-Jinn." In that surah the *jinn* told Muhammad, "Amongst us are some who are Muslims (literal translation) (Surat Al-Jinn 72:14). They also told him that Allah has no son (verse 3).

Ahmad Bahgat in his book, *Prophets of Allah*, page 386, quoted Abdallah Ibn Massoud who said:

> The Messenger of Allah said to his followers, 'Everyone of you is escorted by a jinni and an angel.' 'Even you, Messenger of Allah?' they asked. 'Even me, Muhammad answered, but Allah helped me and he was converted to Islam, since that time he does not order me but to do good.'

Here we have to ask, since Muhammad was escorted by a *jinni*, what kind of suggestions did the *jinni* give to Muhammad before the *jinni* became a Muslim?

The Holy God of the Bible commanded his people not to be associated with the *jinn* or to try to approach them, "For all that do these things are abomination unto the Lord" (Deuteronomy 18:12). A book which recorded a surah for the *jinn* is not God's book.

The challenge of the Koran was met by poets and *jinn* to assure us that the Koran is not the Word of God. Moreover, we read in the Bible:

> The angel of the LORD encamps all around those who fear him, and delivers them.   (Psalm 34:7 NKJ)

True believers in Jesus Christ are escorted by the angel of the Lord, not by a *jinni*.

Chapter Fifteen

Discrepancies in the Koran

If a book is truly inspired by the true God, it should not contradict itself. We see an example of this in the four Gospels in the New Testament as mentioned before. In contrast to the Bible, the Koran is full of discrepancies and many Muslim scholars firmly believe that it has also been altered. There is no doubt that Caliph Uthman tampered with it and that the original Koran was burned. Aisha, Muhammad's wife said:

> Surat Al-Ahzab was 200 verses during the prophet's life; when Uthman wrote the Koran it became what it is now (72 verses). (*Alostora Wa-Altorath - The Legend and the Heritage*, p 274)

The Koran suggests a test for itself in the following verse:

> Do they not ponder the Koran? Had it been from other than Allah, they would surely have found therein much discrepancy. (Surat Al-Nisa 4:82)

The fact is there are many discrepancies in the Koran. The following are some of the many clear contradictions in the Koran.

Discrepancies in the Koran

The Verses	Their Contradictions
Those who believe [in the Koran] and those who follow the Jewish [Scriptures] and the Christians and the Sabians, any who believe in Allah and the last days, and work righteousness, shall have their reward with their Lord, on them shall be no fear, nor shall they grieve. (Surat Al-Baqarah 2:62)	The Jews call Uzair a son of Allah, and the Christians call Christ the son of Allah. That is a saying from their mouth; [in this] they but imitate what the infidels (literal translation) of old used to say. Allah's curse be on them: how they are deluded away from the truth. (Surat Al-Tawbah 9:30)
*************************.	*************************.
Let there be no compulsion in religion: Truth stands out clear from error. (Surat Al-Baqarah 2:256) Unto you your religion and unto me my religion. (Surat Al-Kafirun 109:6 MPT)	Fight those who believe not in Allah nor the last day, nor hold that which hath been forbidden by Allah and His Messenger [Muhammad], nor acknowledge the religion of truth [Islam], from among the people of the book [Jews and Christians] until they pay the Jezia [special taxes paid by the Jews and Christians who do not want to renounce their religion] with willing sub-mission, and feel themselves subdued. (Surat Al-Tawbah 9:29) And fight them on until there is no more sedition (literal translation) and religion [Islam] becomes Allah's in its entirety. (Surat Al-Anfal 8:39)
**********************	*************************.

The Verses	Their Contradictions
To Allah belong the East and the West: whithersoever ye turn, there is Allah's face, for Allah is all-Embracing, All-Knowing. (Surat Al-Baqarah 2:115)	So from whencesoever thou startest forth, turn thy face in the direction of the sacred mosque [the Kaaba]; and wheresoever ye are, turn thy face thither. (Surat Al-Baqarah 2:150)
************************	************************
O Prophet rouse the Believers [Muslim] to fight, if there are twenty amongst you, patient and persevering, they will vanquish two hundred: if a hundred, they will vanquish a thousand of the unbelievers: for these are a people without understanding. (Surat Al- Anfal 8:65)	Now hath Allah lightened your burden, for He knoweth that there is weakness in you. So if there be of you a steadfast hundred they shall overcome two hundred, and if there be of you a thousand they shall overcome two thousand by permission of Allah. Allah is with the steadfast. (Surat Al-Anfal 8:66)
************************	************************
Thy duty (Muhammad) is to make [The Message] reach them. It is our part to call them to account. (Surat Al-Rad 13:40) If it had been Allah's will, they would not have taken false gods but We made thee not one to watch over their doings, nor art thou set over them to dispose of their affairs. (Surat Al-Anam 6:107)	... I will instill terror into the hearts of the unbelievers: smite ye above their necks and smite all their finger-tips of them this because they contended against Allah and His Messenger (Muhammad): If any contend against Allah and His Messenger. Allah is strict in punishment. (Surat Al-Anfal 8:12)
************************	************************

149

The Verses	Their Contradictions
O Prophet! We have made lawful to thee thy wives to whom thou has paid their dowers; and those whom they right hand possesses out of the captives of war whom Allah has assigned to thee; and daughters of thy paternal uncles and aunts, and daughters of thy maternal uncles and aunts, who migrated with thee; and any believing woman who gives herself to the Prophet if the Prophet wishes to wed her - this only for thee, and not for the believers [at large]; We know what We have appointed for them as to their wives and the captives whom their right hands possess - in order that there should be no difficulty for thee. And Allah is Oft Forgiving, Most Merciful. (Surat Al-Ahzab 33:50)	It is not lawful for thee [to marry more] women after this, nor to change them for [other] wives, even though their beauty attract thee, except any thy right hand should possess [as handmaidens]: and Allah doth watch over all. (Surat Al-Ahzab 33:52)
*************************	*************************
And nearest among them in love to the believers [the Muslims] wilt thou find those who say "we are Christians" because amongst these are men devoted to learning and men who have renounced the world, and they are not arrogant." (Surat Al-Maidah5:82)	O ye who believe! Take not the Jews and the Christians for your friends and protectors: they are but friends and protectors to each other. And he amongst you that turns to them [for friendship] is of them. Verily Allah guideth not a people unjust. (Surat Al-Maidah 5:51)

The Verses	Their Contradictions
We sent after them Jesus the son of Mary, and bestowed on him the Gospel; and we ordained in the hearts of those who followed him compassion and mercy. (Surat Al-Hadid 57:27) We did aforetime grant to the children of Israel the Book, the power of command, and prophet-hood; We gave them, for sustenance, things good and pure; and We favoured them above all nations. (Surat Al-Jathiyah 45:16) ************************	************************
To Moses We did give Nine Clear Signs: Ask the Children of Israel: When he came to them, Pharaoh said to him: "O Moses! I consider thee, indeed, to have been worked upon by sorcery." Moses said, "Thou knowest well that these things have been sent down by none but the Lord of the heavens and the earth as eye-opening evidence: and I consider thee indeed, O Pharaoh, to be one doomed to destruction!" So he resolved to remove them from the face of the earth: but	We took the children of Israel across the sea: Pharaoh and his hosts followed them in insolence and spite. At length, when overwhelmed with the flood, he said: "I believe that there is no god except Him Whom the children of Israel believe in: I am of those submit [to Allah in Islam]." [It was said to him]: "Ah now! - But a little while before, wast thou in rebellion! - And thou didst mischief [and violence]! "This day shall We save thee in thy body, that thou mayest be a

The Verses	Their Contradictions
We did drown him and all who were with him. (Surat Al-Isra 17:101-103) *************************	sign to those who come after thee! But verily, many among mankind are heedless of Our signs!" (Surat Yunus 10:90-92) *************************
Adam and Jesus The similitude of Jesus before Allah is as that of Adam; He created him from dust, then said to him: "Be": and he was. (Surat Al-Imran 3:59)	**Adam was not created by the word "Be" but by the breath of Allah** Behold, thy Lord said to the angels: "I am about to create man from clay: when I have fashioned him and breathed into him of My Spirit, fall ye down in prostration unto him." (Surat Sad 38:71-72) **Jesus was not conceived by the word "Be"** And Mary [mother of Jesus] the daughter of Imran, who guarded her virginity (literal translation); and We breathed into [her body] of our spirit; and she testified to the truth of the words of her Lord and of his revelations, and was one of the devout [servants]. (Surat Al-Tahrim 66:12)
.*************************	*************************

152

The Verses	Their Contradictions
Say: O disbelievers! I worship not that which ye worship; nor worship ye that which I worship. And I shall not worship that which ye worship. Unto you your religion, and unto me my religion. (Surat Al-Kafirun 109:1-6 MPT) ************************	Say: "If The Most Gracious Had a son, I would be the first to worship." (Surat Al-Zukhruf 43:81) ************************
It is not fitting for a believer, man or woman, when a matter has been decided by Allah and His Messenger (Muhammad) to have any option about their decision: If anyone disobeys Allah and His Messenger, he is indeed on a clearly wrong path. (Surat Al-Ahzab 33:36). ************************	Say: "Allah knows best - with him is (the knowledge of) the unseen of the heavens and the earth... He makes none to share in His decision and His Rule" (Surat Al--Kahf 18:26). ************************
We have made it a Koran in Arabic, that ye may be able to understand. (Surat Az-Zukhruf 43:3) ************************	He it is Who has sent down to thee the book [the Koran]... no one knows its true meaning except Allah. (Surat Al-Imran 3:7) ************************

This verse indicates that the Koran is exclusively for the Arabic speaking people. It could not be a miracle, because people of other tongues cannot even read it. When the Koran is translated into any

153

other language, it totally loses its poetic rhyme and becomes almost incomprehensible.

It is of great importance to deal with two verses of the Koran at the close of this section. The first verse is:

> Those who follow the Messenger, the unlettered Prophet, whom they find mentioned in their own [scriptures]. In the Torah and the Gospel for he commands them what is just and forbids them what is evil. . .   (Surat Al-Araf 7:157)

The second verse is:

> And remember, Jesus, the son of Mary, said: 'O children of Israel: I am the messenger of Allah [sent] to you confirming the Torah [which came] before me, and giving glad tidings of a messenger to come after me, whose name shall be Ahmad. . .   (Surat Al-Saff 61:6.

I am confident that there is no mention of Muhammad and no prophecy concerning him in the Torah or the Gospel. Muhammad is not the prophet like Moses, as Muslim scholars claim. He is not the comforter, for the comforter is the Holy Spirit. Muhammad is not a spirit. He is not the servant mentioned in Isaiah 42:1, and he is not the stone cut out without hands mentioned in Daniel 2:34.

All these prophecies were fulfilled to the letter in Jesus Christ and in the Holy Spirit who descended from heaven in the day of Pentecost. Jesus is the prophet like Moses (Deuteronomy 18:15-19 and Acts 3:19-23), He is the servant chosen by God (Isaiah 42:1-4 and Matthew 12:17-21), He is the stone cut out without human hands (I Peter 2:6-8) and His kingdom will fill the earth at His second coming (Revelation 11:15).

In short there are no prophecies concerning Muhammad in the sixty-six books of the Bible. When the Koran says that

Muhammad was mentioned in the Torah and the Gospel, and was mentioned by Jesus, the Koran is in error.

One more verse should be dealt with:

> Allah hath purchased of the Believers their persons and their goods; for theirs [in return] is the garden [of paradise]: they fight in his cause, and slay and are slain: a promise binding on Him, in truth through the Torah, the Gospel, and the Koran. And who is more faithful to his covenant than Allah? Then rejoice in the bargain which ye have concluded: that is the achievement supreme.　　　　　(Surat Al-Tawbah 9:111)

Contrary to what the Koran said here, the God of Abraham, Isaac and Jacob did not command the children of Israel to fight so that Judaism would be the only religion. But Allah of Islam commanded them to force people to be Muslims. More importantly, we find no command in the Gospel for Christians to fight. We read that God purchased of the Christians their persons by the blood of Jesus Christ. We read the song which was sung in heaven to the crucified Christ:

> You are worthy to take the scroll and to open its seals, because you were slain, and with your blood you purchased men for God from every tribe and language and people and nation.　　　　　(Revelation 5:9NKJ)

God does not exchange eternal life in paradise with fighting in his cause, or with good works, or any human merits. In fact, in the New Testament God commanded his people:

> Beloved, do not avenge yourselves, but rather give place to wrath; for it is written 'Vengeance is mine, I will repay,' says the Lord. Therefore if your enemy is hungry, feed him; if he is thirsty, give him a drink; for

155

in so doing you will heap coals of fire on his head. Do
not be overcome by evil, but overcome evil with good.
(Romans 12:19-21 NKJ)

**I repeat, God does not command Christians to fight for His
cause. The question is: If the Muslims believe that Islam is
Allah's religion, why don't they leave Allah to protect and
defend his religion?**

When God called Gideon to save Israel from the hand of the
Midianites, He ordered him to tear down the altar of Baal which
his father had and to cut down the wooden image that was beside
it. When the people discovered what Gideon did, they said to his
father, "Bring out your son that he may die, because he has torn
down the altar of Baal." Joash, Gideon's father, answered them:

Would you plead for Baal? If he is a god, let him plead
for himself, because his altar has been torn down...
(Judges 6:31 NKJ)

Certainly, the True and Almighty God does not need anyone to
fight for Him. To fight in the cause of Allah is to make Allah a
powerless torturer and a murderer.

Chapter Sixteen

The Koran Does Not Satisfy Spiritual Needs of Mankind

If the Koran is the true word of God, it must give satisfactory answers to the basic spiritual needs of mankind. If it fails to give these much needed answers, then it is not the true word of God. Are there satisfactory answers in the Koran for these four basic spiritual needs of the human heart?

First: The Need to Love and be Loved

The Koran denies that God is love, rather it introduces Allah who is severe in punishment:

> If only those who do wrong could see, when they will see the torment that all power belongs to Allah and that Allah is severe in punishment. (Surat Al-Baqarah 2:165)

There are many verses in the Koran declaring the severity of Allah. Here are a few of them: Surat Al-Baqarah 2:196, 211; Surat Al-Imran 3:4, 11; Surat Al-Maidah 5:2, 98; Surat Al-Anam 6:124; Surat Al-Anfal 8:13, 25, 48, 52; Surat Al-Rad 13:6.

On the other hand, the New Testament declares that:

God demonstrates His own love toward us, in that while we were still sinners, Christ died for us.

(Romans 5:8 NKJ)

Beloved let us love one another, for love is of God; and everyone who loves is born of God and knows God. He who does not love does not know God, for God is love. In this the love of God was manifested toward us, that God has sent His only begotten Son into the world that we might live through him. In this is love, not that we loved God, but that He loved us and sent His son to be the propitiation for our sins. Beloved if God so loved us, we also ought to love one another. . . If someone says 'I love God,' and hates his brother, he is a liar; for he who does not love his brother whom he has seen, how can he love God whom he has not seen.

(I John 4:7-11, 20 NKJ)

We see the magnificent example of forgiveness and love in Jesus Christ. While Jesus was hanging on the cross in great agony, he prayed for his enemies:

Father, forgive them; for they know not what they do.

(Luke 23:34 NKJ)

Concerning the love of Christ for his own, we read:

. . . having loved His own which were in the world, he loved them unto the end.   (John 13:1 NKJ)

The Apostle John wrote:

We love Him, because He first loved us.(1 John 4:19 NKJ)

158

The Muslims do not believe that "God is love." That name is not mentioned in the Koran among the ninety-nine beautiful names of Allah. You will not find even one verse in the Koran that says that Allah loves sinners. The Koran does not satisfy the need to be loved and to love.

Second: The Need of Total Forgiveness

Sin is a heavy burden. It disturbs man's conscience, robs him of joy and peace and is the cause of many psychological problems. The prophet David cried out:

> For mine iniquities are gone over mine head: as a heavy burden they are too heavy for me.   (Psalm 38:4 NKJ)

Muhammad felt the burden of sin. It was too heavy for him and made him bend under its weight.

> Have We not expounded thee thy breast? And removed from thee thy burden [literally 'iniquity']. The which did gall thy back.   (Surat Al-Inshirah 94:1-3)

The Bible declares that man is a sinner by nature and actions. The Prophet David said:

> Behold, I was shapen in iniquity, and in sin did my mother conceive me.   (Psalm 51:5 NKJ)

The Apostle Paul said:

> For we know that the law is spiritual, but I am carnal, sold under sin.   For what I am doing, I do not understand.   For what I will to do, that I do not practice; but what I hate, that I do.   If, then, I do what I will not to do, I agree with the law that it is good.   But now, it is

159

no longer I who do it, but sin that dwells in me. For I know that in me (that is, in my flesh) nothing good dwells; for to will is present with me, but how to perform what is good I do not find. For the good that I will to do, I do not do; but the evil I will not to do, that I practice. Now if I do what I will not to do, it is no longer I who do it, but sin that dwells in me.

(Romans 7:14-20 NKJ)

The doctrine of original sin or inherited sin has no room in the teaching of Islam. Man, according to the Koran and to Muhammad, is born in a natural state of purity or *fitrah*. Whatever becomes of man after birth is the result of external influences.

This Koranic teaching is false because before there was any external influence Cain, the first son of Adam and Eve, hated his brother Abel and killed him. That act was motivated by his inherited sinful nature.

More importantly, this teaching shows the contradictions in the Koran:

Verily, We created man in the best stature. Then we reduced him to the lowest of low. (Surat At-Tin 95:4-5)

This verse declares that humans are inherently corrupted, and if that is the case, how could humans do any good deeds to please a Holy God? The only way for humans to obtain forgiveness is the shed blood of Jesus Christ on the cross.

Jesus said:

For from within, out of the heart of men, proceed evil thoughts, adulteries, fornications, murders, thefts, covetousness, wickedness, deceit, lasciviousness, an evil eye, blasphemy, pride, foolishness: all these evil things come from within, and defile the man.

(Mark 7:21-23 NKJ)

160

Psychology confirms what the Bible says. There is the "Id:" the dark side of the human psyche where inherited sin resides; the "Ego:" self; and the "Super Ego:" conscience.

The Bible declares that sin is the transgression of the law of God (I John 3:4). It is negligence in doing what is good (James 4:17). It is whatever is not of faith (Romans 14:23). It is an evil or foolish thought (Proverbs 24:9).

In the light of the Biblical definition of sin, we can say with the Apostle Paul:

> . . . All have sinned, and come short of the glory of God.
>
> (Romans 3:23 NKJ)

To deny that all men are sinners, is to deceive ourselves (I John 1:8). The Koran does not offer assurance of forgiveness. Muhammad said to the Muslims:

> Do good things, give alms, but know that none of you will escape judgment by his work. 'Even you Messenger of Allah?' his followers asked. 'Even me, unless Allah bestow his mercy on me.'
>
> (*The Doctrines of Islam*, p 75)

I will explain further in Part III of this book the five Islamic rituals which are called the fundamentals of Islam. Every true Muslim should fulfill them, along with *Jihad*, which is the sixth fundamental. Even with the performance of all these obligations, a Muslim cannot be assured that his sins are forgiven. The Koran declares salvation by works:

> For those things that are good remove those that are evil.
>
> (Surat Hud 11:114)

But at the Day of Judgment scales will be set to weigh the good and evil deeds.

> The balance that day will be true: Those whose scale [of good] will be heavy, will prosper: Those whose scale will be light will find their souls in perdition.
>
> (Surat Al-Araf 7:8, 9)

A Muslim is terrified of the Day of Judgment. He is not sure of the result of weighing his good and evil deeds in the balance.

On April 3, 1991, the Egyptian magazine, *Akher Saa*, recorded a heated debate between four female journalists and Sheik Doctor Abdu-Almonim Al-Nimr who holds a high position at Al-Azhar Islamic University. One of the journalists asked him

> 'Is the hejab [veil] obligatory for women in Islam? If I do not wear the hejab shall I go to hell in spite of my other good deeds. I am talking about the decent woman who does not wear the Hejab?'
>
> 'The ordinances in Islam are many, my daughter, Allah made us accountable to each. It means if you do that ordinance you earn a point. If you neglect one you lose a point. If you pray, you earn a point, if you do not fast you lose a point and so on,' Dr. Al-Nimr answered. Then he continued, 'I did not invent a new theory . . for every man there is a book in which all his good and evil deeds are recorded . . even how do we treat our children.'
>
> The journalist said: 'That means, if I do not wear the Hejab I will not enter the hell fire without taking into account the rest of my good deeds.'
>
> 'My daughter, no one knows who will enter the hell

fire. I might be the first one to enter it' Caliph Abu-Bakr Al-Sadik said: 'I have no trust concerning Allah's schemes, even if one of my feet is inside of paradise who can determine which deed is acceptable and which is not. You do all that you can do, and the accountability is with Allah. You ask him for acceptance.'

(*Akher Saah*, issue 2945)

The Bible clearly shows that sin is rebellion against the Holy God. No one may be granted forgiveness by good deeds. The only way for forgiveness is through faith in the shed blood and the finished work of Jesus Christ on the cross.

> For by grace you have been saved through faith, and that not of yourselves; it is the gift of God, not of works, lest anyone should boast. (Ephesians 2:8, 9 NKJ)

> If you confess with your mouth the Lord Jesus and believe in your heart that God has raised Him from the dead, you will be saved. (Romans 10:9 NKJ)

The Koran offers no assurance of forgiveness, and that is in stark contrast with what is said in the Bible. The Apostle Paul says:

> In Him we have redemption through His blood, the forgiveness of sins, according to the riches of His grace. (Ephesians 1:7 NKJ)

The Apostle John says:

> If we confess our sins, He is faithful and just to forgive us our sins and to cleanse us from all unrighteousness. (I John 1:9 NKJ)

Third: The Need for a Divine Code for a Holy Life

Can we find a code for a holy way of life, a life that pleases God and helps us to deal fairly with our fellow men in the Koran? In his book, *Knowing God*, J.I. Packer wrote on pages 14 and 16:

> Knowing about God is crucially important for the living of our lives. . . Godliness means responding to God's revelation in trust and obedience, faith and worship, prayer and praise, submission and service. Life must be seen and lived in the light of God's Word. This, and nothing else, is true religion.

Man cannot live beyond the attributes of the god he believes in. If his god is cruel he will be cruel. If his god is kind, he will be kind. If his god is holy, he will be holy. The Apostle Peter wrote to the Christians:

> But as he which hath called you is holy, so be ye holy in all manner of conversation; because it is written, be ye holy, for I am holy.   (I Peter 1:15-16)

The Apostle Paul says:

> Be ye therefore followers of God, as dear children; and walk in love, as Christ also hath loved us, and hath given himself for us an offering and a sacrifice to God for a sweet-smelling savour.   (Ephesians 5:1-2)

> For to this you were called, because Christ also suffered for us, leaving us an example, that you should follow His steps. 'Who committed no sin, nor was deceit found in His mouth.'   (I Peter 2:21-22 NKJ)

God is the supreme example for how Christians should live. Now, who is this Allah in the Koran, that the Muslim should imitate? In the Koran:

Allah is the best plotter:

> And when those who disbelieve plot against thee [O Muhammad] to wound thee fatally, or to kill thee or to drive thee forth; they plot, but Allah [also] plotteth; and Allah is the best of plotters. (Surat Al-Anfal 8:30 MPT)

Allah is a deceiver:

> The Hypocrites - they seek to deceive Allah, but it is Allah who deceives them. When they stand up to prayer, they stand without earnestness, to be seen of men, but little do they hold Allah in remembrance.
> (Surat Al-Nisa 4:142)

Allah is a murderer:

> Ye [Muslims] slew them not, but Allah slew them. And thou [Muhammad] threwest not when thou didst throw, but Allah threw, that He might test the believers by a fair test from Him. Lo! Allah is Hearer, Knower.
> (Surat Al-Anfal 8:17 MPT)

Allah is a torturer:

> Fight them and Allah will torture [Author's literal translation] them by your hands, and disgrace them, help you (to victory) over them, heal the breasts of believers.
> (Surat Al-Tawbah 9:14)

165

Allah is unjust and unfair:

> And when we would destroy a township we send
> commandment to its folk who live at ease, and
> afterward they commit abomination therein, and so the
> Word [of doom] hath effect for it, and We annihilate it
> with complete annihilation. (Surat Al-Isra 17:16 MPT)

Allah commands those who live at ease to disobey and commit
abomination, and when they do this he annihilates them. That is
unjust and unfair.

If a Muslim follows the pattern of Allah who is presented in
the Koran, he would plot, deceive, murder, torture non-Muslims,
and be unjust and unfair without any sense of guilt. This is the way
of life the Koran presents to the Muslims, and this is why, when
any Muslim turns to believes that Jesus Christ is his Savior and
Lord, other Muslims will try to persecute, torture and eventually
kill him or her in the name of Allah.

**Fourth: The Need of Total Assurance of Eternal Life in
Heaven**

Does the Koran provide assurance of eternal life with God in
heavenly bliss? The only way by which a Muslim might enter
paradise is to die a martyr's death fighting non-Muslims for the
cause of Allah. The Prophet Muhammad himself was terrified
from the expectation of torture after death.

Sahih Al-Bukhari recorded the following event:

> A Jewess entered Aisha's room and mentioned the
> torture of the dead in the grave and said to her 'may
> Allah save you from the torture of the grave.' Aisha
> [Muhammad's wife] asked him about the torture of the
> grave, 'yes, there is torture in the grave,' he answered.
> Aisha said: 'I never saw the Messenger of Allah praying

after that, but asking for refuge from torture of the grave.' (Vol. 1-2, p 584)

Sahih Al-Bukhari stated also:

Abu-Huraira said 'The Messenger of Allah, was always calling Allah, and saying "I take refuge in you from the torture of the grave, and hell fire, and from the sedition of life and death and from the sedition of the false messiah."' (Sahih Al-Bukhari, Vol. 1, 2 p 585)

The Koran decrees that every Muslim will enter Hell:

Man says: 'What! When I am dead, shall I then be raised up alive?' But does not man call to mind that We created him before out of nothing? So, by thy Lord, without doubt, We shall gather them together, and [also] Satans [with them], then shall We bring them forth on their knees round about Hell; then shall We certainly drag out from every sect all those who were worst in obstinate rebellion against [Allah] Most Gracious. And certainly We know best those who are most worthy of being burned therein. Not one of you but will enter it (Author's literal translation); this is, with thy Lord, a decree which must be accomplished.

(Surat Maryam 19:66-71)

Ibn Katheir the great expositor of the Koran interprets the words "Everyone of you will enter it" by the following stories:

The first story: Abd-Elrazak cited Ibn Ayeena, who cited Ibn Abi Khalid, who cited Qyse Ibn Abi Hazim, who said that Abdullah Ibn Rowaha was putting his head on his wife's lap, he wept, his wife wept, he asked her: 'Why do you weep?' 'I saw you weeping so I wept' she answered. He said, 'I remembered what Allah said 'Not one of you but will enter it (Hell).' I do not know if I will escape from it or not.'

The second story: Ibn Qurair cited Abu-Kareeb, who cited Ibn Yaman, who cited Malik Ibn Magul, who cited Abu-Ishacc, who said: Abu Mysarah used to say every night before he goes to bed, 'I wish that my mother had not given birth of me,' then weep. Someone asked him 'Why do you weep Abu Mysarah?' 'The Koran told us that we shall enter Hell, but we were not told that we will get out of it.'

The third story: Abdu-Allah Ibn Al-Mubarak cited Al-Hasan Al-Basari: A man said to his brother: do you know that you will enter Hell fire? 'Yes,' his brother answered. 'Do you know if you will get out of it?' he asked. 'No' his brother answered. 'Why do you laugh then?' From that time on he was never seen laughing till he died.

(Ibn Katheir on Surat Maryam, Vol. 3, p 129)

There is no hope for the Muslim to escape Hell's fire.
This is in stark contrast with what Christ said in the Bible:

Most assuredly, I say to you, he who hears My word and believes in Him who sent Me has everlasting life, and shall not come into judgment, but has passed from death into life.   (John 5:24 NKJ)

The true Christian is completely assured that he or she will never enter Hell:

There is therefore now no condemnation to them which are in Christ Jesus, who walk not after the flesh, but after the Spirit. (Romans 8:1 NKJ)

These things have I written unto you that believe on the name of the Son of God; that ye may know that ye have eternal life. (I John 5:13)

Chapter Eighteen

The Koran Teaches Polytheism

Polytheism is the belief in, or worship of, more than one god. Muslims accuse Christians of being polytheistic because they believe in a triune God: the Father, the Son, and the Holy Spirit. They ignore the fact that Christians believe in one true God who is triune.

On the contrary, our study of the Koran will clearly show that it teaches polytheism. But before we mention the Koranic verses which teach polytheism, an important question should be answered: from where did we get our knowledge about the true and living god?

The answer is from one of two sources.

First, we can imagine God with our foolish hearts and darkened minds, which is what the pagans did. This is what the Apostle Paul said concerning the pagans:

> Because that, when they knew God, they glorified Him not as God, neither were thankful; but became vain in their imaginations, and their foolish heart was darkened. Professing themselves to be wise, they became fools, and changed the glory of the incorruptible God into an image made like corruptible man, and to birds, and four-footed beasts, and creeping things... who changed the truth of God into a lie, and worshipped and served

171

the creature more than the Creator, who is blessed forever, Amen.   (Romans 1:21-25)

Secondly, we can know the true God by a special revelation from Him, which Christians have received in the Bible. We take God at His word and believe His revelation of Himself. God is everlasting, having no beginning; therefore He must be self-sufficient.

No one can fully comprehend God. The finite human mind cannot contain the infinite God. If we could contain God in our minds, he would no longer be God.

The Bible Reveals a Triune God

The great and true God is eternal, infinite and everlasting. His attributes must also be eternal and everlasting. He should not lose any of His attributes nor acquire new ones. God is immutable in wisdom, in power, in holiness, in justice, in goodness and in truth.

According to the Bible, God is called Father (Malachi 2:10, John 8:41). Eternal fatherhood demands eternal sonship. In the New Testament we read that God is love (1 John 4:16) and love demands someone to be loved. God talks, hears and sees.

Here we have many important questions concerning God that need answers. Before God created angels and men, with whom was he talking? Whom did He hear? Whom did He see? Most importantly, whom did He love? These questions cannot be answered unless we believe in a triune God.

The only true, logical and perfect God must be a triune God to exercise His attributes with no need of His creation. This is the confession of every true Christian, which was expressed in the Westminster Confession of Faith, chapter 2, in the following words.

There is but one living and true God, who is infinite in being and perfection... God hath all life, glory, goodness, blessedness, in and of himself; and is alone in and unto himself all-sufficient, not standing in need of any creatures which he hath made... In the unity of the Godhead there be three persons, of one substance, power, and eternity: God the Father, God the Son, and God the Holy Ghost.

The Old Testament uses the plural name of Deity:

And God said, let us make man in our image, after our likeness... so God created man in His own image.
(Genesis 1:26-27 NKJ)

And the Lord God said behold, the man is become as one of us. (Genesis 3:22 NKJ)

Also I heard the voice of the Lord, saying, whom shall I send, and who will go for us? (Isaiah 6:8 NKJ)

Here we have to notice the two words, "I" and "us." For the One who says "I" says also "us." That indicates the oneness of the triune God.

It is of great importance to notice that God never used the word "we" or "us" to magnify himself in the Bible. It was not the custom of the kings of the great empires to use the word "we" to magnify themselves.

King Nebuchadnezzar, the Emperor of the great Babylonian empire, issued a decree saying, "Therefore I make a decree..." (Daniel 3:29). King Darius issued a decree saying, "I make a decree..." (Daniel 6:26). So when God uses the words "we" or "us," it is not to magnify Himself but to indicate that He is a triune God.

In the book of Numbers, there is a clear demonstration of the triune God. The prophet Balaam came to King Balak upon the request of the King to curse Israel. In that story we read three verses which clearly show the triune God.

The first verse: And God met Balaam
The second verse: And the LORD met Balaam
The third verse : ... and the Spirit of God came upon him.

(Numbers 23: 4, 16; 24:2 NKJ)

Here, we see God the Father, the Lord Jesus Christ, and God the Holy Spirit in clear manifestation. Then we read in Psalm 110:1:

The LORD said unto my Lord, sit thou at my right hand, until I make thine enemies thy footstool.

Jesus asked the Pharisees concerning this passage saying:

'What think ye of Christ? Whose son is He?' They say unto him, 'the son of David.' He saith unto them, 'how then doth David in spirit call him Lord, saying, "the LORD said unto my Lord, sit thou on my right hand, till I make thine enemies thy footstool."'

(Matthew 22:42-44)

The only right answer for this passage is the belief in the triune God. For in this passage we see "The LORD" is God the Father and "my Lord" is God the Son. David, by the Spirit, called Him my Lord and that Spirit is the "Holy Spirit." Again, we read in the book of Proverbs:

Who has ascended into heaven or descended? Who has gathered the wind in his fists? Who has bound the waters in a garment? Who has established all the ends

174

of the earth? What is his name, and what is His son's name, if you know.   (Proverbs 30:4 NKJ)

Dr. Charles Bridges says in his commentary on Proverbs:

. . . and no one knows the Son except the Father. Nor does anyone know the Father except the Son. . . (Matthew 11:27 NKJ). Yet there is a Son in the Eternal Godhead; a Son not begotten in time, but from eternity (Proverbs 8:22-30); his name therefore, not as some would have it, a component part of his humiliation, but the manifestation of his Godhead: co-existent with his Father in the same ineffable nature, yet personally distinct. What is his name? and what is his Son's name? Sovereignty-Omnipresence-Omnipotence are His. He too controls the winds and water, and establishes the earth...   (pp 591, 592)

Concerning Christ, the Son of God, we read in the epistle to the Hebrews:

God, who at sundry times and in diverse manners spake in time past unto the fathers by the prophets, hath in these last days spoken unto us by his Son, whom he hath appointed heir of all things, by whom also he made the worlds; Who being the brightness of his glory, and the express image of his person, and upholding all things by the word of his power, when he had by himself purged our sins, sat down on the right hand of the Majesty on high...   (Hebrews 1:1-3)

The early Christians' Bible was the Old Testament, the book of the Jewish people who believe in monotheism. Clearly, the plurality of God's being was still consistent with the Jewish monotheistic doctrines.

175

We come now to the New Testament. On the occasion of the baptism of Jesus by John the Baptist, we see clearly the triune God.

> When He had been baptized, Jesus came up immediately from the water; and behold, the heavens were opened to him, and he saw the Spirit of God descending like a dove and alighting upon him. And suddenly a voice came from heaven saying, 'This is my beloved son, in whom I am well pleased.'
>
> (Matthew 3:16-17 NKJ)

In this scene we have:

♦ The Father, speaking from heaven, calling Jesus "My beloved Son."
♦ The Son, Jesus Christ, coming up from the water.
♦ The Holy Spirit descending like a dove from heaven and alighting upon the Son.

The Koran also testifies to the existence of the Holy Spirit as a separate manifestation of the godhead.

> We gave Jesus the Son of Mary evidence, clear [signs] and strengthened him with the Holy Spirit.
>
> (Surat Al-Baqarah 2:87)

> To Jesus the Son of Mary We gave clear [signs], and strengthened him with the Holy Sprit.
>
> (Surat Al-Baqarah 2:253)

Ibn Katheir cited Ibn Abbas who said, "The Holy Spirit is the Greatest Name with which Jesus was able to raise the dead." Ibn Katheir also cited Al Zamakhshari who said, "The Holy Spirit here means the Spirit of Jesus Himself" (Ibn Katheir, Volume 1, pp 117-118).

The triune God is the God revealed in the Bible. This profound mystery of the Godhead is summed up in the words of Dr. Boardman, a great theologian:

- The Father is all the fullness of the Godhead invisible.

No one has seen God at any time.   (John 1:18 NKJ)

- The Son is all the fullness of the Godhead manifested.

In the beginning was the Word, and the Word was with God, and the Word was God...and the Word became flesh and dwelt among us, and we beheld His glory as of the only begotten of the Father, full of grace and truth.   (John 1:1-14 NKJ)

No one has seen God at any time. The only begotten Son, who is in the bosom of the father, He has declared Him.   (John 1:18 NKJ)

- The Holy Spirit is all the fullness of the Godhead acting immediately upon the creation.

But as it is written: 'eye has not seen, nor ear heard, nor have entered into the heart of man the things which God has prepared for those who love him.' But God has revealed them to us through His Spirit. For the Spirit searches all things, yea the deep things of God.
          (1 Corinthians 2:9-10 NKJ)

Again, in the last chapter of the last book of the Bible we see the triune God in eternity:

And he showed me a pure river of water of life, clear as crystal, proceeding from the throne of God and of the Lamb. (Revelation 22:1 NKJ)

1. We see the Holy Spirit represented allegorically as "a pure river of water of life, clear as crystal, proceeding from the throne of God and of the Lamb." Christ spoke of the Holy Spirit as "rivers of living water." Here are his words:

> In the last day, that great day of the feast, Jesus stood and cried, saying, 'If any man thirst, let him come unto me and drink. He that believeth on me, as the scripture hath said, out of his belly shall flow rivers of living water.' (But this spake he of the Spirit, which they that believe on him should receive: *for the Holy Ghost* was not yet given; because that Jesus was not yet glorified.
> (John 7:37-39)

Moreover, that pure river of water proceeds from the throne of God and of the Lamb. The Bible declares that the Holy Spirit is the spirit of the Father and the spirit of Christ. That is clear from the words of the Apostle Paul to the Christians in Rome:

> But you are not in the flesh but in the spirit, if indeed the Spirit of God dwells in you. *Now if anyone does not have the Spirit of Christ* (Author's Emphasis) he is not His. (Romans 8:9 NKJ)

> And because you are sons, God has sent forth the spirit of His Son into your hearts, crying out 'Abba, Father.'
> (Galatians 4:6 NKJ)

2. We see God the Father on the throne.

3. We see Christ sharing the same throne with the Father.

If Christ is not God the Son, He would not share the throne in eternity with God the Father.

> I am the Lord, that is my name; and My glory I will not give to another.　　　　　　　　　　　(Isaiah 42:8 NKJ)

In eternity we shall see the triune God face to face (Revelation 22:4).

Though Muslims accuse Christians of worshipping three gods, the Koran itself does not say this. Instead, it clearly states that if God had a son, He should be worshipped:

> Say (O Muhammad) if the Most Gracious (Allah) has a son I am the first to worship.　(Surat Al-Zukhruf 43:81)

The Arabic words are:

> *Kul, (O Muhammad) in kana lilrahmani waladon faana awalo Al-Abedeen.*

That Koranic verse obliged Muslims to worship Christ if there is a proof that He is the Son of God. The proof is authentic and clear.

In addition, the Koran has incarnated Allah in many of its verses:

1 The Koran gave God a face

> Everyone upon it will disappear while your *Lord's face* [Author's emphasis] will remain full of majesty and splendor. (Surat Al-Rahman 55:26-27, T.B. Irving, *The First American Version of the Koran*)

2. The Koran gave God a hand.

> Lo! those who swear allegiance unto thee [Muhammad], swear allegiance only unto Allah. *The Hand of Allah is above their hand.*
>
> (Surat Al-Fath 48:10 MPT)

3. The Koran gave God an eye.

When the Koran mentions Moses' mother, it says:

> Behold! We sent to thy mother, by inspiration, the message: 'Throw [the child] into the chest, and throw [the chest] into the river The river will cast him up on the bank, and he will be taken up by one who is an enemy to Me and an enemy to him:' But I endued thee with love from Me. And [this] in order that thou mayest be reared under Mine eye.
>
> (Surat Ta Ha: 20:38-39)

4. The Koran incarnated Allah in a lamp.

> Allah is the Light of the heavens and the earth. The similitude of His light is as a niche wherein is a lamp. The lamp is in a glass. The glass is as it were a shining star. (This lamp is) kindled from a blessed tree, an olive neither of the East nor of the West, whose oil would almost glow forth (of itself) though no fire touched it. Light upon light, Allah guideth unto His light whom He will. And Allah speaketh to mankind in allegories, for Allah is Knower of all things.
>
> (Surat An-Noor 24:35 MPT)

Allah and his light cannot be separated, the Koran incarnated his light in a lamp set in a window closed from the outside, thus

180

declaring that the light of Allah could be incarnated in a thing we can see, and at the same time he is invisible in a window closed.

5. The Koran seated God on the throne.

> He it is who created the heavens and the earth in six days: then he mounted the throne.
>
> (Surat Al-Hadid 57:4 MPT)

The Koran gave Allah a face, a hand, and an eye, incarnated him in a lamp and seated Him on the throne. This is incarnation, however, Muslims may say this is only allegorical.

Such expressions in the Koran, where it is said that God has a face, a hand, and an eye are to be understood only in the sense that those human expressions are used in order to bring the infinite within the comprehension of the finite. **Incarnation is necessary for human beings to comprehend at least a glimpse of the Divine.**

Christians accept the Biblical revelation concerning the character of God and the incarnation of Christ, the eternal Son of God. It is the only source for knowing the true God - the triune God.

Polytheism In The Koran

God is the supreme Being, no one is greater than Him. No one is associated with Him. In the book of Hebrews we read:

> For when God made a promise to Abraham, because *He could swear by no one greater, He swore by Himself.*
>
> (Hebrews 6:13 NKJ, Author's emphasis)

> For men indeed swear by the greater, and an oath for confirmation is for them an end of all dispute.
>
> (Hebrews 6:16 NKJ)

Every time God swears in the Bible, He swears by Himself because no one is greater than Him.

> *By Myself I have sworn, says the Lord...* in your seed all the nations of the earth shall be blessed.
>
> (Genesis 22:16-18 NKJ)

> *I have sworn by Myself;* the word has gone out of My mouth in righteousness, and shall not return, that to Me every knee shall bow. . . (Isaiah 45:23 NKJ)

> *I swear by Myself,* says the Lord. (Jeremiah 22:5 NKJ)

The true and supreme God could not swear by someone else, let alone anything else. So He swore by Himself.

Christians are not polytheists but the Muslims are. I say that, not to ridicule Muslims, but to set the record straight. Two issues are very clear in the Koran.

> First, the Koran puts Allah in a lesser position than his creation.

> Second, the Koran exalted the prophet Muhammad, even to the place of deity.

First: the Koran puts Allah in a lesser position than His creation since He swore by many things other than Himself.

This is polytheism, which the Muslims call "shirk" in Arabic. Allah swore in the Koran twenty-four times, by the Koran, the angels, the winds, the mount, the star, the pen, the moon, the night, the dawn, the day of resurrection, the sky, the day of judgment, the even and odd numbers, the sun, the earth, the soul, the creation of male and female, the fig, the olive and the city of Mecca. Are these things greater than Allah that He would swear by them? What is the value of the pen, the sun, the moon, the fig or the olive, compared to Allah?

Suppose that you are called as a witness in court, and instead of putting your hand on the Bible or the Koran and saying that you will tell the truth and nothing but the truth, you say, "Your honor, I swear by the fig, the olive, the pen, and the star to tell the truth." Will the judge accept your testimony?

For the Koran to declare that Allah swore by things He had created is to teach heresy and clear polytheism.

1. Allah swore by the Koran five times.

By the Koran full of wisdom.   (Surat Ya Sin 36:2)

By the Koran, full of admonition.   (Surat Sad 38:1)

By the Book that makes things clear, we have made it a Koran in Arabic, that ye may be able to understand.
(Surat Al-Zukhruf 43:2)

By the Book that makes things clear.
(Surat Al-Dukhan 44:2)

By the Glorious Koran.   (Surat Qaf 50:1)

2. Allah swore by different ranks of angels or probably men

By those who arrange themselves in ranks. Those who so are strong in repelling [evil]. Those who thus proclaim the message of Allah.
(Surat Al-Saffat 37:1-4)

183

By the [angels] who tear out [the souls of the wicked with violence] by those who gently draw out [the souls of the blessed] and by those who glide along [on errands of mercy], and then press forward as in race, then arrange to do [the commands of their Lord].

(Surat Al-Naziat 79:1-5)

3. Allah swore by the winds.

By the [winds] that scatter broadcast, and those that lift and bear away heavy weights, and those that flow with ease and gentleness, and those that distribute the affair.

(Surat Al-Zhariyat 51:1-4)

By the [winds] sent forth one after another.

(Surat Al-Mursalat 77:1)

4. Allah swore by the mount, the inscribed book, the Kaaba, and the ocean.

By the mount, by the book inscribed in a parchment unfolded, by the much-frequented house [Kaaba] by the canopy raised high and by the ocean filled with swell. (Surat Al-Tur 52:1-6)

It is of great importance to notice in this verse that Allah swore by the Kaaba, while it was still the shrine of 360 idols.

5. Allah swore by the star.

By the star when it goes down. (Surat Al-Najm 53:1)

6. Allah swore by the pen.

By the pen and by the record which [men] write.

(Surat Al-Qalam 68:1)

7. *Allah swore by the moon, the night, and* the dawn.

Nay, verily: By the moon, and by the night as it retreateth, and by the dawn as it shineth forth.
(Surat Al-Muddathir 74:32-34)

8. *Allah swore by the Resurrection Day and the self-reproaching soul.*

I do swear by the Resurrection Day. And I do swear by the self-reproaching soul. (Surat Al-Qiyamah 75:1, 2)

9. *Allah swore by the sky, the Day of Judgment, and by one that witnesses.*

By the sky, with its constellations, by the promised day [of judgment]. By one that witnesses and the subject of witness. (Surat Al-Buruj 85:1-3)

10. *Allah swore again by the sky.*

By the sky and the night-visitant. (Surat Al-Tariq 86:1)

11. *Allah swore by the dawn, the ten nights, by the even and odd, and by the night.*

By the dawn, by the ten nights; by the even and odd [contrasted]. And by the night when it passeth away.
(Surat Al-Fajr 89:1-4)

12. *Allah swore by the city (Mecca).*

Nay I do swear by this city. (Surat Al-Balad 90:1)

185

13. Allah swore by the sun, the moon, the day, the night, the firmament, the earth, and the soul.

By the sun and his [glorious] splendour: by the moon as she follows him; by the day as it shows up [the sun's] glory; by the night as it conceals it; by the firmament and its expanse: by the soul, and the proportion and order given to it; and its inspiration as to its wrong and its right. (Surat Al-Shams 91:1-8)

14. Allah swore by the night, the day, and the creation of male and female.

By the night as it conceals [the light]; by the day as it appears in glory; by the creation of male and female.
(Surat Al-Layl 92:1-3)

15. Allah swore by the morning light and by the night.

By the glorious morning light, and by the night when it is still, thy Guardian-Lord hath not forsaken thee, nor is He displeased. (Surat Ad-Duha 93:1-3)

Ahmad Abdelwahab, citing Muhammad's biographers, wrote in his book, *Prophecy and Prophets*, the following:

Revelations ceased from coming to Muhammad for a long time (some say two years); some of Muhammad's friends may have said to him 'It seems that your Allah has forsaken you.' The prophet passed through a terrible spiritual crisis. The biographers of Muhammad say: 'During that time Muhammad thought to commit suicide by throwing himself from the top of Mount

186

Hira, or Mount Abi-Qubees, because he felt desperate and lonely.' *(Prophecy and Prophets*, pp 177-178)

Could you imagine the Prophet Muhammad thinking of committing suicide? At that time Allah swore to Muhammad "by the glorious morning light, and by the night that He had not forsaken him, nor was He displeased with him." Who is this Allah, who swore by the glorious morning light, and by the night? How could anyone believe in a promise based on this oath?

16. Allah swore by the fig, the olive, Mount Sinai, and the city of Mecca.

By the fig and the olive, and Mount Sinai, and this City of Security [Mecca].   (Surat Al-Tin 95:1-3)

17. Allah swore by the steeds, which, according to the commentators of the Koran, might be camels, war-horses, or spiritual forces.

By the [Steeds] that run, with panting [breath] and strike sparks of fire, and push home the charge in the morning, and raise the dust in clouds the while, and penetrate forthwith into the midst [of the foe].
(Surat Al-Adiyat 100:1-5)

18. Allah swore by time through the ages.

By the time, verily man is in loss.
(Surat Al-Asr 103:1-2)

Does not the association of Allah with these objects and creatures represent polytheism?

Second: the Koran associated Muhammad with Allah and exalted him even to the place of deity.

In Surat Al-Kahf we read:

> Allah... makes none to share in His Decision and His Rule. (Surat Al-Kahf 18:26)

But in another verse the Koran positioned Muhammad as a counselor with Allah. As I mentioned before, Muhammad wanted Zainab Bint Gahsh to marry his adopted son, Zaid. When Zainab refused Muhammad's proposal, the Koran declared that this proposal was the decision of Allah and Muhammad.

> It is not fitting for a believer, man or woman, when a matter has been decided by Allah and His Messenger, to have any option about their decision. If anyone disobeys Allah and His Messenger, he is indeed on a clearly wrong path. (Surat Al-Ahzab 33:36)

The Bible declares that God does not accept any human counseling:

> Oh, the depth of the riches both of the wisdom and knowledge of God! How unsearchable are His judgments, and His ways past finding out! For who hath known the mind of the Lord? Or who has been His counselor? (Romans 11:33-34 NKJ)

For Muhammad to associate himself as a counselor with Allah is clearly polytheism. Again we read in the Koran:

> Verily, those who give pledge to you (O Muhammad) they are giving pledge to Allah... (Surat Al-Fath 48:10)

He who obeys the Messenger (Muhammad) has indeed obeyed Allah... (Surat Al-Nisa 4:80)

In these verses we see that the Koran places Muhammad on equal footing with Allah. Moreover, we read in the Koran:

And the mosques for Allah (Alone) so invoke not anyone along with Allah. (Surat Al-Jinn 72:18 HK)

But, if you listen to the *Moazin* (the man who calls Muslims to prayer from the top of the mosque) you will hear him saying,

Allaho Akbar, Ashado an la-ilaha illa Allah, washado anna Muhammadan rasoulo Allah.

God is greater, I testify that there is no God but Allah, I testify that Muhammad is the Messenger of Allah.

With that call to prayer the *Moazin* associates Muhammad with Allah, five times a day. More importantly, the Koran positions Muhammad as a center of prayer and praise in heaven and on earth.

When I debated Dr. Jamal Badawi on February 1, 1988 at Saint Mary's University, in Halifax, N.S. Canada, Dr. Badawi asked, "How could Christ be God and pray on the cross, 'My God, my God, why have you forsaken Me?'" (Matthew 27:46 NKJ).

"Dr. Badawi," I answered, "The Koran says that Allah and His angels pray on the prophet. 'O ye who believe pray on him and salute him with a worthy salutation'" (Surat Al-Ahzab 33:56 Author's literal translation).

"If Allah in heaven is praying on the prophet," I continued, "the question is, 'to whom is Allah praying?'" Why do Muslims doubt the deity of Jesus Christ because He prayed to God when He was on the cross? Dr. Badawi did not answer my question.

If the Muslim accepts the Biblical revelation of God he would believe that God is a triune God, he would understand that the one who was incarnated in the person of Jesus Christ is God the Son, and that Jesus "took the form of a servant, came in the likeness of men, and being found in appearance as a man, He humbled Himself and became obedient to the point of death, even the death of the cross" (Philippians 2:7,8 NKJ). Then the Muslim would know that Jesus, as a servant, cried out to God, "My God, my God, why have you forsaken me?" And he would understand why Christ said "for my Father is greater than I" (John 14:28). The Father was not incarnated, nor crucified, but the Son was.

Charles Haddon Spurgeon commented on that verse saying:

> In order that the sacrifice of Christ might be complete, it pleased the Father to forsake his well-beloved Son. Sin was laid on Christ, so God must turn away his face from the Sin-Bearer. To be deserted of his God was the climax of Christ's grief, the quintessence of his sorrow. See here the distinction between the martyrs and their Lord; in their dying agonies they have been divinely sustained; but Jesus, suffering as the Substitute for sinners, was forsaken of God. Those saints who have known what it is to have their Father's face hidden from them even for a brief space, can scarcely imagine the suffering that wrung from our Savior the agonizing cry, 'My God, my God, why has thou forsaken me?'
>
> (*Matthew: The King has Come*, p 406)

Nevertheless, the first word Christ uttered while on the cross was:

> Father forgive them, for they do not know what they do.
> (Luke 23:34 NKJ)

Then he committed his human spirit to the Father, saying:

Father, into your hands I commit My spirit.

(Luke 23:46 NAS)

He was always the Son calling on His Father. In addition, He offered that prayer, "My God, My God, why have You forsaken me?" to demonstrate that He was the one whom the prophet David spoke about in Psalm 22. All the prophecies in that Psalm were fulfilled perfectly in Christ when He died on the cross.

We have to see in Christ's prayer Jesus as the Son of Man, praying to God the Father, and, in that hour of darkness, God is still the God Christ reveals.

But in the Koran Allah, who is absolute, prays to himself on the prophet. The Muslims accept that. They should not question Christ's deity because of his prayer on the cross. **More importantly, if Allah and his angels in heaven are praying on the Prophet, and on earth Muslims are praying on the prophet, then Muhammad is the center of praise and worship in heaven and on earth.** This is also the conclusion arrived at by some intellectual Muslims.

The daily Egyptian Newspaper, *Alwafd*, (September 9, 1992), recorded the following question sent to Sheik Hassan Mamoun, one of the prominent clerics in Egypt:

What is your judgment concerning prayer on Muhammad, the messenger of Allah? Doesn't that mean worshipping him?

Muslims never mention the name of Muhammad without saying peace be upon him or in Arabic *Salla Allaho Alihe Wasalaam* or *Alayhe Alsalaato Wasalaam* which means "Allah's prayer and salutation on him." Look at any Islamic inscribed sign, and you will read the name "Allah" at the same level with the name "Muhammad."

Mahmoud Al-Saadani, the well known Egyptian journalist, wrote a critical article in the August 9, 1996 issue of *Almussawar*, an Egyptian weekly magazine, saying:

> On the memorial birthday of the Messenger [Muhammad] I listened to the Friday message on an Arabic television. The speaker was a young man... he said while shedding tears over the decline of Muslims in this age... 'the only cause for the Muslims' demise in this age is that they do not glorify the master of creatures, Muhammad Ibn Abdullah, as they should glorify this glorious Messenger, who is the beginning and the last of all creation... the early Muslims used to glorify the Prophet to the point of drinking his urine...'

This is clear polytheism in Islam.

Do you see how the Koran and the Muslims exalt Muhammad, even to the place of deity, while he lived a sinful life, and rejected the biblical revelation which confirm that Christ is the sinless savior, the eternal Son of God?

Some Christians think the Allah of Islam is the same God revealed to Jews and Christians in the Bible. They refer to Judaism, Christianity, and Islam, as the three great monotheistic religions.

The Koran declares to the Jews and the Christians:

> Our God and your God is one.
>
> (Surat Al-Ankabut 29:46)

> Say (O Muhammad to the Jews and Christians), Dispute you with us about Allah while He is our Lord and your Lord? (Surat Al-Baqarah 2:139)

Here we have an important question: If Allah of the Muslims is the same God of the Jews and Christians, why do

Jews and Christians need Islam at all? Why do the Muslim clerics propagate Islam to Christians in Christian countries? The fact is that the Allah of Islam is not the same God as the God of the Christians and the Jews revealed in the Bible.

Clearly, the Koran and Islamic traditions fall short of monotheism. Instead, they teach polytheism by their representation of Allah swearing by lesser creatures and objects, and by raising the level of created things to that of Allah as well as associating the praise and superiority of Muhammad with that of Allah.

Chapter Nineteen

The Bible and the Koran

The Bible was written in a period of 1500 years by forty different writers but with amazing unity among its sixty-six inspired books. It is the story of the plan of God for man, from his fall and deterioration to his redemption and glorification.

The late Robert Chapman of England wrote the following statement concerning the Bible:

> This book contains the mind of God, the state of man, the way of salvation, the doom of sinners, and the happiness of believers. Its doctrines are holy, its precepts are binding, its histories are true, and its decisions are immutable. Read it to be wise, believe it to be safe, and practice it to be holy. It contains light to direct you, food to support you, and comfort to cheer you. It is the traveler's map, the pilgrim's staff, the pilot's compass, the soldier's sword, and the Christian's charter. Here paradise is restored, heaven opened, and the gates of hell disclosed. Christ is its grand subject, our good its design, and the glory of God its end. It should fill the memory, test the heart, and guide the feet. Read it slowly, frequently, prayerfully. It is a mine of wealth, a paradise of glory and a river of pleasure. It is given you in life, will be opened at the judgment, and be remembered forever. It involves the

highest responsibility, rewards the greatest labor, and condemns all who trifle with its sacred contents.

(*The Bible Has the Answer*, p 31)

Contrary to the Koran, the Bible is arranged in chronological order. It begins with the book of Genesis and ends with the book of Revelation. Dr. Lehman Strauss wrote in the introduction of his book, *The Book of The Revelation*, pp 17, 18:

> One careful reading of the Bible will convince anyone that this inspired volume forms a complete cycle. Genesis is the book of commencement; Revelation is the book of consummation. Revelation is an excellent finish to the divine library.
>
> Genesis - The commencement of Heaven and earth (1:1)
> Revelation - The consummation of Heaven and earth (21:1)
>
> Genesis - The entrance of sin and the curse (3:1-19)
> Revelation - The end of sin and the curse (21:27; 22:3)
>
> Genesis - The dawn of Satan and his activities (3:1-7)
> Revelation - The doom of Satan and his activities (20:10)
>
> Genesis - The tree of life is relinquished (2:9; 3:24)
> Revelation - The tree of life is regained (22:2)
>
> Genesis - Death makes its entrance (2:17; 5:5)
> Revelation - Death makes its exit (21:4)
>
> Genesis - Sorrow begins (3:16)
> Revelation - Sorrow is banished (21:4)

The first book of the Bible knows no completion apart from the last book of the Bible, and all the rest of the sixty-four books in between are dependent upon each other. No one book in the Bible is an independent contribution to be divorced from the other books. Dr. Sidlow Baxter of Scotland commented in one of his sermons on the first five books of the Bible. Here is what he said:

Genesis: The earth became ruin through the sin of man.
Exodus: Redemption through the blood of the lamb.
Leviticus: Communion with God through the sacrificial offerings.
Numbers: Direction to the people of God through the pillar of cloud by day and the pillar of fire by night.
Deuteronomy: Destination, the faithfulness of God demonstrated in leading his people to the promised land.

Moreover, the focal point of every book of the Bible is Christ the Savior.

In Genesis: Christ the seed of the woman and the ram offered in the place of Isaac (Genesis 3:15 & 22:13)
In Exodus: Christ the Passover Lamb (Exodus 12:6, 7)
In Leviticus: Christ the High Priest (Leviticus 9:7, 24)
In Numbers: Christ the stricken rock and the bronze serpent (Numbers 20:11 and 21:8)
In Deuteronomy: Christ the prophet like Moses (Deuteronomy 18:15)

We continue in every book to see Christ. From the book of Isaiah where we see him as the suffering Redeemer (Isaiah 53), to the book of Jonah where we see the buried and risen Christ (Jonah 1:17 and 2:10), to the book of Micah where we see Christ born in Bethlehem (Micah 5:2) until the book of Revelation where we see Christ as the Lamb slain, the King of Kings and Lord of Lords (Revelation 19:15).

Could that magnificent book, with that wonderful design, be written apart from inspiration of the Holy Spirit?

In the great library of the Bible we read books dealing with the question: "Why do righteous people suffer?" We find the answer in the book of Job. We read Ecclesiastes to discover that life under the sun is "vanity of vanities." We read Psalms to see believers talking to God in an intimate fellowship. We read also prophetic Psalms and discover new attributes of the Eternal God.

The Bible is a solid foundation, upon which you can safely build your faith. The Bible is like a piece of gold. It carries in itself the proofs of its purity and authenticity. I will mention the proofs without elaboration:

1. The prophetic proof
2. The scientific proof
3. The source of commandments proof
4. The Messiah as the focal point of Scripture proof
5. The archaeological proof
6. The experiential proof
7. The amazing unity proof
8. The Koranic proof of the Bible

(For a complete discussion of these proofs, order the author's book, *God's Last Messenger*).

This is not the case with the Koran. Its opening surah is a prayer which must be repeated five times a day by every Muslim, followed by Surat Al-Baqarah which contains many verses that were abrogated in other surahs, and it ends with the following surah:

In the name of Allah, the Beneficent, the Merciful. Say: I seek refuge in the Lord of mankind, the King of mankind, The Ilah of mankind, from the evil of the sneaking whisperer, who whispereth in the hearts of mankind, of the jinn and of mankind.

(Surat Al-Nas 114:1-6 MPT)

This is how the Koran ends, with fear of *jinn*, fear of the sneaking whisperer, and of men, while the Bible ends with the hope of the second coming of Christ and with the grace of Christ on the believers (Revelation 22:20-21). The Koran is completely different from the Bible in its language, style, and setting.

The Bible was Never Corrupted

A major stumbling block preventing Muslims from believing in the Lord Jesus Christ to obtain God's free gift of forgiveness and eternal life is their belief in the false claim that the Bible was corrupted by the Jews and Christians and that the Koran abrogated the Bible.

For Muslims to believe this erroneous claim is to insult the Koran itself, for it declares that the Bible was given by God to the prophets and the apostles and demands the belief in its authenticity.

Because of the many contradictions between the Bible and the Koran, and because the Bible does not mention any prophecies concerning Muhammad, Muslim scholars claim that the Bible has been altered and corrupted. Such a claim is in opposition to several clear verses of the Koran.

First: the Koran states explicitly that the Old and the New Testaments are the inspired word of God.

Here we have to emphasize the fact that we have at least five thousand ancient manuscripts of the entire Bible which are called codices. These codices go back to the year 350 A.D. that is almost 250 years before the birth of Muhammad. One of these ancient codices is kept in the British Museum in London, others are kept in France and in the Vatican at Rome.

1. The Codex Vaticanus (325-350 AD) is kept at the Vatican Library in Rome.
2. The Codex Sinaiticus (350 AD) is kept in the British Museum.

3. The Codex Alexandrinus (400 AD) is kept in the British Museum.
4. The Codex Ephraemi (400 AD) is kept in the French Library.
5. The Codex Bezac (450 AD) is kept in the Cambridge Library.

Because these ancient codices were in existence before the Koran, which came more than six hundred years after Christ, what the Koran declares in its verses is a proof that these codices are inspired by God.

The Old Testament

This is what the Koran declares concerning the Old Testament which was in the hands of the Jews and the Christians.

♦ We gave Moses the Book, and made it a guide to the children of Israel...   (Surat Al-Isra 17:2)

♦ We did indeed aforetime give the Book to Moses: Be not then in doubt of its reaching [thee]: And We made it a guide to the children of Israel.
(Surat Al-Sajdah 32:23)

♦ How can they choose you as a judge when they have the Torah, which contains God's judgment?...We have sent down the Torah containing guidance and light. (Surat Al-Maidah 5:43, 44 T.B. Irving - *The First American Version of the Koran*)

Would Allah refer those Jews to a corrupted Torah?

It is clear from these Koranic verses that it was not necessary for the Jews to go to Muhammad for judgment because they had the Torah which came down from heaven and contained all the needed guidance and light. They had no need for Muhammad or his Koran.

The New Testament

Again we read in the Koran:

> And had Jesus the son of Mary follow in their footsteps in order to confirm what had come before him from the Torah and we gave him the Gospel which contains guidance and light, to confirm what he already had in the Old Testament, and as guidance and lesson for those who do their duty. Let the people of the Gospel judge by what God has sent in it. Those who do not judge by what God has sent down are perverse.
>
> (Surat Al-Maidah 5:46-47 T.B. Irving - *The First American Version of the Koran*)

According to this Koranic verse, Jesus confirmed the Torah, which He actually did on many occasions as stated before. He proclaimed the Gospel. More importantly, the people of the Gospel - the Christians - should judge by the Gospel. They are not in need of the Koran. The Koran says, "Those who do not judge by what God has sent down in the Gospel are perverse."

The New Testament also teaches that Jesus confirmed the Torah:

> Do not think that I will accuse you to the Father: there is one that accuseth you, even Moses, in whom ye trust. For had ye believed Moses, ye would have believed me: for he wrote of me. But if you believe not his writings, how shall ye believe my words?   (John 5: 45-47)

It is clear from the two previous Koranic verses that the Torah and the Gospel were sent down from God.

201

What is the "Gospel" the Koran refers to?

A Muslim friend said to me, "The Koran mentions only one Gospel which was given to Jesus Christ, but in the New Testament there are four gospels, Matthew, Mark, Luke and John. How do you explain that?"

First of all, let me say that the word "Gospel" is the translation of the Greek word "Evangelion" which means the Good News or the Joyful News.

The Good News which was given to Jesus is that God loves us so much that He sent His Son Jesus to "demonstrate His love toward us, in that while we were still sinners, Christ died for us" (Romans 5:8). The Apostle Paul defines the Gospel in the following words:

> Moreover, brethren, I declare to you the gospel which I preached to you... that Christ died for our sins according to the Scriptures, and that He was buried, and that He rose again the third day according to the Scriptures, and that He was seen by Cephas, then by the twelve. After that He was seen by over five hundred brethren at once.
>
> (I Corinthians 15:1-6 NKJ)

In this passage we see that the death of Jesus Christ was to fulfill the Scriptures, and that His burial and resurrection were also to fulfill the Scriptures. The crucifixion, burial, and resurrection of Jesus Christ were not a man made story. It was a Biblical and historical reality, foretold in the Old Testament and fulfilled in the New Testament.

The Gospel was given in four books, Matthew, Mark, Luke and John. The four books were in reality one gospel in different settings, but their focal point was the crucifixion, burial, and resurrection of Jesus Christ.

The Gospel of Matthew is the Gospel of Jesus the King.
The Gospel of Mark is the Gospel of Jesus the Servant.
The Gospel of Luke is the Gospel of Jesus the Perfect Man.
The Gospel of John is the Gospel of Jesus the Son of God.

Let us go back to the Koran. In Surat Al-Maidah 5:68 we read:

> Say: 'People of the book, you will not make any point until you keep up the Torah and the Gospel' (T.B. Irving - *The First American Version of the Quran*).

It is clear from this Koranic verse that the Koran does not supersede the Torah or the Gospel, because if the Koran superseded them, why is it that the people of the book will not make any point or have any guidance until they keep up the Torah and the Gospel?

Second: God would not allow His Word to be changed.

The Koran says:

> Lo! We even We, reveal the reminder [that is the Word of Allah] and Lo! we verily are its guardian.
> (Surat Al-Hijir 15:9 MPT)

> No changes can there be in the Words of Allah.
> (Surat Yunus 10:64 HK)

It is very clear from these verses that Allah promised to guard His word. There is no way to alter or change it.

If God is immutable, unchangeable, and most certainly He is, then this principle must be applied to all His books. He cannot guard one of His books and leave the other to be tampered with. No one would trust a God who allows His Word to be corrupted. The conclusion is, since the Bible is the Word of God, then it is guarded and kept pure throughout history by the power of God. We have no choice but to accept it as such without any dispute, and receive it as a solid foundation to build our faith on.

The Koran commands Muslims to believe in the Scriptures which were sent down before Muhammad and clearly declares that these Scriptures came from above, from Allah, not from any human or spiritist sources:

> O you who believe (Muslims), believe in Allah, and His Messenger (Muhammad) and the Book (the Koran) which he has sent down to His Messenger, and the Scripture which He sent down to those before (him); and whosoever disbelieves in Allah, His Angels, His Books, His Messengers, and the Last Day, then indeed he has strayed far away.   (Surat Al-Nisa 4:136)

Would Allah ask Muslims to believe in the Scripture which was sent down before Muhammad, while these books according to the false claim of the Muslim clerics are corrupted?

A Muslim friend said to me, "The Jews and the Christians tampered with the Bible, they corrupted it. We Muslims cannot trust your Bible." I answered him with the following words:

1. If the Torah and the Gospel were tampered with by Jews and Christians, then the testimony of the Quran to their authenticity is false.

If you say that the Bible was tampered with after Muhammad, that means that the Allah of the Quran did not know that the Bible would be corrupted. In that case, we have to conclude that the Quran is not trustworthy.

2. There were thousands of manuscripts of the Bible in more than one language in the hands of many Jews and Christians.

If anyone wanted to corrupt the Bible, he must have access and authority to collect all these manuscripts to corrupt them, and that is impossible.

3. The honesty of the Bible declares it never was tampered with. The Bible is absolutely honest.

It shows how Abraham, the great grandfather of Israel, for fear of being killed, told Sarah to lie about her relationship to him. It shows Jacob, the father of Israel, to be a deceiver. It shows how Moses, the great prophet of Israel, in his first attempt to help his own people, killed a man and then ran for his life into the desert. It records the sin of David, Israel's beloved king and spiritual leader, when he committed adultery with Bathsheba, the wife of a great officer of Israel's army and then conspired to kill him to cover his sin.

The Old Testament speaks about the people of Israel as "rulers of Sodom, people of Gomorah" (Isaiah 1:10). The New Testament speaks about the Apostle Peter and how he denied Jesus three times (Luke 22:54-62). It speaks about the sins in the Corinthian Church (I Corinthians 5:1) and it teaches that the way to heaven is narrow, and demands honesty in searching, while the road to Hell is wide open. A book with such honesty is not corrupted.

4. The integrity of those whom God entrusted to keep His Word pure was great.

The Quran declares:

It was we who revealed the Torah [to Moses]: therein was guidance and light. By its standard have been judged the Jews, by the Prophets who bowed to Allah's will, by the rabbis and the Doctors of law: For to them was entrusted the protection of Allah's Book, and they were witnesses thereto: Therefore fear not men, but

205

fear Me, and sell not my signs for a miserable price. If any do fail to judge by what Allah hath revealed, they are unbelievers (literally infidels).

(Surat Al-Maidah 5:44)

This verse declares that the Torah was revealed to Moses, that it gives guidance and light, and that the prophets, rabbis and doctors of law were entrusted the protection of Allah's book.

The important question is, "Will God entrust His word to people who would corrupt and alter it?" Obviously not. Moses said to the children of Israel:

Ye shall not add unto the word which I command you, neither shall ye diminish aught from it, that ye may keep the commandments of the LORD your God which I command you. (Deuteronomy 4:2)

The Apostle Paul declares:

What advantage then hath the Jew? or what profit is there of circumcision? Much every way: Chiefly, because that unto them were committed the oracles of God. (Romans 3:1-2 NKJ)

God committed His oracles to the Jewish prophets. They were trustworthy. They kept His Word pure throughout history. If the Jews had altered the Old Testament, they would have taken out the story of the fall of their King David (II Samuel 11:1-26); the hard words directed to them (Isaiah 1:21); and the terrible prophecies concerning their future (Zechariah 14:1-2).

The existence of these and other stories related to them indicate the truthfulness of the Old Testament.

5. Biblical prophecies have been fulfilled to the letter.

This we have seen in the fulfillment of the prophecies concerning Jesus and the prophecies mentioned in the book of Daniel and other prophetic books.

6. Most of the New Testament writers were martyred.

No one will die for a lie.

7. To claim that the Bible was corrupted, we have to give satisfactory answers to the following questions:

> When was the Bible corrupted?
> Who corrupted the Bible?
> Why should anybody corrupt the Bible?
> What portions of the Bible were corrupted?
> Where is the uncorrupted Bible to give evidence of the corruption of the Bible we have?

To prove that the dollar somebody holds is forged, you have to have the authentic dollar to compare it with. The question is, "Do you have the true Bible to compare with the corrupted Bible?" If the answer is "no," then to claim that the Bible was corrupted is totally false.

The truth is, the Bible is the gold standard by which the Koran should be examined.

In addition, the New Testament ends with these solemn words:

> For I testify unto every man that heareth the words of the prophecy of this book, if any man shall add unto these things, God shall add unto him the plagues that are written in this book: And if any man shall take away from the words of the book of this prophecy, God shall take away his part out of the book of life, and out of the holy city, and from the things which are written in this book. (Revelation 22:18-19 NKJ)

Who would dare to add or take away from the Word of God after such a warning?

We are assured that the God of the Bible is immutable, unchanging, and most certainly He, blessed be His name, guarded the Bible and kept it pure.

> Forever, O Lord, thy word is settled in heaven.
>
> (Psalm 119:89 NKJ)

The Koran or the Bible?

Which one is the true Word of God, the Koran or the Bible? The truth is the Bible is the original Word of God. It was in the hands of the Jews and the Christians 600 years before the Koran. The Koran must be the altered document because of the clear contradictions between it and the Bible.

The Bible is self-interpretive. It can be understood by comparing its verses to interpret scripture with scripture. When anyone receives the Lord Jesus Christ as his or her savior, the Holy Spirit illuminates his or her heart and mind to understand and enjoy the Bible.

Concerning the Koran we read:

> No one knows its true meaning except Allah.
>
> (Surat Al-Imran 3:7)

The Koran is a book the meaning of which no one can know. Would God give us a book that no one can understand?

Contrary to what the Koran says, we read in the Bible:

> Open my eyes, that I may see wondrous things from your law. (Psalm 119:18 NKJ)

Your Word I have hidden in my heart, that I might not sin against you. (Psalm 119:11 NKJ)

How sweet are your words to my taste, sweeter than honey to my mouth. (Psalm 119:103 NKJ)

It is of great importance to read and understand the Bible. Jesus Christ says "search the scriptures" (John 5:39).

Chapter Nineteen

Contradictions Between the Bible and the Koran

If the Koran is truly God's word and the continuation of His revelation to mankind, why did the Koran repeat the stories of the Bible in this distorted manner? Why do we read the story of the two sons of Adam while the Koran did not even mention their names? Why the repetition of the stories concerning Abraham in more than one surah of the Koran? Why do we read a distorted repetition of the story of Joseph?

If the Koran is the continued revelation of God, there was no need of repeating these and other stories. Because the New Testament is the continuation of God's revelation, the New Testament refers to, and comments on, the Old Testament stories without repeating them.

It is amazing how Muslims and Muslim countries fear the Bible. Some Muslim countries do not allow Bibles to be brought into their countries while they distribute thousands of copies of the English translation of the Koran in the United States and other western countries.

Christians do not fear the Koran, in fact thousands of them are reading it to discover the many unnecessary repetitions in it and how boring it is.

Muslim countries are afraid of the Bible because the Bible is true. When people know the truth, they will ask for freedom in every area of their lives. Christ said:

211

And you shall know the truth, and the truth shall make
you free.   (John 8:32 NKJ)

If Muslims read the Bible and believe it, they will ask for
democracy and Islam and democracy cannot co-exist.

If your religion is true, you have nothing to fear. Serious
questions deserve serious answers; the sincere researcher will
follow the truth regardless of the consequences.

The Story of the Cow

A good example of inconsistencies between an original Bible
story and its version found in the Koran is the story of the Cow
found in Surat Al-Baqarah (The Cow), the second and longest
surah of the Koran. Here is the story of the cow as recorded in that
surah:

> And (remember) when Musa (Moses) said to his
> people: 'Verily, Allah commands you that you
> slaughter a cow.' They said, 'Do you make fun of us?'
> He said, 'I take Allah's Refuge from being among Al-
> Jahilun (the ignorant or the foolish).'
>
> They said, 'Call upon your Lord for us that he may
> make plain to us what it is!' He said, 'He says, 'Verily,
> it is a cow neither too old nor too young, but (it is)
> between the two conditions,' so do what you are
> commanded.'
>
> They said, 'Call upon your Lord for us to make plain
> to us its colour.' He said, 'He says, "It is a yellow cow,
> bright in its colour, pleasing the beholders."'
>
> They said, 'Call upon your Lord for us to make plain
> to us what it is. Verily, to us all cows are alike. And
> surely, if Allah wills, we will be guided.'

He [Musa (Moses))] said, 'He says, "It is a cow neither trained to till the soil nor water the fields, sound, having no other colour except bright yellow."' They said, 'Now you have brought the truth.' So they slaughtered it though they were near to not doing it.

(Surat Al-Baqarah 2:67-71 HK)

This story is taken from the book of Numbers in the Old Testament and is recorded in the Koran with great distortion. The Koran changes the color of the cow from "red" in the Bible to "yellow" in the Koran. In the Bible that cow was chosen for purification but in the Koran there is no reason for the slaughter of that cow.

Here is the story of the cow as recorded in the Bible:

Now the Lord spoke to Moses and Aaron, saying, 'This is the ordinance of the law which the Lord has commanded, saying: "Speak to the children of Israel, that they bring you a red heifer without blemish, in which there is no defect and on which a yoke has never come. You shall give it to Eleazar the priest, that he may take it outside the camp, and it shall be slaughtered before him; and Eleazar the priest shall take some of its blood with his finger, and sprinkle some of its blood seven times directly in front of the tabernacle of meeting. Then the heifer shall be burned in his sight: its hide, its flesh, its blood, and its offal shall be burned. And the priest shall take cedar wood and hyssop and scarlet, and cast them into the midst of the fire burning the heifer. Then the priest shall wash his clothes, he shall bathe in water, and afterward he shall come into the camp; the priest shall be unclean until evening. And the one who burns it shall wash his clothes in water, bathe in water, and shall be unclean until evening. Then a man who is clean shall gather up the ashes of the heifer, and store them outside the camp in a clean place; and they shall be kept for the congregation of the children of Israel for the water of purification; it is for purifying from sin."' (Numbers 19:1-9 NKJ)

Do you see the difference between the inspired word of God and the distorted story in the Koran?

If the Koran is the true inspired book of the latest major religion revealed to mankind, then it must be completely consistent with the Bible and its principles, because God would not contradict Himself. In addition, should not its principles and morality be superior to Judaism and Christianity? But that is not the case. The fact is, the Koran is in total contradiction to the Bible. Let us consider some examples:

First: Noah's wife and son - perished or saved?

The Koran declares that Noah's wife entered Hell, and that one of his sons was drowned by the flood:

> Allah cited an example for those who disbelieve: The wife of Noah and the wife of Lot, who were under two of our righteous slaves yet betrayed them so that they [the husbands] availed them naught against Allah and it was said [unto them]: Enter the fire along with those who enter. (Surat Al-Tahrim 66:10 MPT)

> And it sailed [the ark] with them amid waves like mountains, and Noah cried unto his son and he was standing aloof - O my son! Come ride with us, and be not with the disbelievers. He said: I shall betake me to some mountain that will save me from the water. [Noah] said: This day there is none that saveth from the commandment of Allah save him on whom He hath had

mercy. And the wave came in between them, so he was among the drowned. (Surat Hud 11:42,43 MPT)

These Koranic verses contradict the Bible which says:

In the selfsame day entered Noah, and Shem, and Ham, and Japheth, the sons of Noah, and Noah's wife, and the three wives of his sons with them, into the ark.
(Genesis 7:13)

Whom should we believe, the Koran or the Bible? The Bible tells us that the human race descended after the flood from Shem, Ham and Japheth. Since none of them drowned, the Koran is in error.

Second: The throne of God - is it on water or in heaven?

The Koran declares that the throne of God is upon the water:

And He it is Who created the heavens and the earth in six days and His Throne was upon the water.
(Surat Hud 11:7 MPT)

The Bible declares that the throne of God is in heaven:

Swear not at all, neither by heaven, for it is God's throne. (Matthew 5:34 NKJ)

Third: How are the dead resurrected?

In the Koran we read that Abraham asked Allah to show him how He gives life to the dead:

Behold! Abraham said: 'My Lord! Show me how thou givest life to the dead.' He said: 'Dost thou not then

215

believe?' He said: 'Yea! but to satisfy my own heart.' He said: 'Take four birds, tie them [cut them into pieces], then put a portion of them: on every hill, and call to them: they will come to thee [flying] with speed. Then know that Allah is exalted in power, wise.'

(Surat Al-Baqarah 2:260)

This story is a distortion of the biblical story where Abraham asked God to show him how he would inherit the land of Canaan:

And he said unto him, 'Take me...a turtledove, and a young pigeon.' And he took unto him all these...

(Genesis 15:9-10 NKJ)

The biblical story continues to relate how God told Abraham about the future of his descendants (Genesis 15:9-21). It has nothing to do with the resurrection of the dead.

Now, concerning Abraham's belief in the resurrection of the dead we read in the Bible:

By faith Abraham, when he was tried, offered up Isaac; and he that had received the promises offered up his only begotten son, of whom it was said, that in Isaac shall thy seed be called: accounting that God was able to raise him up, even from the dead; from whence also he received him in a figure. (Hebrews 11:17-19)

There was no magic. Giving life to birds is no assurance of the resurrection of the dead. After all, birds will not be resurrected. The Bible gives us this assurance of life after death in the inspired word:

But someone will say, 'How are the dead raised up? And with what body do they come?' Foolish one, what you sow is not made alive unless it dies.

216

So also is the resurrection of the dead. The body is sown in corruption, it is raised in incorruption. It is sown in dishonor, it is raised in glory. It is sown in weakness, it is raised in power. It is sown a natural body, it is raised a spiritual body. There is a natural body, and there is a spiritual body. And so it is written, 'The first man Adam became a living being.' The last Adam became a life-giving spirit. However, the spiritual is not first, but the natural, and afterward the spiritual. The first man was of the earth, made of dust; the second Man is the Lord from heaven. As was the man of dust, so also are those who are made of dust; and as is the heavenly Man, so also are those who are heavenly. And as we have borne the image of the man of dust, we shall also bear the image of the heavenly Man. Now this I say, brethren, that flesh and blood cannot inherit the kingdom of God; nor does corruption inherit incorruption. (1 Corinthians 15:35-36; 42-50 NKJ)

Because the true believers in Christ will be raised in spiritual bodies, they will not engage in sex or need one hundred virgins in paradise!

Fourth: Was Christ crucified or not?

I will elaborate on this point in the coming part of this book. Here I will only write what the Bible says and what the Koran says to show the great contradiction between the two. Here is what the Apostle John says as an eye witness:

> … so they took Jesus and led Him away. And he bearing His cross went out to a place called the place of a Skull, which is called in Hebrew, Golgotha, where they crucified Him, and two others with Him, one on either side, and Jesus in the center. (John 19:16-18 NKJ)

217

Now read what Muhammad says in his Koran:

> ... they killed him not, nor crucified him, but the resemblance of Jesus was put over another man (and they killed that man). For surely, they killed him not.
>
> (Surat An-Nisa 4:157 HK)

By this false verse the Koran is saying that all the books of the New Testament, indeed all the books of the Bible are fabricated, because all these books prophesy and focus on the crucifixion of Christ.

The truth is that Christ was crucified. Christianity was built on that fact and true Christians are called not to kill innocent people by suicide bombers or any other means, but to sacrifice even themselves for others. The Apostle Peter says:

> For this you were called, because Christ also suffered for us leaving us an example, that you should follow His steps. (I Peter 2:21 NKJ)

This is why Christian countries help Muslim countries with food and medicine, and send physicians to treat their sick people.

The Koran, by its denial of the crucifixion, makes the Holy God a deceiver, as well as unjust because it says that Allah put the resemblance of Jesus on another man, and that man was crucified in his place. The Holy God would not commit such deception!

Fifth: Love or revenge, retaliation and racism?

Jesus Christ commanded Christians:

> Love your enemies, bless them that curse you, do good to them that hate you, and pray for them which

despitefully use you, and persecute you; that ye may be the children of your Father which is in heaven. . .

(Matthew 5:44, 45 NKJ)

The Apostle Paul says:

Bless them which persecute you: bless, and curse not...

Recompense to no man evil for evil. Provide things honest in the sight of all men...

Dearly beloved, avenge not yourselves, but rather give place unto wrath: for it is written, Vengeance is mine; I will repay, saith the Lord. Therefore if thine enemy hunger, feed him; if he thirst, give him drink: for in so doing thou shall heap coals of fire on his head. Be not overcome of evil, but overcome evil with good.

(Romans 12:14, 17, 19-21)

The Koran says:

There is the law of equality. If then any one transgresses the prohibition against you, transgress ye likewise against him. (Surat Al-Baqarah 2:194)

O ye who believe! Take not the Jews and the Christians for your friends and protectors: They are but friends and protectors to each other. And he amongst you that turns to them [for friendship] is of them. Verily Allah guideth not a people unjust. (Surat Al-Maidah 5:51)

Could any Muslim honestly and sincerely befriend any Jew or Christian if he or she obeys the Koran? (Read also Surat Al-Maidah 5:33.)

Sixth: Peace and forgiveness or sword and brutality?

Jesus Christ said to Peter, His disciple:

> Put up again thy sword into his place: for all they that take the sword shall perish with the sword.
>
> (Matthew 26:52)

The Koran says:

> O Prophet! rouse the believers to fight.
>
> (Surat Al-Anfal 8:65)

It is recorded in Al-Tabari's history that Muhammad said:

> I was sent by the sword, the good is with the sword, the good is in the sword, the good is by the sword. My followers will be always good as long as they carry the sword. (*Islamic Caliphate*, p 144)

In another chapter of this book we mentioned many verses in the Koran commanding Muslims to fight and to kill non-Muslims. A Muslim writer said in an article that Christ also came by the sword, mentioning the following verse from the book of Matthew:

> Think not that I am come to send peace on earth: I come not to send peace, but a sword. (Matthew 10:34 NKJ)

Here we have to realize that when Christ, who is called in the Bible "The Prince of Peace" (Isaiah 9:6) uttered these words, he did not mean that he would come with a sword like Muhammad's sword, but that sword was not the sword to kill but the sword of division. This is clear from His words:

220

Do you suppose that I came to give peace on earth? I tell you, not at all, but rather division. For from now on five in one house will be divided: three against two, and two against three. Father will be divided against son and son against father, mother against daughter and daughter against mother, mother-in-law against her daughter-in-law and daughter-in-law against her mother-in-law. (Luke 12:51-53 NKJ)

This often happens when one member of the family becomes a Christian, the rest of the family will be against him or her. The sword Christ mentioned is not the sword to kill, but a sword of division between those who believe in Him and those who do not.

The Koran upholds the use of the sword for killing and for shedding the blood of anyone who does not believe in Muhammad and his Koran.

One example of brutality in Islam is seen in the beheading of Sadeq Abdul Kareem Malallah in Saudi Arabia. *The Washington Post* recorded that beheading in an article by Carlyle Murphy on Thursday, October 1, 1992:

KUWAIT CITY, Sept. 30 - Saudi Arabian authorities, in a case that has drawn protests from human rights groups and questions from other Muslims, have beheaded a 23-year-old Saudi man convicted of insulting the prophet Muhammad and Islam's holy book, the Koran.

Sadeq Abdul Kareem Malallah was publicly executed in a marketplace in the town of Qatif on Sept. 3, according to a statement the next day by the Interior Ministry.

The statement said Malallah, a member of Saudi Arabia's minority Shiite Muslim sect who was convicted in 1988 and imprisoned since, had 'insulted God, the holy Koran and Muhammad the prophet.'

His conviction, upheld by two Islamic law appeal courts, was confirmed by King Fahd in August, it added.

Malallah called Muhammad 'a liar and swindler' and accused him of using 'witchcraft' and 'help from devils,' the government said. He allegedly termed the Koran, which Muslims believe is a revelation from Allah, 'a product of the prophet,' and said Islam is 'a fabricated religion.'

'This is not mere apostasy,' the government said. 'Indeed, it is a crime calling for death, but even death will not pardon Sadeq in front of Muhammad and the Koran.'

A London-based human rights group supported by Saudi dissidents quoted a witness to the execution as saying that those gathered at the scene experienced a 'massive shock' at the sentence, and that just before his death Malallah was shouting: 'I am innocent. You are oppressive.'

The case highlights the importance of religious orthodoxy in Saudi society, whose Sunni Muslim leaders base much of their political legitimacy on the claim to be custodians of the original intent of Muhammad's teachings as well as of Islam's holy places.

But the secretive proceedings against Malallah, allegations of mistreatment in prison and the fact that he belonged to the Shiite minority have raised questions about his execution.

'I've never heard of such a case in Saudi Arabia because it's very rare for a Saudi to say [such things] in Saudi society,' said Fahmy Howeidy, an Egyptian journalist specializing in Islamic affairs.

'The question is not what the Koran says about apostasy and its punishment,' he added. 'The point is, is it true that he said such a thing? And was he given a legal trial and given justice, and a lawyer to defend him? We cannot discuss the [matter] from an official Saudi statement only.'

Amnesty International has protested to the Saudi government over the execution of a 'possible prisoner of conscience.'

The organization said it has asked the Riyadh government to release details of the charges and legal proceedings against Malallah, citing reports that he was held in solitary confinement for long periods and beaten in prison.

Aziz Abu Hamad, a human rights investigator with the New York based Middle East Watch, cited Malallah's execution in recent testimony he gave to the U.S. Congress on Saudi Arabia's human rights record.

'This is the first time in Saudi history where a man was killed for such a crime,' Hamad said in a telephone interview. 'My reading is that the government wants to seize the moral high ground from the [Islamic] fundamentalists.'

The London-based International Committee for the Defense of Human Rights in the Gulf and the Arabian Peninsula, which is supported by exiled Saudi dissidents, including Shiites, also protested the execution.

Based on interviews with his relatives and former inmates of Mababeth prison in Dammam, Saudi Arabia, where Malallah was held for a time, the committee said he was arrested in April 1988 for allegedly 'throwing stones at a police car.'

Later, a judge in Qatif 'accused him of smuggling a Bible into the country' and asked him to convert to Wahhabi Islam, the puritanic sect prevailing in Saudi Arabia, which harbors deep suspicions about Shiite

Muslims, the committee alleged. When Malallah refused, he reportedly was placed in solitary confinement and physically abused, the committee said.

To criticize Muhammad, the prophet of Islam, or to say that the Koran is "a product of the prophet," or that Islam is a "fabricated religion," or to smuggle a Bible into a country ruled by the Koran, is a crime punishable by beheading. *It should be noted also that Islam is a prison with no exit. Once you enter that prison, you can not come out of it alive. Once a Muslim, always a Muslim.*
According to Islamic law, the Muslim who converts to Christianity from Islam is an apostate and must be killed.

The International Christian Concern, in its press release of October 2, 1996, wrote under the title, *"Apostate" Christian Pastor Murdered in Iran*:

> News of another murder of an Iranian Christian pastor reached the West seven days after his body was found on September 25 hanging from a tree in a secluded forest. Rev. Mohammed Ravanbaksh was killed shortly after he had reportedly been detained and questioned by the Iranian police. He is the fourth Christian leader to have been murdered in less than three years.
>
> Since the 35 year old pastor had converted from Islam to Christianity 11 years ago, he has been labeled by the Iranian authorities and Muslim leaders as an 'apostate' who was deserving of death. He was ordained by the Assemblies of God Church under the leadership of the late Bishop Haik Hovespian-Mehr, who was brutally murdered after being abducted in January 1994. Rev. Ravanbaksh has been pastoring an underground church since 1988, after the Iranian authorities forcibly closed down the three churches he had been pastoring.

Another martyred pastor and former Muslim, Mehdi Dibaj, served as mentor to Rev. Ravanbaksh. Mehdi Dibaj was murdered in 1994 shortly after serving more than nine years in prison on charges of apostasy. Rev. Mehr was outspoken on behalf of Mehdi Dibaj during his imprisonment, which led to an international campaign that resulted in Mehdi Dibaj's release in late 1993. Since the time of Pastor Dibaj's death, Rev. Ravanbaksh has been caring for Dibaj's young children. In addition to Dibaj's children, Rev. Ravanbaksh's wife, Akhtar, is left to care for two small children of their own who are now without a father.

Rev. Ravanbaksh is said to have been willing to follow in the footsteps of Mehdi Dibaj who wrote these words a short time before his death: 'I have always envied those Christians who were martyred for Christ Jesus our Lord. What a privilege to live for our Lord and to die for Him as well... I am ready to give my life for the sake of Jesus Christ.'

A protest campaign has been launched by International Christian Concern (ICC) for the purpose of drawing international attention to the intense persecution against evangelical Christians in Iran and to condemn the Iranian government's continued detention, imprisonment, torture, and murder of Christian leaders. Numerous pastors have received death threats. Christians who dare to openly practice their faith fear government harassment and even death.

America, as well as many European Christian nations, went to war, shed the blood of their soldiers and billions of dollars to rescue Muslims in Kuwait, Bosnia and Somalia. Yet, Islamic fanaticism is spreading all over the world. An Islamic invasion is taking place in America with hundreds of thousands of Muslims given visas and green cards to migrate to America. Their hidden agenda is to ultimately convert this country to Islam.

In the West, as well as in Islamic States, Muslim clerics have the right to convert Christians to Islam without any threat or danger to them. But once a Muslim is converted to Christianity he is threatened, persecuted, tortured, and ultimately executed.

This proves just how dangerous and brutal Islam is.

Seventh: Should a divorced woman marry another man in order to remarry her first husband again?

What the true God called abomination, the Koran called limits ordained by Allah. The Bible states that remarriage of the divorced wife to the same husband, after marrying another man, is an *abomination* in the sight of God. In the book of Deuteronomy we read:

> When a man takes a wife and marries her, and it happens that she finds no favor in his eyes because he has found some uncleanness in her, and he writes her a certificate of divorce, puts it in her hand, and sends her out of his house, when she has departed from his house, and goes and becomes another man's wife, if the latter husband detests her and writes her a certificate of divorce, puts it in her hand, and sends her out of his house, or if the latter husband dies who took her to be his wife, then her former husband who divorced her must not take her back to be his wife after she has been defiled; for that is an abomination before the Lord, and you shall not bring sin on the land which the Lord your God is giving you as an inheritance.
>
> (Deuteronomy 24:1-4 NKJ)

This is a very clear commandment of God.

The Koran however, sanctions remarriage of the divorced wife to her husband upon the condition that the woman must first marry another man. Without first marrying another man and then getting divorced from him, she cannot marry her first husband again. This is what the God of the Bible calls an *abomination*, yet the Koran calls it the limits ordained by Allah. Read what the Koran says:

> If a husband divorces his wife [irrevocably], he cannot, after that, remarry her until after she has married another husband and he has divorced her. In that case there is no blame on either of them if they re-unite, provided they feel that they can keep the limits ordained by Allah. Such are the limits ordained by Allah, which He makes plain to those who know.
>
> (Surat Al-Baqarah 2:230)

There is a clear contrast here between the Bible and the Koran. These two conflicting commandments could not be from the same source. Surely, the Bible's command is God's command, the Koran is not!

Eighth: Amazing grace or severe punishment?

The New Testament is the book of the new covenant of God, the covenant of grace:

> For the law was given through Moses, but grace and truth came through Jesus Christ. (John 1:17 NKJ)

Grace means unmerited favor of God to the undeserving sinner.

If the Koran were the Word of God, we would have seen in it more grace, but the Koran thunders with the severity and wrath of Allah in almost every chapter. We see that severity in the punishments in the Koran.

227

(a) The punishment of those who wage war against Muhammad

> ... be killed or crucified or their hands and their feet be cut off from opposite sides.
>
> (Surat Al-Maidah 5:33 HK)

(b) The punishment of the thief - male or female

> And (as for) the male thief and the female thief, cut off (from the wrist joint) their (right) hands as a recompense for that which they committed, a punishment by way of example from Allah. And Allah is All-Powerful, All-Wise.   (Surat Al-Maidah 5:38)

Imagine that London, New York, Washington, D.C., Athens, Paris and Sydney became Muslim cities, and thiefs there are wandering with their right hands cut off and having to beg as they are handicapped. What kind of a society is that? There is no place for mercy in Islam!

(c) The punishment of the adulterer and adulteress.
Here is what the Koran says:

> The woman and the man guilty of illegal sexual intercourse, flog each of them with a hundred stripes. Let not pity withhold you in their case, in a punishment prescribed by Allah, if you believe in Allah and the Last Day.   And let a party of believers witness their punishment.   (Surat Al-Nur 24:2)

Now see the grace of Jesus Christ in the following story:

> But Jesus went to the Mount of Olives. But early in the morning He came again into the temple, and all the people came to Him; and He sat down and taught them.

Then the scribes and Pharisees brought to Him a woman caught in adultery. And when they had set her in the midst, they said to Him, 'Teacher, this woman was caught in adultery, in the every act. Now Moses, in the law, commanded us that such should be stoned. But what do You say?' This they said, testing Him, that they might have something of which to accuse Him. But Jesus stooped down and wrote on the ground with his finger, as though He did not hear. So when they continued asking Him, He raised Himself up and said to them, 'He who is without sin among you, let him throw a stone at her first.' And again He stooped down and wrote on the ground. Then those who heard it, being convicted by their conscience, went out one by one, beginning with the oldest even to the last. And Jesus was left alone, and the woman standing in the midst. When Jesus had raised Himself up and saw no one but the woman, He said to her, 'Woman, where are those accusers of yours? Has no one condemned you?' She said, 'No one, Lord.' And Jesus said to her, 'Neither do I condemn you; go and sin no more.'

(John 8:1-11 NKJ)

Ninth: Women and married life in the Bible and the Koran

Women have an honored place in the Bible. The name of the first woman, "Eve," is mentioned with Adam. When God brought Eve to Adam, Adam said:

> This is now bone of my bones and flesh of my flesh; she shall be called woman, because she was taken out of man. (Genesis 2:23 NKJ)

229

Names of women are mentioned all through the books of the Bible. Two books are named after women in the Old Testament, Ruth and Esther. Many women were mentioned by name in the New Testament.

In the Koran, women are totally degraded. They are considered impure; **they have no value.** No women's names are mentioned in the Koran except Mary the mother of Jesus, not even Khadija, Muhammad's first wife, or the rest of his wives.

When Zainab Bint Ghahs refused to marry Muhammad's adopted son, Zaid, Muhammad recited to her a revelation he received as follows:

> It is not for a believer, man or woman, when Allah and His Messenger (Muhammad) have decreed a matter that they should have any option in their decision. And whoever disobeys Allah and His Messenger, he has indeed strayed into a plain error.
>
> (Surat Al-Ahzab 33:36)

By this revelation, Zainab was robbed of her freedom of choice and obeyed Muhammad against her will. This is terrible bondage.

a.) One wife at one time, or two, three or four - and sex with your slaves?

The Bible declares that God created one woman for Adam when the earth was empty and needed to be populated, with no permission for divorce except for adultery.

Christ said to the Pharisees who came to test Him, saying, "Is it lawful for man to divorce his wife for just any reason?"

> And He answered and said to them, 'Have you not read that He who made them at the beginning made them male and female, and said, 'For this reason a man shall leave his father and mother and be joined to his

wife, and the two shall become one flesh?' So then, they are no longer two but one flesh. Therefore what God has joined together, let no man separate.

They said to Him, 'Why then did Moses command to give a certificate of divorce, and to put her away?' He said to them, 'Moses, because of the hardness of your hearts, permitted you to divorce your wives, but from the beginning it was not so. And I say to you, whoever divorces his wife, except for sexual immorality, and marries another, commits adultery; and whoever marries her who is divorced commits adultery.' (Matthew 19:4-9 NKJ)

The Apostle Paul wrote:

Nevertheless, because of sexual immorality, let each man have his own wife, and let each woman have her own husband. (1 Corinthians 7:2 NKJ)

The Koran permits Muslim men to marry two, or three, or four women at one time, making the woman a sex object, and making marriage only to satisfy man's sexual desire. Here are the words of the Koran:

Marry women of your choice, two, or three, or four; but if ye fear that ye shall not be able to deal justly [with them] then only one, or that which your right hands possess. . . (Surat Al-Nisa 4:3)

This verse in the Koran gives the right to the Muslim to marry two or three or four women, especially if the Muslim follows the example of Muhammad who married fourteen wives. Muhammad is the excellent example for every Muslim. No Muslim will fear that he will be unjust. Here we have to mention the double standard of Islam. The Quran permits the Muslim man to marry a

Christian or a Jewish woman, but forbids the Muslim woman to marry a Christian or a Jew.

The above mentioned verse also permits the Muslim to have sex with his slave girls, which the Koran call "that which your right hands possess." By this permission, the Koran justifies sex outside of marriage, and makes adultery acceptable. Polygamy - one man marrying more than one woman - demonstrates inequality and female subservience. It invites exploitation of the wives and degrading competition among them.

The Koran declares also that men "excel" women:

> Men are the protectors and maintainers of women, because Allah has made one of them to excel the other...   (Surat An-Nisa 4:34)

That is a clear contradiction of what the Bible says (read Genesis 2:18; I Corinthians 11:11-12; Galatians 3:28).

Dr. Moody Adams recorded the following true story in his book, *The Religion that is Raping America*:

> A friend of mine was brought face to face with the Muslim sexual practices which are so attractive to men and so deplorable to women. She told me that thirty years ago in England she had a very beautiful female cousin, whose name was Sylvia. She said: 'Sylvia was ten years older than me; I always admired her and wanted to be like her, she had beautiful blonde hair, blue eyes and a peach complexion. She was always full of life and had an unquenchable thirst for adventure. When she was eighteen she went on a vacation to the Middle East. On this vacation she met a handsome Lebanese sheik and fell in love. She told her parents that she was going to marry him, but they were very afraid for her; they said they had heard stories that Muslim men had many wives and harems full of

concubines. They had heard that the wives were kept as virtual prisoners with very few rights. They also had heard that Middle Eastern men coveted the blonde hair and blue eyes of a European woman; it was like a trophy.

Sylvia told them not to be afraid; her future husband was a very modern Muslim and did not think and behave like that. She also told them that he had said he would never take another wife, as with Sylvia he only needed the one. Sylvia was married in a small civil ceremony in London with her parents in attendance and then taken by her husband back to Lebanon, where she converted to Islam and was married in an Islamic ceremony.

She seemed to be happy for a few years and had two handsome sons. Then without any warning, her parents did not hear from her for quite a few months; they began to worry. Her parents tried to call her in Lebanon, but her husband took the phone calls and told them she was ill and could not talk; but that they were not to worry as she had good doctors attending her and would be fine.

Three more months passed and they still had not heard from her. No-one would take their phone calls; then finally Sylvia's husband called to say she had died suddenly. Her parents felt there was more to this story than an illness. They were poor and could not go to Lebanon themselves; but they got in touch with their local politician. This man was a very caring individual who had known Sylvia as a child. He assured her parents that he would make discreet inquiries.

After about a month they received the most heartbreaking news. Sylvia's life in Lebanon in this strict Muslim home was bondage; she had been one of four wives and, indeed, her husband did have concubines. Her parents worst predictions had been correct.

Her parents learned Sylvia had tried to escape from her husband with her two sons. She was caught by her husband's 'guards' and returned to him. A few weeks later she had taken one of her husband's cars and tried to escape again. Her husband had anticipated this and set a trap by tampering with the brakes. Sylvia lost control of the car and went over a cliff to her death. The crash decapitated her.

Sylvia's sons remained in Lebanon; her parents never had a chance to see them and they were told that they would not be able to bring her husband to justice; he was only subject to Islamic law and under the law he had done nothing 'wrong.'

(pp 77, 78 & 79, Printed by permission)

We must not forget that a Muslim can divorce his four wives and marry another four and another four with no end. A Muslim can therefore marry a large number of women during his lifetime.

b.) Wife's sexual satisfaction: Is it an obligation or irrelevant?

The Bible clearly says that a husband should satisfy his wife, and a wife should satisfy her husband in their sexual relationship.

Let the husband render to his wife the affection due her, and likewise also the wife to her husband. The wife does not have authority over her own body, but the husband does. And likewise the husband does not have authority over his own body, but the wife does. Do not deprive one another except with consent for a time, that you may give yourselves to fasting and prayer; and come together again so that Satan does not tempt you because of your lack of self-control.

(1 Corinthians 7:3-5 NKJ)

Again the Bible says:

> For this is the will of God, your sanctification: that you should abstain from sexual immorality; that each of you should know how to possess his own vessel in sanctification and honor, not in passion of lust, like the Gentiles who do not know God; that no one should take advantage of and defraud his brother in this matter, because the Lord is the avenger of all such, as we also forewarned you and testified. For God did not call us to uncleanness, but in holiness.
>
> (1 Thessalonians 4:3-7 NKJ)

Now read what the Koran says:

> Your wives are a tilth for you, (a land to plough) so go to your tilth, when or how you will.
>
> (Surat Al-Baqarah 2:223)

Woman's satisfaction is not important, only man's is.

c.) Love, be kind, understand and honor your wife - or beat her.

The Bible commands the husbands to be kind to their wives, to honor them and to love them.

> Husbands, love your wives, and be not bitter against them. (Colossians 3:19)

> Likewise, ye husbands, dwell with them according to knowledge, giving honor unto the wife, as unto the

235

weaker vessel, and as being heirs together of the grace
of life; that your prayers be not hindered.　(I Peter 3:7)

Husbands, love your wives, even as Christ also loved
the church, and gave himself for it . . . (Ephesians 5:25)

A virtuous woman is a crown to her husband.
(Proverbs 12:4)

The crown is over the head, that is how the Bible honors women.
What does the Koran say?

As to those women on whose part ye fear disloyalty and
ill-conduct, admonish them, refuse to share their beds,
and beat them.　　　　　　(Surat Al-Nisa 4:34)

Just a suspicion of disloyalty on the part of a wife is justification
for the husband to beat her.

The above mentioned verse describes stages in dealing with the
wife when her husband fears disloyalty or ill conduct on her part.
First: admonish her, second: refuse to have sex with her, and third:
beat her. We have to admit that, if the first two stages fail, beating
will not be light but severe. Any other conclusion is not logical.

d.) Is a woman clean or impure?

When Christ arose, Mary Magdalene and the other Mary were
the first to meet the risen Christ:

...Jesus met them, saying, 'Rejoice!' So they came and
held Him by the feet and worshipped Him.
(Matthew 28:9 NKJ)

Christ let the women hold his feet; they were clean. But a Muslim cannot pray if he touches a woman, because women are unclean. Here is what the Koran says:

> O ye who believe (Muslims)! Approach not prayers... if you are ill, or in a journey... or you touched women.
> (Surat Al-Nisa 4:43 - Author's translation)

Touching a woman prevents Muslims from prayer. This is how women are degraded in Islam, and why they are treated in Muslim countries as nothing.

e) The testimony of one woman with a man is not accepted in Islamic courts.

> ... and get two witnesses out of your own men. And if there are not two men then a man and two women.
> (Surat Al-Baqarah 2:282 HK)

f) The daughter only inherits half as much as the son does.
The Koran says:

> 'If there are two sisters, they shall have two thirds of the inheritance. If there are brothers and sisters, the male will have twice the share of the female.
> (Surat An-Nisa 4:176 HK)

It is clear from this documented analysis of the Bible and the Koran that the Muslim cannot practice Islam in a civilized or western country. He cannot marry four wives at one time. He cannot beat his wife, because if she calls the police, he will be arrested. He cannot legally have sex with women other than his wife.

The Koran is not for civilized people. It is time for intellectual Muslims to admit that the Koran is outdated and is less applicable now than ever.

Chapter Twenty

The Fruit of Believing the Koran

If the Koran was the inspired word of Allah to Muhammad, it would have resulted in building a great and decent life in all the areas of human society. Jesus Christ instituted this test when he instructed us to test prophets by their fruit:

> Beware of false prophets, who come to you in sheep's clothing, but inwardly they are ravenous wolves. You will know them by their fruits. Do men gather grapes from thornbushes or figs from thistles? Even so, every good tree bears good fruit, but a bad tree bears bad fruit. A good tree cannot bear bad fruit, nor can a bad tree bear good fruit. Every tree that does not bear good fruit is cut down and thrown into the fire. Therefore by their fruits you will know them. (Matthew 7:15-20 NKJ).

What kind of life do we have when we apply the Koran's principles and commandments?

Muhammad's Household

To judge the fruit of the Koran let us first examine Muhammad's household. Dr. Aisha Abd-Alrahman, known as "Bint Al-Shati," in her book, *Wives of the Prophet*, portrays a vivid picture of life in Muhammad's home. It is a sordid tale of plotting and deception.

Aisha, the youngest and the most beautiful of his wives, was accused of committing adultery with Safwan Ibn Almouatal Alsalmi. When rumors spread concerning that accusation, Muhammad became disturbed and treated Aisha harshly. The crisis between them continued until Muhammad received a revelation that Aisha was innocent.

> Verily, those who like that illegal sexual intercourse should be propagated among those who believe, they will have a painful torment in this world and in the hereafter. And Allah knows and you know not.
>
> (Surat Al-Nur 24:19 HK)

Another event took place in Muhammad's home when he married Asma, daughter of Al-Namam, who was a very attractive woman. Aisha conspired with Hafsa and one of Muhammad's other wives to abort his marriage to Asma. They went to Asma and advised her to say to Muhammad when he came in to her, "I seek refuge in Allah from you," if she wanted to please him. The naive bride believed them. When Muhammad came into her room, she said "I seek refuge in Allah from you." Hearing that, Muhammad sent her back to her parents. The conspiracy of his wives was successful (*Wives of the Prophet*, p 77-78).

Once, all of his wives conspired against him, so he threatened to divorce all of them (Surat Al-Tahrim 66:5). More examples concerning the troubles and conspiracies in Muhammad's home are recorded in the book, *Wives of the Prophet*. This is the fruit of the Koran in Muhammad's household.

Society Built On The Koran

If one examines the impact of Islam on the society Muhammad created by the dictates of his Koran, one discovers a society full of corruption, bloodshed, lack of individual freedom, and brutality.

First: Corruption

Caliph Omar Ibn-Alkhataab acquitted Al-Mugherah Ibn Shuba who committed adultery with a woman named Omm Jameel. He hinted to Zyad Ibn Samila, one of four witnesses, to testify in support of Al-Mugherah. Zyad testified against three other eye witnesses Abi-Bakra, Nafi Ibn Alharith, and Shibl Ibn Maabad who testified that they saw Al-Mugherah in the act. Caliph Omar accepted the witness of Zyad and acquitted Al-Mugherah and ordered him to beat the three eye witnesses who testified against him (*Al Ostorah Waltorath, The Legend and Heritage*, p 266). Caliph Alwathic, the last Caliph of Abaseieen was homosexual. His partner was "Muhag," an attractive young man. It is said: If Muhag gets angry with Alwathic and refuses to have sex with him, the Caliph would suspend all the government activities until Muhag resumes his relationship with him (*The Hidden Truth*, pp 124-126).

Many of the Muslim governors during the Caliphate period robbed the countries they governed and became very rich. When they died they left an enormous amount of wealth.

Second: Bloodshed

A cruel example of the bloodshed under Islam is found in the succession of Caliphs who came after Muhammad. Caliph Omar was assassinated, and Caliph Ali Ibn Abu Talib was assassinated. Caliph Uthman Ibn Affan, who ordered the writing of the new Koran, was also assassinated. The Muslims refused to bury him in the Muslim cemetery and after his death two Muslims jumped on his dead body and broke one of his ribs (*The Hidden Truth*, pp 25, 26).

This was the society Muhammad created with his Koran; Muslims killed Muslims. The first century of Islamic history is stained with blood and characterized by brutality. And consider modern Islamic societies. Little difference can be seen.

Third: Lack of individual freedom

Muslims who leave their own countries to seek a better way of life enjoy total freedom in the Christian nations of Europe, Australia and North America. Many take advantage of that freedom to promote Islam by means of television, radio, books, tracts, and financial aid to those who embrace Islam. They are also building mosques with oil dollars coming from Libya, Saudi Arabia, Kuwait, and the United Arab Emirates.

They do not permit the preaching of the gospel in their own countries. In some Islamic states there is not even one church building. It is a crime to smuggle a Bible into these countries and if a Muslim accepts Jesus Christ as his Savior and Lord, he is considered apostate and should be executed. A Muslim can not express his opinions freely if they are critical of Islam.

On August 9th, 1996, *Al-Ahram*, the semi-official daily newspaper in Egypt, reported:

> The High Court of personal affairs announced its verdict in the case of Dr. Nasr Hamid Abu Zaid, professor at Cairo University, and demanded that he divorce his wife, Ibtihal Yunus, because, as the court stated, Dr. Abu Zaid was an apostate and that was clear from what he wrote in his books mocking Muhammad and the Koran, and saying that the *Shariah* (Koran's laws) is the reason for the demise of the Muslim countries.

Mrs. Abu Zaid did not wish to divorce her husband. Abu Zaid and his wife fled from Egypt. *The New York Times* on August 6, 1996, quoted a human rights advocate who said "The ruling is a slap in the face of civil society."

The situation in Afghanistan, under the Taliban Islamic movement, is another example. *Newsweek Magazine* (October 14,

1996) printed a report by Rod Nordland and Tony Clifton under the title "The Islamic Nightmare." Here is a part of what they wrote:

> The Mullahs who took over that week in Kabul, the conquered capital of Afghanistan, made Iran's ayatollahs look like Western playboys. The fundamentalist Taliban movement issued decree after decree through its six-member ruling council, the Shura. Television stations and movie theaters were shut down, and music was banned from the radio. Kabul's one million people were ordered to pray five times a day - including two visits to the local mosque, where attendance would be taken. Criminals were threatened with beatings, mutilation and death. Men were given 45 days to grow proper Muslim beards - which are left untrimmed - and were told to shed their Western clothes in favor of traditional Afghan dress.
>
> Women were chastised even more severely. They were sent home from their schools and jobs and were instructed to veil themselves from head to toe, preferably in the suffocating burqa, in which even the opening for the eyes is screened with mesh. Violators of the female dress code were beaten on the streets by Taliban fighters. In a sermon last Friday, the Muslim Sabbath, Syed Ghiasuddin, the acting education minister in the new theocracy, explained that a woman is like 'a rose - you water it and keep it at home for yourself to look at and smell. It is not supposed to be taken out of the house to be smelled.'
>
> The establishment of a severely fundamentalist regime in Kabul set off alarm bells all over the region. Amnesty International accused the Taliban of conducting 'a reign of terror.'

With all the restrictions against individual freedom in Islam, fundamentalists stir up a tempest if you attempt to expose the truth about Islam. *The Washington Post* reported on June 20, 2000 that Rev. Jerry Vines, former President of the Southern Baptist Convention made some remarks on the Prophet of Islam which caused Muslims to become outraged. Dr. Jerry Falwell commented concerning the Muslims' reaction to what Rev. Vines said and wrote to subscribers of his *Falwell Confidential* e-mail newsletter:

> If you want to raise the ire of the mainstream press and the swarm of politically correct organizations in this nation, just criticize Islam (as Dr. Vines learned).

While Muslims deprive anyone living in Muslim countries from expressing his or her ideas concerning Islam, they demand the same attitude in the United States and the western countries.

Fourth: Blind Hatred

The Washington Post Magazine in its August 25, 1996 issue wrote the story of David Belfield, a young Baptist man from a small town on Long Island, who went to Washington to study at Howard University. Under the influence of an Iranian Muslim, David embraced Islam, changed his name to Daoud Salahuddin and became increasingly devout. His Iranian handler had little trouble persuading him to kill a man he had never met; Daoud saw the act as an Islamic duty.

The late Ayatollah Ruhollah Khomeini had ordered the assassination of Ali Akbar Tabatabi who lived in Bethesda, Maryland and was the chief spokesman in the United States for the counter-revolutionary forces against the Khomeini government. Daoud Salahuddin assassinated Tabatabai, fled to Canada and then to Tehran. The Iranian government had agreed to send him to

China to study medicine, but never did. Here is what the *Post Magazine* wrote on page 22:

> The community Salahuddin had chosen to enter was international in scope but driven by sectarian and political feuds, despite heady talk of Arab and Muslim world unity. In the early '70s, Shiite Iran and Sunni Iraq were supporting Kurdish rebellions in each other's countries; radical Palestinians and royalist tribes, all Sunni Muslims, were fighting for control of Jordan; the Muslims of Pakistan were splitting into two separate nations, and the Arab countries - under competing Muslim monarchist, socialist and nationalist rulers - were plotting constantly against one another.   (p 22)

This is a true picture of what Islam has done for Islamic countries. And this is how they turn some of those who are converted to Islam into assassins in the name of Allah.

Fifth: Brutality

In 1995 the Sudanese Islamic government tried to assassinate President Hosny Mubarak of Egypt in Ethiopia. There has also been a great deal of turmoil in recent times in Egypt, Algeria, Afghanistan, Yemen, Israel, Uganda, and Iran. The source of this trouble is the fundamentalist Muslims who strictly obey the Koran. *The Washington Times* said in an article printed on August 25, 1996:

> The Sudanese government proceeded to escalate the war. They even redefined the war. It was no longer a civil war between the state and a group of dissenting citizens but a Jihad by Muslims against 'Infidels.' Every non-Muslim and non-Arab became an enemy of the state. . . . It is in this context that the massive aerial

and ground bombardments of innocent civilians have been and are being conducted . . . to them war is heaven. Their warriors are taught that if they kill an 'infidel' they get a place in heaven. If they are killed by an 'infidel' they are wedded to one hundred of Allah's pretty virgins in heaven. A rosy portrait indeed. The slave market is as thriving as never before. Thousands of women and children captured in slave raids remain in captivity.

Add to that the many Sudanese Christians who were tortured and crucified and the boys and girls who were captured and forced to be Muslims and trained to fight Christians. In addition, in Egypt many Coptic Christians were killed, and many girls were kidnapped and raped, and forced to marry Muslims. This is the society that the Koran has created.

Dr. Christian Goforth wrote the following story which portrays how Christians are suffering and are martyred under Islamic regimes.

The Story of Zia Nodrat

In Kabul, Afghanistan, during 1964, a fourteen year old boy, Zia Nodrat, enrolled in the NOOR Institute for the Blind. He already knew the whole Koran by heart. In Western terms that would be like an English speaker memorizing the complete New Testament in Greek, since Arabic was not Zia's mother tongue. He completed the six primary grades of the Institute in three years.

While attending his classes in Braille in the Institute for the Blind, Zia also mastered English. He did this by listening and repeating what he heard on a transistor radio. With the help of a small ear plug, he heard programs coming into Afghanistan from other countries. He eventually started asking questions about what he had heard, such as, 'What do you mean by the substitutionary atonement?' He had heard such theological concepts during Christian radio broadcasts like the *Voice of the Gospel* coming from Addis Ababa in Ethiopia, Africa.

Finally, he shared with a few persons that he had received Jesus the Messiah as his personal Savior. They asked him if he realized that he could be killed for this, since the Islamic Law of Apostasy for anyone leaving Islam is death. He answered, 'I have counted the cost and am willing to die for the Messiah, since He has already died on the cross for me.'

Zia then became the spiritual leader of the few Afghan Christians. In the Institute for the Blind in Kabul, the students elected him as the president of their association. But the next year after it was known that he had become a Christian, he lost the election for this position. One of his Christian teachers told him how sorry she was that he lost. He replied, quoting the prophet John the Baptist who said of Jesus, 'He must become greater, I must become less' (John 3:30). His goal in life was not to seek prominence for himself, but to be a humble servant of his Lord. Zia's father said that before he had entered the Institute for the Blind, he had been like a cold and unlit piece of charcoal. After his experience there, he had become like a red hot, brightly burning coal.

Once he borrowed an English Braille copy of the Gospel of John. He opened it and read with his fingers. He then returned it and said that his question had been answered. When asked what his question was, he replied that in John 13:34 Jesus said, 'A new commandment I give you that you love one another.' He wondered why the Lord Jesus called it 'new,' since the commandment 'love your neighbour as yourself' had already been given to Moses, as recorded in the Old Testament book of Leviticus 19:18. But now he understood. He explained that until the incarnation of the Messiah the world had never before seen love personified. He went on to state that the Bible reveals that God is love, and that Jesus as God in human flesh is love incarnate. This was what made the command new. Jesus said, 'A new commandment I give you that you love one another as I have loved you.' In his perfect life Jesus has now given us a new model to follow.

Zia was the first blind student to attend regular sighted schools in Afghanistan. There he had a small recorder with which he taped everything his teachers said, so that he could go over it and learn it thoroughly. He thus became the number one student out of hundreds at his grade level. Those who failed in their classes were given a second chance to take examinations after the three month vacation. He studied the next year during this break and passed the tests. In this way he completed high school, finishing two grades each year.

Zia wanted to study Islamic Law so that he could defend Christians who might be persecuted for their faith. He therefore entered the University of Kabul, from which he graduated with his law degree. He also studied Calvin's Institutes on the side since he wanted to grasp the concepts of this Reformation leader.

The Christoffel Blind Mission in Germany gave the Institute for the Blind in Afghanistan an extensive library of Braille books in German. Since Zia wanted to read these, along with his other classes, he went to the Goethe Institute in Kabul and learned German. As the top student there too, he won a scholarship to go to Germany to study advanced German. When the

Germans found out that he was blind, they withdrew the fellowship since they did not have the arrangements or accommodations for a blind person. He asked them what he would have to do. They replied that he would have to travel alone and take care of himself. When he agreed to do that, they finally accepted him. While studying there with top students from Goethe Institutes around the world, he was number one in this advanced course as well.

Zia also translated the New Testament from Iranian Persian into his own Afghan Dari dialect. This was published by the Pakistan Bible Society in Lahore. Its third edition was published by the Cambridge University Press in England in 1989. He also traveled to Saudi Arabia where he won a memory contest on the Koran. The Muslim judges were so amazed and chagrined that a non-Arabic speaker had taken first place, that they also awarded another prize for the best Arab in the competition.

Because earlier blind students like Zia had become Christians, the Muslim government in Afghanistan sent a written order closing the two Institutes for the Blind in March 1973, one of which was in Kabul and the other seven hundred miles to the west in Herat. All the expatriate teachers of the blind along with their families were ordered to leave Afghanistan within one week. As these dedicated teachers left, God gave them a promise from Isaiah 42:16, *'I will lead the blind by ways they have not known, along unfamiliar paths I will guide them; I will turn the darkness into light before them and make the rough places smooth. These are the things I will do: I will not forsake them.'*

The Muslim Government then destroyed the Christian Church building in Kabul, after previously having given permission to build it. President

Eisenhower had requested permission for construction of this building from King Zahir Shah on his visit to Afghanistan in 1959, since a mosque had been built in Washington, DC, for the Muslim diplomats there, and Christian diplomats and other Christians needed a place to worship on a reciprocal basis in Kabul. Christians from nations all around the world contributed toward its construction. At its dedication, the cornerstone carved in beautiful Afghan alabaster marble read: 'To the glory of God "Who loves us and has freed us from our sins by the blood of Jesus" this building is dedicated as a "house of prayer for all nations" in the reign of H. M. Zahir Shah, May 17, 1970 A.D., "Jesus Christ Himself being the Chief Cornerstone."'

When troops arrived and started knocking down the wall between the street and the Church property preparatory to destroy it, a German Christian businessman went to the mayor of Kabul, who had given the order, and said, 'If your Government touches that House of God, God will overthrow your Government.' This proved to be a prophecy. The mayor then sent a letter to the congregation ordering them to give the Church for destruction, since that would mean that the government would not have to pay compensation. They replied that they could not give it to anyone since it did not belong to them. It had been dedicated to God. They also added that if the Government took it and destroyed it, they would be answerable to God.

Police, workmen and bulldozers were sent to destroy the Church. The congregation, instead of opposing, offered them tea and cookies. Christians all around the world prayed and many of them wrote letters to Afghan embassies in various nations. Billy Graham and other world Christian leaders signed a statement of concern and sent it to the King.

On July 17, 1973 the destruction of the Church building was completed. That very night the Afghan government responsible for the destruction was overthrown in a coup. Afghans who are quick to see omens in events say that Jesus the Messiah came down from heaven and overthrew the government because the government had overthrown His Church. It had been a monarchy for 227 years. That night it became a Republic under President Daoud. In 1978 this government was toppled by a Communist coup, followed by the Russian invasion just after Christmas in 1979. Millions of Afghans had to flee their country as refugees. One of them was heard to say, 'Ever since our government destroyed that Christian Church, God has been judging our country.'

Under the Communists, the Institute for the Blind in Kabul was reopened and Zia was put in charge. He did a fine job of reorganizing it. Then pressure was brought on him to join the Communist party. He refused. One official told him that if he did not join, he might be killed. He replied that he was not afraid to be killed because he was sure he was going to heaven. He asked the Communist if he knew where he would go when he died.

Finally Zia was arrested on false charges and put in the Puli Charkhi political prison outside of Kabul, where thousands were executed. There was no heat in the jail to protect the prisoners from the cold winter weather. He had to sleep on the freezing mud floor in his overcoat. A prisoner next to him was trembling with cold since he did not even have a jacket. Zia knew John the Baptist had said, 'The man who has two coats should share with him who has none' (Luke 3:11). He took off his only coat and gave it to the neighbour. From then on, the Lord miraculously kept him warm every night. He slept as if he had a comforter over him.

In prison the Communists gave Zia shock treatments to try to brainwash him. The electric burns left scars on his head. But he did not give in. When he was offered the opportunity to study Russian in prison, he mastered this language also. The Communists finally freed him in December 1985.

Following his release from prison Zia read Genesis 12:1-3 in his Braille Bible, 'The Lord said to Abram, "Leave your country, your people and your father's household and go to the land I will show you. I... will bless you... and you will be a blessing. I will bless those who bless you, and whoever curses you I will curse; and all peoples on earth will be blessed through you."' Zia felt God was calling him to leave Afghanistan to go as a missionary to Pakistan. He therefore got in touch with a friend, a blind beggar. He then dressed himself in rags. On their way out of the country, he let his friend do all the talking, thereby concealing his identity or detection from the soldiers. They thus were able to get through the Soviet check points along the main highway from Kabul. It took them twelve days to travel the 150 miles to the Khyber Pass and then on into Pakistan

After Zia arrived in Pakistan, he was offered an opportunity to travel to the United States to study Hebrew since he was also working on a translation of the Old Testament into his Dari language. He declined saying he had so much to do among the Afghan refugees that he could not leave. He started an Institute for the Blind for them. He learned the main language of Pakistan, Urdu, preaching in this language in Christian churches. He furthermore completed a book of New Testament stories in Dari for children.

On March 23, 1988, Zia was kidnapped by a fanatical Muslim group, *Hisbe Islami*, ('The Party of Islam') and was accused of being a CIA agent because he knew English, a KGB or Khad spy because he knew Russian, and an apostate from Islam because he was a Christian. He was beaten for hours with rods. A sighted person can brace and flinch when the blow comes. But a blind person cannot see the club coming and thus gets the full force, even like the torture the Lord Jesus Christ experienced when he was blindfolded and then struck (Luke 22:64). His wife and three daughters had been able to get out of Afghanistan and were with him in Pakistan at the time he was kidnapped. Soon after his wife gave birth to a beautiful boy who looks much like his father. No one knows whether Zia ever heard that he had a son.

The latest word, though not absolutely definite, is that *Hisbe Islami* murdered Zia. Before he was kidnapped, he had told a friend that if this party ever captured him they would kill him. This same party caught two Pakistani Christians taking relief items to needy Afghans and tortured them. Before releasing them, one of the captors stated, 'We are not going to kill you the way we killed Zia Nodrat.' In addition, an Afghan news reporter on the Northwest Frontier of Pakistan claims to have evidence that *Hisbe Islami* murdered Zia in a cruel way.

The United Nations Universal Declaration on Human Rights in article 13 states, 'Everyone shall have the right to freedom of thought, conscience and religion; freedom to manifest one's religion or belief.' The story of Zia is a story of infringement of human rights. Zia has been denied his freedom and has probably been martyred for his faith.

Before his capture, he asked a Christian friend that if anything happened to him, his friend would take care of his family. The friend answered in the affirmative, not realizing that a short time later Zia would be kidnapped. He was able to arrange for Zia's wife and two of his children to be brought to North America.

God does not force a belief system upon people. He has given them liberty to choose. Therefore what right does an earthly regime or group have to impose a certain belief system?   (Printed by permission)

The story of Oswaldo "Wally" Magdangal

In 1992, December 25th fell on Friday, the Muslim day of rest, when Pastor Oswaldo 'Wally' Magdangal was to be hanged in the Saudi capital of Riyadh for blaspheming Islam. Shari'ah law requires beheading for 'apostates' - those who renounce Islam - as well as for murderers. No Friday passes without at least one such execution in the public square following the noon prayers, rights organizations say. Hangings are reserved for 'blasphemers' like Magdangal. Foreigners of non-Islamic faiths can worship legally in private in Saudi Arabia, but the 42-year-old Filipino pastor was arrested after his growing house church had become too noticeable. On December 23, Magdangal wrote out his last will and testament for his wife and young daughter.

Religious police had tortured every part of his body in trying to force him to renounce his faith in Christ. Embracing Islam would have won his immediate release. Initially the religious police, or *muttawin* - (a vigilante force with a hierarchy and membership extending into government and other sectors) beat him throughout 210 minutes of mocking interrogation. They handed him a pencil and paper and demanded names of other Christians he knew. He refused.

'Eventually I was so weak, they placed the pad of paper in my lap, and they forced the pencil into my hand,' Magdangal told CT. 'I was weeping, and I said, 'Lord, you've got to help me here,' and I began to write the names of Billy Graham, Charles Spurgeon, and others. After a few days, they were so mad, because they'd been all over Saudi Arabia looking for those people.'

During interrogations - which included flogging of his back, his palms, and the soles of his feet - the *muttawa'in* did not state charges against him. Only when he answered that he agreed with an article predicting the ultimate fall of Islam *in Christ for the Nations magazine* (which the *muttawa'in* found in his home) was the basis for the eventual blasphemy charge established.

Magdangal was not allowed to speak during his high court trial, which Muslim clerics held in secret. 'I was shaking with pain; I was trembling with fear,' Magdangal says. 'I kept asking them to get my wife, but that led them to tell me in strong words to stand silent - not to say a word or I would suffer the consequence of every word I spoke. That's when I just broke down, and I just wept and wept.'

By then the lower court had read some charges - preaching a message different from the Koran, 'building' a church - but only hinted at the blasphemy charge. Magdangal would learn of the blasphemy verdict before he knew the charge itself: a *muttawa'in* officer interrogating him, Lt. Bader Alyaya, said his case had become 'very serious' and that he was going to be hanged.

'He motioned around his neck like a noose, and then he pulled the noose above his head in a motion with his hand,' he recalls. 'I knew that people guilty of blasphemy are hanged to death for three days, to send a strong warning to the Muslims not to turn to another religion, and for Christians to not try to reach the Muslims.'

Magdangal describes a sensation of fire or lightning striking him in the chest. 'It felt like there was something within me that was getting ready to explode, and as I opened my mouth, the words came out: "I shall not die but live and declare the works of my Lord, for no weapon formed against me shall prosper, for greater is he who is in me than he who is in the world,"' Magdangal says. 'That's all I said. And then I bent over, and I wept, and I wept, and I wept.'

Normally Saudi authorities do not tell the condemned of their sentence until the day of their execution, so as to forestall appeals and protests, Magdangal says. Sometimes the authorities go to the extra step of leading prisoners to believe they are being released just before executing them.

Magdangal knew only that the Philippine embassy had filed protests of his detention, which went unheeded, though soon Amnesty International was also monitoring his case. As executive secretary to the Saudi director of Defense and Civil Aviation, Magdangal had close friends high in the Saudi government, including members of the royal family - and even in the muttawa'in - who had only gradually become aware of his arrest. Muttawa'in officers warned each of Magdangal's high-level friends to stop advocating for him.

The threats worked. But a general secretly told Magdangal's wife to inform Fidel Ramos, then president of the Philippines, that the case had become 'very serious.'

Having freshly achieved victory from Saudi soil in the Gulf War, the U.S. Congress and the White House joined with human rights organizations to appeal for Magdangal's life - unbeknownst to him. By December 23 he had settled in his heart that he was going to be executed.

Magdangal then prayed that if he were spared, he would be a voice for the persecuted. Shortly before midnight, the prison commander arrived with orders to deport Magdangal. 'Even at that point, from the prison to the airport, I was very terrified because the two officers with me were interrupted on their radio by Muslim clerics who were yelling, fighting my release, and telling them to divert the car and bring it somewhere else to kill me,' he says.

Now president of Christians in Crisis, an advocacy group based in Sacramento, California, Magdangal later learned from a friend high in the muttawa'in that military advisers were vying with clerics for the ear of King Fahd bin Abdul al-Aziz Al Saud - whose mandate in Saudi Arabia, the clerics reminded him, was to uphold Shari'ah.

'The war was still very fresh, and Saddam Hussein was still a major threat,' Magdangal recalls. 'The military advisers were saying, in essence, "King, we are under such pressure from the friendly nations - what is one person compared to what we are facing from Saddam Hussein, and all the benefits that might be diminished as a result of executing this person?"'

King Fahd ordered Magdangal to be expelled within 24 hours. According to Magdangal's muttawa'in contact, 500 Muslim clerics resigned their state posts in protest. (*Christianity Today*, July 8, 2002)

Brutality and suicide bombing are taught to the Muslim children in Palestine at a very early age. Here is an example of a song little girls sing on the Palestinian television:

> I am the voice of the exalted martyr...
> And we shall march as warriors of *Jihad.*
> Oh, my exalted martyr, you are my example.
> Oh my companion, you are beside me.
> Oh, my sister, sing constantly about my life as a suicide warrior.

Anyone who encourages people to kill innocent people under any circumstances is of the devil. Christ says concerning the devil:

> He was a murderer from the beginning, and does not stand in the truth, because there is no truth in him.
>
> (John 8:44 NKJ)

Sixth: Deceit

If Allah of the Koran abrogates his word, how much easier is it for the Muslims to cancel and terminate any treaty or agreement they make? I once heard Ibn Baz, the late chief imam of Saudi Arabia, on the radio. Someone asked him if it was right for the Palestinians to make peace with the Jewish state according to the Islamic *Shariah.* "Yes," answered Imam Ibn Baz, "until they become strong enough to defeat them."

Remember the treaty of *Al-Hudaybiyah*? Hudaybiyah is a small fertile area between Mecca and Al-Madina where Muhammad fought a battle in the early years of Islam. When he saw he was fighting a losing battle, Muhammad signed a ten year peace treaty with the tribe of Quraish who lived in Mecca. Years later, when his army became stronger and the Meccans were living securely and off their guard, Muhammad led his army into Mecca and captured it with no regard of the treaty. That is Islam.

There is a principle in Islam called *takiya*. It means the right to pretend that Muslims want peace when they are weak so they can later defeat their enemy when they are stronger. This principle shows the deceit in Islam. An email dated June 20, 2002, recorded the following, under the title, *Scholar warns West of Muslim Goals*:

> A leader of the small worldwide Muslim reform movement warned the West Tuesday against wishful thinking as the U.S. government promotes an intensive dialogue with Islam.
>
> 'The dialogue is not proceeding well because of the two-facedness of most Muslim interlocutors on the one hand and the gullibility of well-meaning Western idealists on the other,' said Bassam Tibi, in an interview with United Press International.
>
> Syrian-born Tibi, who claims to be a direct descendant of the prophet Muhammad and teaches political science at Goettingen University in Germany, appealed for intellectual honesty between both parties in these exchanges.
>
> 'First, both sides should acknowledge candidly that although they might use identical terms these mean different things to each of them. The word 'peace,' for example, implies to a Muslim the extension of the *Dar al-Islam* - or 'House of Islam' - to the entire world,' explained Tibi, who is also a research scholar at Harvard University.
>
> 'This is completely different from the Enlightenment concept of eternal peace that dominates Western thought, a concept developed by 18th century philosopher Immanuel Kant.'
>
> 'Similarly, when Muslims and the Western heirs of the Enlightenment speak of 'tolerance' they have different things in mind. In Islamic terminology, this

term implies abiding non-Islamic monotheists, such as Christians, Jews and Zoroastrians, as second-class believers. They are *dhimmi*, a protected but politically immature minority.'

According to Tibi, the quest of converting the entire world to Islam is an immutable fixture of the Muslim world view. Only if this task is accomplished - if the world has become a *Dar al-Islam* - will it also be a *Dar a-Salam*, or a "House of Peace."

Tibi appealed to his co-religionists to 'revise their understanding of peace and tolerance by accepting pluralism.' 'Furthermore,' he said, 'Muslim leaders should give up the notion of Jihad in the sense of conquest - as opposed to Jihad as an internal struggle of the individual.'

Tibi's advice comes at a time when the U.S. government is urging American Muslim leaders to promote understanding for the United States in the Islamic world. To Tibi, this is more of a diplomatic endeavor than the promotion of a more profound theological understanding between Islam and the Judeo-Christian worldview prevalent in the West.

In an article in the prestigious Hamburg weekly, *Die Zeit*, Tibi gave anecdotal evidence of how daunting a task this dialogue with Islam can be.

The bishop of Hildesheim in Germany paid an imam a courtesy visit in his mosque. The imam handed the Catholic prelate a Koran, which he joyfully accepted. But when the bishop tried to present the imam with a Bible, the Muslim cleric just stared at him in horror and refused to even touch Christianity's holy book.

'The bishop was irritated because he perceived this behavior as a gross discourtesy,' wrote Tibi, 'but the imam had only acted according to his faith. For if an imam gives a bishop a Koran, he considers this a *Da'Wa*, or "call to Islam."'

'This,' explained Tibi, 'must be borne in mind when one engages in a dialogue with Muslim scholars.'

The Contributions of the Koran to Mankind

What did Muslims contribute to mankind? What are their achievements and inventions? We recognize Muslim philosophers such as Ibn Al-Haytham and Ibn Sina, who practiced primitive medicine, and one who formulated algebra, but where is the modern contribution of Islam today other than suicide bombers? What kind of life would the Muslim countries be living if they had not discovered oil in their lands and used American engineers, and other westerners along with foreign technology to pump it?

A Muslim asked the late Sheik Al-Sharawy, a well-known Muslim imam and television speaker in Egypt, "Why do we see great inventions such as computers and medical technology in the Christian countries, while Islamic countries do not have any modern achievements?" "Allah," Sheik Sharaway answered, "gave the Islamic countries oil to have great wealth, so they can hire those Christians. Christians toil and invent and Muslims use them and enjoy their inventions."

What a strange answer!

It is a fact that all the comforts Muslims enjoy today are the products of Christian minds. There is a sharp contrast between the social and economic conditions of the many countries in Europe and North America where societies were founded on Judeo-Christian principles, and the corrupted social and economic conditions in many Islamic countries.

The Fruit of a Bible Believing Society

When we speak about fruit the Bible produces in the life of those who believe, we mean that wherever the Bible is preached

261

and accepted, it changes lives, homes become more secure, children are raised in the fear of God and crime almost disappears.

Several years ago, my wife and I went to England to attend the Keswick Convention. We realized that there were no policemen in the village. When we asked a friend who used to attend that convention to explain this, she replied, "During the convention, people sense the presence of Christ. In fact, they leave their homes unlocked. No burglary was reported to the police for many years." To test this statement, my wife and I decided to go to a few homes to see if their doors truly were unlocked. We opened the first door, noting that the cabinets were full of silver plates and precious china. We opened the door to another house, to discover the same reality. Then, to the third. And we came to the conclusion that because of the effect of the Word of God and the presence of Christ during Keswick weeks, there were no crimes committed.

The Word of God has the power of regenerating the sinful individual, as the Apostle Peter says:

> Having been born again, not of corruptible seed but incorruptible through the Word of God, which lives and abides forever.   (I Peter 1:23 NKJ)

The Apostle Paul wrote:

> For I am not ashamed of the gospel of Christ, for it is the power of God to salvation for everyone who believes, for the Jew first and also for the Greek.
> (Romans 1:16 NKJ)

> Therefore, if anyone is in Christ, he is a new creation; old things have passed away; behold, all things have become new.   (2 Corinthians 5:17 NKJ)

Christ changed the Pharisee Saul and he became the Apostle Paul. He commanded seven demons to come out of Mary

Magdalene, changed her life and sent her to announce His resurrection to the disciples (Luke 8:2 and John 20:17).

The book of Acts recorded the history of the first century Christians; there was no bloodshed, no conspiracies, and no corruption among the apostles of Jesus Christ. Paul did not kill Peter, none of them killed anyone. Many of the first century Christians were martyred, not in fighting each other, but they were persecuted, tortured, and murdered because of their faith in Christ, His crucifixion, and His resurrection. They lived in the catacombs of Rome for the sake of Christ. But with all these afflictions, they conquered the world, not by the sword but by being Spirit-filled people preaching the gospel of Jesus Christ.

Here is a vivid picture of the early Christian community as written in the book of Acts:

> And the multitude of them that believed were of one heart and of one soul: neither said any of them that aught of the things which he possessed was his own; but they had all things common. And with great power gave the apostles witness of the resurrection of the Lord Jesus: and great grace was upon them all. Neither was there any among them that lacked: for as many as were possessors of lands or houses sold them, and brought the prices of the things that were sold, and laid them down at the apostles' feet: and distribution was made unto every man according as he had need.
>
> (Acts 4:32-35)

In the name of the living Christ, many miracles were also done (Acts 3:6; 9:34; 16:18). Christ said:

> I am the light of the world, he who follows me shall not walk in darkness, but have the light of life.
>
> (John 8:12 NKJ)

He also said to His disciples:

Ye are the light of the world.   (Matthew 5:14)

Christ not only gives spiritual light to the believers but also intellectual light. No one can deny the scientific, medical, and technological achievements of Christians as we see them in the western world.

Dr. D. James Kennedy, president of Evangelism Explosion International, with Jerry Newcombe mentioned on page 101 of their book *What if Jesus Had Never Been Born* a list of some outstanding Bible-believing scientists, who were pioneers of science and committed Christians. We will mention but a few of them:

Antiseptic Surgery, Joseph Lister
Bacteriology, Louis Pasteur
Chemistry, Robert Boyle
Comparative Anatomy, Georges Cuvier
Computer Science, Charles Babbage
Dimensional Analysis, Lord Rayleigh
Dynamics, Isaac Newton
Electronics, John Ambrose Fleming
Electrodynamics, James Clerk Maxwell
Electromagnetics, Michael Faraday
Energetics, Lord Kelvin
Galactic Astronomy, Sir William Herschel
Gas Dynamics, Robert Boyle
Genetics, Gregor Mendel
Glacial Geology, Louis Agassiz
Gynecology, James Simpson
Hydrography, Matthew Maury
Hydrostatics, Blaise Pascal
Isotopic Chemistry, William Ramsey
Model Analysis, Lord Rayleigh

Natural History, John Ray
    Non-Euclidean Geometry, Bernard Riemann
    Oceanography, Matthew Maury
    Optical Mineralogy, David Brewster

It is a historical fact that most of the inventions that made life more comfortable came from the minds and thoughts of Christian inventors and manufacturers. Electric current was discovered by the French mathematician, Andre-Marie Ampere, who formulated Ampere's law. The SI unit of electric current is named after him. Thomas Alva Edison invented the incandescent lamp, the carbon telephone transmitter, and the first central electric power plant in the world. Alexander Graham Bell invented the telephone. Henry Ford built the automobile. There are many others. All these achievements were the fruit of Biblical preaching.

Add to all these achievements, the inspiring Christian songs and music that fill the heart with praise to God and divine joy. Think about the German composers and musicians Johann Sebastian Bach (1685-1750) who composed over 200 Christian cantatas; Ludwing Van Beethoven (1770-1827) the composer who wrote music of all genres including nine symphonies, five piano concertos and thirty-two piano sonatas; George Frederick Handel (1685-1759) who wrote the *Messiah* in 1742 which still to this day is an inspiring Biblical musical; and Wolfgang Amadeus Mozart (1756-1791) the Austrian composer who enriched music with his symphonies and operas.

There are no similar songs, symphonies or music like these in Islamic culture - no joy of the Lord in Islamic worship. Islam did not produce even one musician of the standard of the great Christian ones.

Looking at the Islamic countries, you see people who are afraid of evil spirits and *jinn*, afraid of even touching a Bible, and afraid of building churches in their countries. Authorities do not permit Christians to preach the gospel, because Islam is a religion that is not open to research, criticism, discussion or freedom of choice. It is a religion which keeps the illiterate masses in Islamic countries living in ignorance and fanaticism a stark contrast to living life in a civil western culture. Islam is built on the primitive culture of Arabia in the year 600 - the culture which orders Muslims to circumcise their daughters. This brutal mutilation which ruins the sex life of the woman is all because Muslim men are obsessed by sex and the female sex organs. This is not God's religion.

Conclusion

As I conclude Part II of this book, I call the dear Muslim reader to make an honest research and compare between Christianity and Islam with an open mind and heart for the sake of his or her eternal life.

The Koran says that Allah gave the Jews the prophethood (Surat Al-Jathiya 45:16). He spoke through their prophets. Those prophets foretold the coming of Jesus Christ His eternal Son, to die on the cross to save all who believe in Him.

When the fullness of time had come, God sent forth His eternal son, born of the Virgin Mary. He has no human father, for He is the Son of God, not by sexual intercourse, for God never had a wife. God is a spirit; there is none comparable to Him. The Son of God died on the cross of Calvary, was buried and rose from the dead. He calls all the people with open arms saying:

> Come to Me, all who labor and are heavy laden, and I will give you rest.   (Matthew 11:28 NKJ)

No human being can give rest to all who labor and are heavy laden, only God can do that. Buddha can not do that. Confucius can not do that. Muhammad never claimed that he could give rest to anyone.

Jesus Christ offers rest to every one who feels the heavy burden of sin, every one who is tired of life and oppressed by afflictions. Will you believe in Him, open your heart and receive Him to become a child of God instead of being a slave of sin? The Bible says concerning Christ:

> But as many as received Him, to them He gave the right to become children of God, even to those who believe in His name: who were born, not of blood, nor of the will of the flesh, nor of the will of man, but of God.
>
> (John 1:12, 13 NKJ)

It is a sad fact that the majority will always believe the lie rather than the truth. This is why Jesus said:

> Enter by the narrow gate; for wide is the gate and broad is the way that leads to destruction, and there are many who go in by it. Because narrow is the gate and difficult is the way which leads to life, and there are few who find it. (Matthew 7:13, 14 NKJ)

There are two key words in these verses: "go" and "find." The way that leads to destruction does not need any thinking, any investigation. Just "go" with the crowd. The way that leads to life needs a diligent investigation and an honest decision for Jesus Christ.

Which way shall you choose?

PART THREE

UNDERSTANDING ISLAM

Chapter Twenty One

Islam Is Not A Religion Of Peace

The barbaric terrorist attacks on Tuesday, September 11, 2001, on America's World Trade Center in New York City and the Pentagon in Washington, DC, shocked the American people, and caused them to ask, "Why did it happen? Who did it? And why do those who did it hate us?"

Investigation by the CIA and FBI concluded that the attackers were Muslims. Does that mean that every Muslim is a terrorist? By no means. There are many decent Muslims; to be sure they are not true Muslims as we will explain. While many news commentators and politicians are proclaiming that Islam is a religion of peace, voices come warning that Islamic *Jihad*, or Holy War, has begun against Jews and Christians.

These conflicting descriptions of Islam can be explained by examining the three types of Muslims: Secularists, Moderates, and Fundamentalists.

Secularists are Muslims by culture and tradition and have only a vague knowledge of the Koran. Many secular Muslims believe that the Koran was given to the Arabs of the Arabian peninsula in the sixth century and cannot be applied to present day sophisticated societies. Therefore, it has little significance to them.

Moderates know and study the Koran but seek to make their faith relevant to modern life. They try to reconcile the contradictory verses in the Koran in such a way that Islamic society may tolerate Jews and Christians living among them. They emphasize the verses that the prophet Muhammad uttered when he tried to win Jews and Christians to Islam and when he was weak militarily and in need of their support.

Here are some of these kind verses concerning Jews and Christians:

> O Children of Israel! Remember My Favour which I bestowed upon you and that I preferred you to mankind.
> (Surat Al-Baqarah 2:47)

> Verily, those who believe and those who are Jews and Christians, and Savians, whoever believes in Allah and the Last Day and does righteous good deeds shall have their reward with their Lord, on them shall be no fear, nor shall they grieve. (Surat Al-Baqarah 2:62)

When needed, Muslim clerics quote these and other select verses to paint a glowing picture of Islam as a religion of peace, brotherhood, modesty, morality, self-discipline and family values. Many Americans and westerners are deceived by such claims. Barnabas Fund in England wrote the following:

> The Muslim prophet Muhammad, the founder of Islam, was a complex character whose attitudes and opinions changed and evolved during his lifetime in response to events around him. It is not surprising to find that Islam is a complex faith.

Fundamentalists are those who are true Muslims, who want to follow the verses of the Koran precisely. This includes verses calling Muslims to wage war against Jews and Christians known as "infidels." Muhammad received these verses after he became strong militarily and after he realized that the Jews and the Christians rejected his new religion.

Muhammad's anger and hatred against Jews and Christians is clearly shown in the following Koranic verses which abrogate and terminate the earlier kind verses. These later verses are the root of violence and terrorism which saturates and captures the mind of fundamentalists.

Most assuredly, Islam is not a religion of peace, rather it is a religion of terror and bloodshed. Following is the proof.

First: Islam is not a religion of peace according to the testimony of the Koran itself.

The Koran is the final authority for true Muslims. The following verses of the Koran call Muslims to fight, torture, and kill Jews, Christians, and non-Muslims. Some of these verses I have mentioned before, but I must repeat them here to give the reader an organized list of them.

The Koran commands the prophet Muhammad to incite Muslims to fight in the cause of Allah:

O prophet Muhammad urge the believers (Muslims) to fight. (Surat Al-Anfal 8:65)

The Koran commands Muslims to fight Jews and Christians:

Fight against those who believe not in Allah, nor in the Last Day, nor forbid that which has been forbidden by Allah and His Messenger (Muhammad) and those who acknowledge not the religion of truth (Islam) among the people of the Scripture (Jews and Christians) until they pay the Jizyah with willing submission, and feel themselves subdued. (Surat Al-Taubah 9:29)

Jizyah is a special high tax to be paid only by Jews or Christians who do not want to renounce their religion and convert to Islam.

The Koran commands Muslims to fight non-Muslims until they destroy all other religions and Islam is the only religion in the world:

> And fight them until there is no more Fitnah (disbelief and worshipping of others along with Allah) and (all and every kind of) worship is for Allah (alone).
>
> (Surat Al-Baqarah 2:193)

Fundamentalists divide the world's population into two camps, Dar Al-Harb (House of War) where Jews and Christians live, and Dar Al-Islam (House of Islam) where Muslims live. They believe that Holy War should continue against those who live in the House of War until they are all exterminated or converted.

Fundamentalists dream of a global Islamic empire. They believe that if they destroy America and western countries they will achieve this dream.

The Koran declares that fighting is ordained by Allah for Muslims:

> Jihad (holy fighting in Allah's cause) is ordained for you. (Surat Al-Baqarah 2:216)

The Koran declares that Allah loves those who fight in His cause:

> Verily, Allah loves those who fight in his Cause in rows as if they were solid structures. (Surat Al-Saff 61:4)

The Koran commands Muslims to convert non-Muslims to Islam by force:

> Kill the Mushrikun (polytheists, Christians and non-Muslims), wherever you find them, and capture them and besiege them, and lie in wait for them in each and every ambush. But, if they repent and perform Al-Salat (public prayer with Muslims) and give Zakat (Islamic alms), then leave their way free. Allah is oft-forgiving, most merciful.   (Surat Al-Taubah (9:5)

Blaise Pascal, a mathematician who lived in 1670 said, "Men never do evil so completely and cheerfully as when they do it from religious conviction." The heart of man is naturally evil. You can ignite that evil with religious gasoline. The Koran's verses ignited that evil in the hearts of those terrorists and will ignite evil in many more Muslims' hearts.

The Koran declares that those who wage war against Allah and Muhammad must be crucified and tortured in a sadistic manner:

> The recompense of those who wage war against Allah and His Messenger and do mischief in the land is only that they shall be killed or crucified or their hands and their feet be cut off from opposite sides, or be exiled from the land. That is their disgrace in this world, and a great torment is theirs in the Hereafter.
>
>   (Surat Al-Maidah 5:33)

> Fight them and Allah will torture [author's literal translation] them by your hands and disgrace them, help you to (victory) over them.   (Surat Al-Taubah 9:14)

275

The Koran commands Muslims to fight the infidels who are neighbors and close to them:

> O you who believe (Muslims)! Fight those of the infidels who are close to you, and let them find harshness in you; and know that Allah is with those who are the pious.   (Surat Al-Taubah 9:123)

The Koran commands Muslims to terrorize and strike the necks and smite the fingers and toes of the infidels (Jéws and Christians):

> I will cast terror into the hearts of those who are infidels, so strike them over the necks and smite over all their fingers and toes. This is because they defied and disobeyed Allah and His Messenger (Muhammad). And whoever defies and disobeys Allah and His Messenger, then verily, Allah is severe in punishment. This is (the torment), so taste it; and surely, for the infidels is the torment of the Fire.
>   (Surat Al-Anfal 8:12-14)

The Koran declares that Muslims who fight in the cause of Allah are preferred over those who do not fight:

> Not equal are those of the believers who sit (at home), except those who are disabled (by injury or are blind or lame), and those who strive hard and fight in the Cause of Allah with their wealth and their lives. Allah has preferred in grades those who strive hard and fight with their wealth and their lives above those who sit (at home). Unto each, Allah has promised good (Paradise),

but Allah has preferred those who strive hard and fight, above those who sit (at home) by a huge reward.

(Surat Al-Nisa 4:95)

The Koran warns Muslims that the wrath of Allah will be upon them if they do not fight the infidels (Jews, Christians and non-Muslims) until death:

O you who believe (Muslims)! When you meet those who are infidels in a battlefield, never turn your backs to them. And whoever turns his back to them on such a day - unless it be a stratagem of war, or to retreat to a troop (of his own) - he indeed has drawn upon himself wrath from Allah. And his abode is Hell, and worst indeed is that destination.   (Surat Al-Anfal 8:15-16)

The Koran commands Muslims not to befriend Jews or Christians:

O ye who believe (Muslims) take not the Jews or the Christians for your friends and protectors. They are but friends and protectors to each other. And he among you that turns to them (for friendship) is of them.

(Surat Al-Maidah 5:51)

With these words, the Muslims look to the Jews and Christians as their enemies who should never be trusted but rather be killed.

After reading all these Koranic verses, and there are more in the Koran, how can anyone claim that Islam is a religion of peace?!

The Koran promises the Muslim who fights and kills Jews, Christians and non-Muslims, forgiveness and a sensual, luxurious life in paradise:

> And if you are killed or die in the Way of Allah, forgiveness and mercy from Allah are far better than all that they amass (of worldly wealth).
>
> (Surat Al-Imran 3:157)

> Verily, Allah has purchased of the believers their lives and their properties for (the price) that theirs shall be the Paradise. They fight in Allah's Cause, so they kill (others) and are killed. It is a promise in truth which is binding on Him. (Surat Al-Taubah 9:111)

The Koran describes life in paradise in the following verses:

> Eat and drink with happiness because of what you used to do. They will recline (with ease) on thrones arranged in ranks. And We shall marry them to Hur (fair females) with wide lovely eyes. And We shall provide them with fruit and meat such as they desire.
>
> (Surat Al-Tur 52:17-20,22)

> Water flowing constantly and fruit in plenty whose supply is not cut off and reclining on couches raised high, verily we have created them (women) of special creation and made them virgins of equal age.
>
> (Surat Al-Waqiah 56:31-37)

> Gardens and vineyards and young full-breasted virgins of equal age and a full cup of wine.
>
> (Surat Al-Naba 78:32-34)

Adel Abd-Elmonum Abu-Al-Abass, a Muslim Egyptian author, wrote in his book, *Marriage and Sex in Islam*, in the chapter dealing with sex in paradise:

Muhammad the Messenger of Allah said: 'The Muslim will be given in paradise the strength of a hundred men to enable him to have sex there. The Muslim will have sex with a hundred virgins every day.' He also said, 'By Allah, we will have thrilling sex in paradise. And women in paradise will be made virgins again after every intercourse.' These sayings of Muhammad were documented by Tarmazi and Tabarai

(Marriage and Sex in Islam, pp 133-134).

Such a portrait of paradise captivates the minds of suicide bombers, and motivates them to die as martyrs so they can go immediately to paradise to be married to the beautiful virgins with wide lovely eyes awaiting their arrival. A martyr is guaranteed total forgiveness of his sins and eternal life in paradise where he can drink wine and will be married to a great number of beautiful sensual virgins.

Some prominent Muslim clerics call the suicide bombers martyrs. In its issue dated February 7, 2002, the daily official Egyptian newspaper, *Al-Ahram*, reported what Dr. Sayed Tantawi, the grand sheik of Al-Azhar mosque in Egypt, said answering a question from a reporter who met him in London.

'What is your opinion concerning the suicide bombers?' the reporter asked.

'I say,' sheik Tantawi answered, 'that every one who fights for his rights and explodes himself as a suicide bomber to kill his enemies is a martyr, not a terrorist.'

President Bush told cadets at the Virginia Military Institute in Lexington on April 17, 2002: "The suicide bombers are not martyrs but murderers."

We can certainly conclude after reading all these Koranic verses, that Islam is not a religion of peace.

Second: Islam is not a religion of peace according to the testimony of its own history.

In Chapter Eight I mentioned Muhammad's battles, and it shows how pitiless he was. Muhammad brutally tortured and killed Jews and Christians to eradicate Judaism and Christianity from the Arabian peninsula. Paul Fregosi wrote in his book *Jihad*:

Just before his death Muhammad had ordered Zeid's half-Ethiopian black son, Usama, whose mother was a former slave, to lead a Muslim army back north and defeat the Christian dogs who had killed his father. Usama, obeying the Prophet's last military instructions, set out two weeks after the Prophet's death for the Land of War to the north. Khalid, ordered to conquer Iraq, set out originally with five hundred men, won the battle of the River of Blood and, near Baghdad, captured a few dozen terrified Christians seminarians hiding in a church, who chose apostasy into Islam rather than decapitation into eternity. One of them, a young Yemenite, was to become the father of Musa, governor of North Africa, who launched the first Muslim invasion force from Tangiers across the Mediterranean into Spain.

All the fighting in the first decades of Islam was, for geographically obvious reasons, either in Arabia itself or in the Near and Middle East. The success of Muslim arms in those regions and in those years was due in a large part to Arab military ability: Arab cavalry was swifter and more enterprising than that of their Persian and Byzantine foes. The Arab warriors frightened the Greeks and the Persians with hideous battle cries and, for tactical reasons, always chose to fight on flat, level ground, ideal for charging horses and camels. The Arabs, most importantly, knew what they wanted. Allah, Muhammad, and Islam were the battle cries. Plunder, however, was most probably the primary target; or for some, the houris [beautiful women with wide lovely eyes] in Paradise with wide lovely eyes.

(*Jihad*, pp 72-73)

Another reason for the success of the Arab armies was the Persian and Byzantine empires' exhaustion after more than twenty-five years of warfare against each other. They did not have the strength to fight.

From its beginning Islamic society was a bloody society. After Muhammad's death, a large number of Muslims separated from Islam, and Abu-Bakr, the first caliph, fought and defeated them. Omar Ibn-Al-Khatab became caliph, and then he was murdered by a Persian slave. Othman became caliph and was also assassinated.

In the meantime, Islam continued invading country after country and the conquered peoples were given three choices: embrace Islam, be killed, or pay high taxes. It was a case that could be summarized in the words, "your money or your life." The Christians in Egypt at the present time are descendants of those who chose to sacrifice their money rather than denounce their faith in Christ.

To cover the bloody history of Islam I would need to write an entire volume just on that subject. Others have already done that however, so I would advise my readers to read *Jihad*, by Paul Fregosi, and *The Dagger of Islam* by John Laffin.

The words of Sir. Robert Anderson present another example of why Islam is not a religion of peace according to its

281

own history. On pages 2-4 of his book, *The Silence of God*, Anderson describes the Muslim-Turkish massacres of the Armenians in 1885:

> Every new chapter in the story of Turkish misrule raises a fresh storm of indignation throughout Europe. The conscience of Christendom is outraged by tales of oppression and cruelty and wrong inflicted on the Christian subjects of the Porte.
> Here is a testimony to the Armenian massacres of 1895: Over 60,000 Armenians have been butchered. In Trebizond, Erzeroum, Erzinghian, Hassankaleh, and numberless other places the Christians were crushed like grapes during the vintage. The frantic mob, seething and surging in the streets of the cities, swept down upon the defenseless Armenians, plundered their shops, gutted their houses, then joked and jested with the terrified victims, as cats play with mice. The rivulets were choked with corpses; the streams ran red with human blood; the forest glades and rocky caves were peopled with the dead and dying; among the black ruins of once prosperous villages lay roasted infants by their mangled mothers' corpses; pits were dug at night by the wretches destined to fill them, many of whom, flung in when but lightly wounded, awoke underneath a mountain of clammy corpses, and vainly wrestled with death and with the dead, who shut them out from light and life forever.
> A man in Erzeroum, hearing a tumult, and fearing for his children, who were playing in the street, went out to seek and save them. He was borne down upon by the mob. He pleaded for his life, protesting that he had always lived in peace with his Moslem neighbours, and sincerely loved them. The statement may have represented a fact, or it may have been but a plea for

pity. The ringleader, however, told him that that was the proper spirit, and would be accordingly rewarded. The man was then stripped, and a chunk of his flesh cut out of his body, and jestingly offered for sale: 'Good fresh meat, and dirt cheap,' exclaimed some of the crowd. 'Who'll buy fine dog's meat?' echoed the amused bystanders. The writhing wretch uttered piercing screams as some of the mob, who had just come from rifling the shops, opened a bottle and poured vinegar or some acid into the gaping wound. He called on God and man to end his agonies. But they had only begun. Soon afterwards two little boys came up, the elder crying, 'Hairik, Hairik, (Father, father) save me! See what they've done to me!' and pointed to his head, from which the blood was streaming over his handsome face, and down his neck. The younger brother - a child of about three - was playing with a wooden toy. The agonizing man was silent for a second and then, glancing at these his children, made a frantic but vain effort to snatch a dagger from a Turk by his side. This was the signal for the renewal of his torments. The bleeding boy was finally dashed with violence against the dying father, who began to lose strength and consciousness, and the two were then pounded to death where they lay. The younger child sat near, dabbling his wooden toy in the blood of his father and brother, and looking up, now through smiles at the prettily dressed Kurds and now through tears at the dust-begrimed thing that had late been father. A slash of a saber wound up his short experience of God's world, and the crowd turned its attention to others.

These are but isolated scenes revealed for a brief second by the light, as it were, of a momentary lightning flash. The worst cannot be described.

(*Contemporary Review*: January, 1896)

These are some scenes from the history of Islam, and they certainly declare that Islam is not a religion of peace. It is worthy to note that this happened long before there was a state of Israel, and an Israeli-Palestinian conflict to blame. This massacre represents the raw brutality of Islam and its hatred for Christians.

Third: Islam is not a religion of peace according to current events.

Who attacked the World Trade Center and the Pentagon? Were they Germans, Italians, French? They were Muslims, who wanted to obey their Koran literally.

For Muslims to claim that the attacks on the World Trade Center and the Pentagon were in response to the United States policy concerning the Israel-Palestinian conflict is a hoax. Muslims are jealous of the advanced technology of America and the West, and instead of building up their own countries and providing a better life for their people, they decided to try and destroy Western civilization in the name of Allah.

In January 2000 Muslims massacred more than twenty Coptic Christians in the village of Kosheh in Upper Egypt. Were these persons associated with Israel? Absolutely not.

Bin Laden, who established his headquarters of Al Qaeda in Afghanistan, issued his orders to Muslims around the world: "Kill Americans." Sheik Omar Abd-Alrahman, who is now in prison, conspired to destroy the World Trade Center in 1993.

The American Embassies in Kenya and Tanzania were bombed in 1998, and in 2000 the USS Cole was attacked in Yemen killing 17 Americans. In Beirut, Lebanon, in 1982, Hezbollah sent a suicide bomber to attack American Marines and 241 of them were killed. The list goes on and includes Nigeria, Sudan, Lebanon, Saudi Arabia, Indonesia and the Philippines.

Nineteen educated Muslims committed suicide and killed thousands of innocent men, women and children in the World

Trade Center, the Pentagon and the four planes they flew on that black Tuesday in September 2001. Those nineteen Muslims did that because of their deep conviction they would go directly to paradise to enjoy sensual pleasures.

Muhammad Atta, who flew the first plane into the World Trade Center, was a devout Muslim. He was born in Egypt to a lawyer and was a highly intelligent person who communicated with ease with children, old men, professors and people in government. As a student in Germany he was known to be quiet and very religious. Atta regularly prayed on the floor of his office and founded an Islamic prayer and study group at the University in January 1999.

Atta lived and moved easily in Western society while secretly hating it. He was a man on a mission and on the front of his thesis, presented in October 1999, he wrote the following words: 'My prayer and my sacrifice and my life and my death belong to Allah, the Lord of the worlds' (*The Washington Post* - 09/22/01). The West needs to know that many other Muhammad Attas may quietly be living among us.

It was not poverty that led those nineteen to commit suicide and kill Americans. They were all educated and financially secure, but their minds were saturated with the verses of the Koran calling them to kill the infidels, and the verses promising a paradise with all its sensual pleasures.

The Washington Post reported in its issues of September 22 and 28, 2001:

> Muhammad Atta, one of the key organizers among the 19 hijackers who carried out the September 11 attacks, left behind a five page handwritten document in Arabic that includes Islamic prayers, instructions for a last night of life and practical reminders to bring 'knives, your will, ID's, your passport. Obey Allah and his messenger and stand fast, Allah will stand with those who stand fast. You should pray, you should fast, you should ask Allah for help... continue to pray throughout

285

this night. Continue to recite the Koran. Remember the battles of the prophet... against the infidels, as he went on building the Islamic state... you have to be convinced that those few hours that are left you in your life are very few. From there you will begin to live a happy life, the infinite paradise. Be optimistic. The prophet Muhammad was always optimistic. You will be entering paradise. You will be entering the happiest life, everlasting life.'

USA Today printed on April 16, 2002, the words of Ahmed Alhazanawi who was on United Flight 93 which crashed in Pennsylvania. He said in a video tape:

The time of humiliation and subjugation is over. It's time to kill Americans in their heartland. Lord, I regard myself as a martyr for you, so accept me as such.

In the same video, Ayman Al-Zawahiri, an Egyptian physician and the top deputy of Osama Bin Laden and Al Qaeda, said:

The nineteen brothers who sacrificed their lives for Allah, Allah granted this conquest that we enjoy today. The great victory was achieved because of Allah's help.

It is a spiritual conflict between good and evil, between Allah, the moon god, and the true God of the Bible. Here is an article from *The Washington Post* on February 25, 2002 about a Muslim school in the Washington, DC area:

On world maps that hang every day in the classrooms, Israel is missing. Upstairs in Al-Qalam girls school, the word is blackened out with a marker, with 'Palestine' written in its place.

In a history class at Al-Qalam, Jill Fawzy teaches events from the Revolutionary War to the Civil War. But even before September 11, a major topic of conversation had been what Muslims consider the U.S. government's unfair treatment of Muslims abroad, particularly in the West Bank and Iraq. Given their distrust of U.S. policy, some students question the government's claim that Bin Laden is responsible for the terrorist attacks - disputing that videotapes actually show him taking credit.

The Islamic Saudi Academy does not require that U.S. history or government be taught, offering Arabic social studies as an alternative. Officials there said that only Saudis who intend to return home do not take U.S. history, though a handful of U.S. born students who plan to stay in this country said they opted against it, too.

School officials would not allow reporters to attend classes. But a number of students described the classroom instruction and provided copies of textbooks. The 11th-grade textbook, for example, says one sign of the Day of Judgment will be that Muslims will fight and kill Jews, who will hide behind trees that say: 'Oh Muslim, Oh servant of God, here is a Jew hiding behind me. Come here and kill him.'

These textbooks are being used in schools here in the United States of America!

The *Voice of the Martyrs* reported the following event which took place in Pakistan on October 28, 2001 under the title, "Terror at Bahawalpur". The report says:

Just before 9 a.m. on October 28, 2001, three terrorists dressed in black 'shalwars' (a long, loose fitting shirt that is common among Pakistani males) and armed with Kalishnikov automatic weapons forced their way into

287

St. Dominic's Church. Catholics share the church building with the Protestant Church of Pakistan. The Protestant praise and prayer time had been so joyful; the service was running a bit late. The start of the Catholic mass would be delayed.

Pastor Emmanuel Allah Atta had just concluded his sermon on the importance of prayer during the tumultuous times facing Pakistani Christians. One of the gunmen stormed up to the pulpit and ordered the pastor to throw his Bible to the ground. 'I will not!' insisted Pastor Emmanuel. He turned away from the terrorist and embraced his Bible, pressing it close to his heart. The gunman shouted, 'Allah Ahkbar!' (God is great) and opened fire on Pastor Emmanuel, shooting him in the back, the bullet piercing his heart. As his body plummeted to the floor, Pastor Emmanuel captured one last glance into the almond-shaped eyes of his precious four-year-old daughter Kinza. Later, Kinza said she saw her daddy lovingly look at her before he fell to the ground and 'went to sleep.' When asked to explain where their daddy was, little Kinza said, 'He's in heaven with Jesus.' The radical Islamic terrorists opened fire on the congregation for six minutes, emptying more than 500 rounds on the Christians. Fifteen of the seventy-five congregants attending the service perished in the attack.

(Voice of the Martyrs - February 2002)

The gruesome murder of *Wall Street Journal* reporter Daniel Pearl tells the world all it needs to know about Islam. Pearl was murdered because he was an American and a Jew. *The Washington Post* reported that Daniel Pearl had been cut in the chest and was probably already dead when Islamic extremists sliced his throat in front of a camera (*The Washington Post* - February 24, 2002).

Pearl's abductors made him testify that he was a Jew before they murdered him. The last words he uttered were, "I am a Jew. My father is a Jew." The heinous crime was recorded on video as proof of the extremists ritual murder.

We continue to read about today's events:

> Muslim cleric charged in Britain - Police said a Muslim cleric was charged with incitement to murder two weeks after *The Times* of London reported he had urged his followers to kill Jews.
>
> Abdullah el-Faisal, 38, was arrested Monday at a house in East London. He was being detained pending a hearing today at Bow Street Magistrates Court.
>
> When he was apprehended, police said they were searching other addresses in East London but refused to say why.
>
> Lawmakers called for action to be taken against el-Faisal, a Jamaican, after *The Times* reported that he had toured Britain calling for the killing of Jews and non-Muslims. The newspaper said he was selling audiocassettes instructing all Muslim males to train for battle and calling on boys to learn to use Kalashnikov assault rifles.
>
> The Home Office Minister, Angela Eagle, told the House of Commons this month that police were taking 'a very close look' at el-Faisal. The Simon Wiesenthal Center, which monitors attacks on Jewish organizations and people, said it was 'relieved' el-Faisal had been arrested. (*The Washington Post* - February 21, 2002)

We come now to the Islamic Nations Conference in Malaysia held in the first week of April 2002. In an editorial dated April 4, 2002 in *The Washington Post* we read:

Islamic nations held a conference in Malaysia this week in an effort to refute the connection between the Muslim world and terrorism. Sadly, they managed to accomplish the opposite. Despite appeals from the Malaysian and Bosnian representatives, the 57 assembled states adopted a resolution that specifically rejected the idea that Palestinian 'resistance' to Israel has anything to do with terrorism. As the Muslim governments would have it, the Palestinian who killed himself and 26 Israeli civilians who were sitting down to a Passover Seder in an Israeli coastal city last week was not practicing terrorism; neither were those who organized and dispatched dozens of other young people to kill themselves and scores of innocent Israelis in recent months. In effect, the Islamic conference sanctioned not only terrorism but also suicide as legitimate political instruments.

The refusal of Muslim states, particularly those in the Arab Middle East, to separate themselves from the suicide bombers demonstrates the magnitude of the challenge faced by the United States in combating international terrorism. Arab governments say they reject the September 11 attacks against the United States and support the campaign against al Qaeda. But they are unwilling to renounce either terrorism itself or the extremist Islamic ideology that underlies it. On the contrary, their schools and media help feed the terrorist cause with anti-Western and anti-Semitic incitement, and their governments often help pay for it with donations to radical Islamic groups. Even now, Arab states are subsidizing the families of Palestinian suicide bombers, rewarding them for their acts of savagery and thereby encouraging others to follow them.

Another current portrayal of the real spirit of Islam was shown in a poem titled *The Martyrs*, written by Ghazi Algosaibi, Saudi Arabia's ambassador to Britain. The poem is full of thanks and praise for Palestinian suicide bombers, saying they "died to honor My Allah's word," and that the White House is a place of idols and is "filled with darkness."

The poem appeared in *Al-Hayat*, an Arabic language newspaper published in London on Saturday, April 13, 2002. In a *Washington Post* translation, the poem begins,

> God is witness that you are martyrs.
> The prophets are witness... and the Holy men.
> You died to honor My Allah's word
> In lands where the dearest are prisoners.

The poem also seems to criticize those who do not join with the suicide bombers:

> You committed suicide?
> We are the ones who committed suicide
> by living like the dead.

According to a translation of another section in the *London Observer* newspaper, the ambassador's poem praises Ayat Akhras, the 18-year-old Palestinian girl who killed herself and two Israelis when she detonated a bomb strapped to her body at a supermarket in Jerusalem on March 29, 2002. The poem refers to her as "Ayat, the bride of loftiness."

> She embraced death with a smile
> while the leaders are running away from death.
> Doors of paradise are open for her.

The poem seems to condemn the United States' role in the Middle East:

We complained to the idols
of a White House
whose heart is filled with darkness.

This is Islam today, the same Islam of yesterday.

Fourth: There is no Freedom of thought in Islam.

Islam is a prison with no way out. Once a person enters that prison, he cannot leave it alive. The Koran says:

> Then what is the matter with you that you are divided into two parties about the apostates? Allah has cast them back (to disbelief) because of what they have earned. Do you want to guide him whom Allah has made to go astray? And he whom Allah has made to go astray, you will never find for him any way (of guidance). They wish that you reject Faith, as they have rejected (Faith), and thus that you all become equal (like one another). So take not Aouliya (protectors or friends) from them, till they emigrate in the Way of Allah (to Muhammad). But if they turn back (from Islam), take (hold of) them and kill them wherever you find them, and take neither Aouliya (protectors or friends) nor helpers from them. (Surat Al-Nisa 4:88-89)

This verse means that if a person says the Islamic *Shahada* (creed): "I testify that there is no God but Allah, I testify that Muhammad is the Messenger of Allah," he cannot change his mind. If he does change his mind, he will be executed or beheaded as has happened many times in Saudi Arabia, Afghanistan, and other Islamic countries.

Islam is a religion of intellectual censorship.

In Islam the democratic right to free thought and individual decisions concerning religious matters is totally denied. There are many examples of intellectual censorship, but I will list only a few.

The first concerns Salman Rushdie. Rushdie was born to a Muslim family in Bombay but has spent much of his life in London, England. He wrote a book entitled *The Satanic Verses.* Muslims thought this book was an insult to the Prophet Muhammad and Islam, so Ayatollah Khomeini issued an order to assassinate Rushdie and promised $5 million to the one who would kill him. Khomeini, Iran's spiritual leader at that time, said in a statement read for him on the radio in 1989, "anyone who died attempting to kill Rushdie," he promised, "will go straight to paradise."

A second example is Dr. Farag Foda, the great author who was assassinated in Cairo, Egypt in 1993 because he wrote many books exposing the true face of Islam and Islamic society. He was accused of being an apostate Muslim and was shot and killed in front of his son.

The third example is Professor Nasr Hamid Abu Zeid, who was accused of being an apostate Muslim because of his books about the Koran. The court in Egypt ruled that he must divorce his wife, Ibtihal Younes. He fled from Egypt and is now living with his wife in Holland.

A fourth is the well-known Egyptian writer Naguib Mahfouz, who became the first Egyptian to win the Nobel Prize in literature. Muslims stabbed him in front of his house in an attempt to kill him. The man was over 80 years old. They wanted to kill him because they thought that he insulted Muhammad in his novel, *The Children of Gabalawi.*

It is of great importance for any American or any secular Muslim to know what kind of society he or she will live in if fundamentalist Muslims rule. The Taliban, Afghanistan's ruling Islamic movement, was an example of this fundamentalist militant faith which is based on a literal interpretation of the Koran, and it shows in their way of life.

In Afghanistan any woman who shows more than her eyes will be flogged. In Saudi Arabia a woman is banned from driving a car or from walking down the street without covering all of her body except for her eyes.

Christians who went to Afghanistan to help the poor and the sick with food and medicine were arrested and jailed because they had Bibles and Christian cassette tapes. In Sudan more than one million Christians were killed by the Islamic government in Khartoum. In Algeria, thousands of Muslims were slaughtered by militant Muslims.

Today we hear on radio and television many Muslim clerics saying that Islam means "peace." But the word Islam means "submission," and a Muslim is one who is in submission to Allah. Their goal as stated in the Koran is to bring the entire world into submission to Allah and the Koran under a Muslim caliph and to have a global Islamic empire.

This is Islam today, the same Islam of yesterday. Americans Jews and Christians should be aware of this.

This war against terrorism is not a physical war. Most certainly it is a spiritual war.

I am quite sure that God will have the final victory. In His Word He gave us the last chapter of the human drama:

> Then the seventh angel sounded: And there were loud voices in heaven, saying, 'The kingdoms of this world have become the kingdoms of our Lord and of His Christ, and He shall reign forever and ever!'
> (Revelation 11:15 NKJ)

Islam may be the fastest growing religion in the USA and other countries, but that will only be for a short time. In God's timing Islam will diminish and the Kingdom of God and His Christ will be established forever!

Chapter Twenty Two

Islam is not a Divine Religion

Muslims brag that Islam is the fastest growing religion in the world with more than one billion adherents. They say that the growth of Islam is proof that it is a divine religion.

But Islam's fast growth does not necessarily indicate that. Here are the words of Christ on this matter:

> ... wide is the gate and broad is the way that leads to destruction and there are many who go in by it....
>
> (Matthew 7:13 NKJ)

A divine religion has special qualifications. None of these qualifications can be applied to Islam.

First: A divine religion must be established by God and authenticated by the manifestation of His glory.

God Himself established Judaism. He called Moses to be with him on Mount Sinai for forty days and forty nights (Exodus 24:18). During that time God gave Moses the full description of the tabernacle. He gave him "two tablets of the testimony, tablets of stone, written with the finger of God" (Exodus 31:18 NKJ). There can be no doubt that God revealed to Moses all the events he wrote in the Torah. The Torah came from above, from God Himself.

God set His seal on Judaism by the manifestation of His glory by fire. When the children of Israel erected the tabernacle the book of Leviticus records:

> And Moses and Aaron went into the tabernacle of meeting, and came out and blessed the people. Then the glory of the LORD appeared to all the people, and fire came out from before the LORD and consumed the burnt offering and the fat on the altar. When all the people saw it, they shouted and fell on their faces.
> (Leviticus 9:23-24 NKJ)

In Judaism God laid the foundation for Christianity. The Old Testament prophecies, types, and offerings spoke about the coming Messiah and His death on the cross. On this solid foundation Christianity was built.

We find no foundation whatsoever for Islam. Islam was founded on the testimony of one man Muhammad. One testimony for such a serious matter is not valid.

God established Christianity by His Son, Jesus Christ, who is the founder and foundation of the Christian Church (Matthew 16:18, I Corinthians 3:11). God set His seal on Christianity by the manifestation of His glory when He filled the Christian Church at Jerusalem with the Holy Spirit who appeared in divided tongues, as of fire and filled each one of the members of the church gathered in the upper room. The Christians became the temple of God.

> Now when the Day of Pentecost had fully come, they were all with one accord in one place. And suddenly there came a sound from heaven, as of a rushing mighty wind, and it filled the whole house where they were sitting. Then there appeared to them divided tongues, as of fire, and one sat upon each of them. And they

were all filled with the Holy Spirit and began to speak with other tongues, as the Spirit gave them utterance.

(Acts 2:1-4 NKJ)

God set His seal first on Judaism and then also on Christianity. No divine appearance or glory whatsoever was seen on the Kaaba, the holy shrine of Islam in Mecca. Muhammad entered Mecca with his army not by the power of God but by the power of his sword and made the Kaabah a holy shrine for Muslims.

Second: A divine religion must be protected and promoted by God's power, not by the sword.

It is a historical fact that Jews never fought to force people to embrace Judaism. The Jewish person does not associate the name of Moses with the name of God. He would not say, "I testify there is no god but Jehovah, and I testify that Moses is the messenger of Jehovah."

However, anyone who wants to become a Muslim must say, "I testify that there is no god but Allah, and I testify that Muhammad is the messenger of Allah." Thus Muhammad is always associated with Allah in the testimony of every Muslim. This is polytheism.

The Jews were protected by God. When the children of Israel left Egypt, Pharaoh and his army followed, striking terror in their hearts. So Moses said to the people:

Do not be afraid. Stand still, and see the salvation of the LORD, which He will accomplish for you today. For the Egyptians whom you see today, you shall see again no more forever. The LORD will fight for you, and you shall hold your peace. (Exodus 14:13-14 NKJ)

But, as I wrote in the last chapter, the Koran commands Muslims to declare *Jihad* (Holy War) to promote Islam. Nobel

297

laureate Elie Wiesel wrote in one of his articles, "The fanatic who kills in God's name makes his God a murderer." I add to that, that fighting in the cause of Allah makes Allah appear weak and handicapped because He cannot fight for himself.

It is a logical assumption that the strong fight for the weak. We read in the Old Testament that when Gideon tore down the altar of Baal, the men of the city wanted to kill him. They said to his father, "Bring out your son, that he may die, because he has torn down the altar of Baal" (Judges 6:30 NKJ).

Joash, Gideon's father, answered them, "Would you plead for Baal? Would you save him? Let the one who would plead for him be put to death by morning! If he is god, let him plead for himself because his altar has been torn down." (Judges 6:31 NKJ).

Christianity spread by the power of the Holy Spirit, never by the sword. Christ said to His disciples:

> You shall receive power when the Holy Spirit has come upon you; and you shall be witnesses to Me in Jerusalem, and in all Judea and Samaria, and to the end of the earth.   (Acts 1:8 NKJ)

Christ built His church with a few ordinary people, even simple fishermen. The book of Acts records how Christianity spread, in spite of severe persecution, to all the Roman empire. When the Apostle Paul went to Corinth, a city where many adulterers, homosexuals, sodomites, drunkards and idolaters lived, he won them to Christ by the power of the cross, not by a sword.

This is what Paul wrote to the Corinthians:

> And I, brethren, when I came to you, did not come with excellence of speech or of wisdom declaring to you the testimony of God. For I determined not to know anything among you except Jesus Christ and Him crucified. I was with you in weakness, in fear, and in much trembling. And my speech and my preaching

were not with persuasive words of human wisdom, but in demonstration of the Spirit and of power, that your faith should not be in the wisdom of men but in the power of God. (I Corinthians 2:1-5 NKJ)

By contrast, Islam spread by force and terror. It invaded Egypt, Syria, Iraq, Iran, Libya, Spain and other countries all by terror and sword.

Third: A divine religion must give assurance of eternal life with God to those who believe in it.

Norman L. Geisler and Abdul Saleed wrote:

There is no assurance of salvation in Islam. From the very beginning of Islam, Muslims have feared for their eternal destiny. (*Answering Islam*, p 126)

There is no assurance of salvation in Islam. On the other hand there is total assurance of eternal life for the true Christian. We read in the gospel of John:

He who believes in the Son has everlasting life; and he who does not believe the Son shall not see life, but the wrath of God abides on him. (John 3:36)

We also read in the epistle to the Hebrews concerning Christ:

Therefore He is also able to save to the uttermost those who come to God through Him, since He always lives to make intercession for them. (Hebrews 7:25)

The Apostle John said:

If we receive the witness of men, the witness of God is greater; for this is the witness of God which He has testified of His Son. He who believes in the Son of God has the witness in himself; he who does not believe God has made Him a liar, because he has not believed the testimony that God has given of His Son. And this is the testimony: that God has given us eternal life, and this life is in His Son. He who has the Son has life; he who does not have the Son of God does not have life.

(1 John 5:9-12 NKJ)

These verses declare a complete assurance of eternal life to the person who believes in Christ. Islam lacks this kind of assurance. Instead, the Koran assures every Muslim that he or she must enter Hell:

There is not one of you but will enter it (Hell) [Author's literal translation]. This is with your Lord; a decree which must be accomplished.

(Surat Maryam 19: 71)

Dr. Mustafa Mahmoud, a renowned Egyptian author, wrote in his book, *Intercession*, that the Koran declares that the prophet Muhammad will not be able to save any Muslim from Hell and those who will enter Hell will be there forever. Here is what Allah says to Muhammad in the Koran:

If we pronounced the word of torture in fire on someone, will you (O Muhammad) rescue him who is in the fire? [Author's literal translation]

(Surat Az-Zumar 39:19)

The Koran says concerning those who will enter Hell:

They will long to get out of the fire, but never will they get out therefrom, and theirs will be a lasting torment.

(Surat Al-Maidah 5:37)

I feel sad for every Muslim, I want to shout out to them, "Believe in the power of the shed blood of Christ for the forgiveness of your sins, and you will not enter Hell!"

The Almighty God fulfilled his plan for the salvation of mankind through the crucifixion and resurrection of His Son, Christ Jesus. After His plan was completed, there is no place whatsoever for a new religion; there is no place for Islam.

Thus, we can conclude that Islam is not a divine religion.

Chapter Twenty Three

Jihad

Islam has five ceremonial obligations for every Muslim plus a sixth obligation which is *Jihad.* These ceremonial obligations are:

1. Al-Shahada

Al-Shahada means "the testimony." Every Muslim must utter the following *shahada* in Arabic: *Ashadu anna la ilaha illa Allah. Wa anna Muhammad rasulu Allah.* This testimony means "I testify that there is no god but Allah, and I testify that Muhammad is the messenger of Allah."

The mere uttering of this testimony makes the reciter a Muslim. There is no necessity for the person to be born again or to repent of his sins.

2. Al-Salah

Al-salah, which means "prayer," is an essential obligation for the Muslim without it one ceases to be a true Muslim.

Prayer in Islam is not like prayer in Christianity as it does not invoke fellowship with God. Islamic prayer means public worship with readings from the Koran from memory and commencing with the Fatihah, the first surah of the Koran, followed by other short verses from the Koran and confession of *Shahadah.*

The Muslim must pray five times a day: at dawn, midday, mid-afternoon, sunset, and nightfall. The *Muezzin* is the man who calls Muslims to prayer from a special balcony in the mosque. The only time the Muslim is obligated to pray with his fellow Muslims is at the noon service on Friday.

The required number of daily Islamic prayers is not mentioned in the Koran. The number of five daily prayers was decided by the jurists as a compromise allegedly made between Allah and Muhammad when, according to Islamic legend, Muhammad visited the seventh heaven. At that time Allah prescribed forty prayers each day for Muslims, but at last he settled for five.

3. Al-Zakah

Zakah means "giving to the poor." *Zakah* literally means giving back to Allah a portion of his bounty as a way of escaping suffering in the afterlife.

4. Al-Sawm

Sawm means "fasting;" it is an obligation decreed by the Koran for Muslims. The fast is to be observed in the month of *Ramadhan*:

> *Ramadhan* is the (month) in which was sent down the Koran, as a guide to mankind, also clear (signs) for guidance and judgment (between right and wrong). So every one of you who is present (at his home) during that month should spend it in fasting, but if anyone is ill, or on a journey, the prescribed period (should be made up) by days later. Allah intends every facility for you. He does not want to put you to difficulties. (He wants you) to complete the prescribed period, and to

304

glorify Him in that He has guided you; and perchance ye shall be grateful.   (Surat Al-Baqarah 2:185)

During the fast Muslims may not eat any food or have any drink, nor may they smoke, or have sexual intercourse from sunrise to sunset.

The fast is ended each day immediately after sunset. Then Muslims may eat and drink until dawn. The most delicious and elaborate meals are served during the nights of this month-long fast.

The beginning of the fast is determined by the appearance of the new moon, and the end is also determined by similar astronomical observations. The relation between the moon and the month of *Ramadhan* may possibly be explained if Allah was in fact the moon god of Arabia. There is strong historical evidence to this which I will discuss in chapter twenty-four.

5. Al-Hajj

Al-Hajj means "pilgrimage" to the sacred monuments of Mecca. Every able Muslim must make this pilgrimage at least once in his or her lifetime. *Al-Hajj* is commanded by the Koran:

... pilgrimage thereto is a duty men owe to Allah.
                              (Surat Al-Imran 3:97)

The ceremony of *Al-Hajj* includes the following steps:

1) A visit to the Kaabah (the sacred mosque)
2) Kissing the black stone

Hamid Elsaid Ali wrote in his book, *Great Mysteries of the Honoured Kaaba and the Sacred Ceremonies*, under the title *The Black Stone:*

It is recorded that the prophet Muhammad said, 'The Black Stone is the right hand of Allah on earth, with it He shakes hands with his creation as a Muslim shakes hand with a Muslim.'

Ibn Abbas said 'The prophet received the black stone with his hand and put his lips on it, kissing it, and crying for a long time. He looked and there was Omar Ibn Al-Khafal standing. "Here man should cry," Muhammad said to Omar. The prophet Muhammad said, "The black stone descended from paradise as white as milk, but was made black by the sins of the children of Adam."'

Al-Azraki said 'The black stone will ascend to heaven, for nothing taken from paradise will remain on earth.'

(pp 81-84)

3) Walking around the Kaabah seven times three times at a run and four at a quick pace

4) A visit to the sacred stone where Abraham allegedly climbed to lay the upper part of the Kaaba

5) Ascension to Mount Safa, and from there the pilgrim runs to Mount Marwa seven times

6) Going to Mount Arafat on the ninth day of the pilgrimage. This is a "station before Allah." This is the culminating point of pilgrimage without which the whole pilgrimage would be null and void.

7) Throwing 21 little stones at Satan. It is said that Muhammad declared to the Muslims, "The first one who threw stones at Satan was Abraham."

Professor Khalil Abd-AlKareem wrote in his *book The Historical Roots of the Islamic Sharia*:

> Arabs before Islam used to perform the Hajj in the month of Zealhega every year... they used to perform all the ceremonies the Muslims perform in the present day.
>
> (pp 16,17)

What Muhammad did was to sanctify the pagan rituals of the *Hajj* and include them in Islam.

6. Al-Jihad

> The word *Jihad* is an Arabic word which means "striving hard." It is an incumbent religious duty established in the Koran and the Hadith as a divine institution and enjoined especially for the purpose of advancing Islam and repelling evil from Muslims.
>
> (*Dictionary of Islam* by Thomas Patrick Hughes)

Muslims call *Jihad* "holy war" because it is done in the way of Allah to promote Islam. That shows that Islam uses force to convert people. *Jihad* should be called unholy war because of the innocent blood Muslims shed in their *Jihad*.

What makes *Jihad* a binding institution in Islam is the fact that it is a communal, not an individual, obligation. The verses of the Koran calling for *Jihad* are synonymous to the verses calling for fighting:

> O prophet (Muhammad) strive hard against the infidels and the hypocrites, and be harsh against them, their abode is Hell, and worst indeed is that destination.
>
> (Surat Al-Taubah 9:73 HK)

Those who believe, and emigrate and strive with might and remain, in Allah's cause, with their goods and their persons, have the highest rank in the sight of Allah: They are the people who will achieve.

(Surat Al-Tauba 9:20)

There are many more verses calling for *Jihad* in the Koran: Surat Al-Baqarah 2:218, Surat Al-Imran 3:142, Surat Al-Anfal 8:74, Surat Al-Tauba 9:16,88, Surat Al-Nahl 16:110, Surat Al-Hujurat 49:15, Surat Al-Saff 61:11, Al-Maidah 5:54, Al-Tahrim 66:9, Surat Al-Furqan 25:52, Surat Al-Taubah 9:41, Surat Al-Nisa 4:95.

Muhammad directed his hatred toward Jews and Christians:

Verily, you will find strongest among men in enmity to the Muslims, the Jews... (Surat Al-Maidah 5:82)

O you who believe (Muslims)! Take not the Jews and the Christians as friends. (Surat Al-Maidah 5:51)

All the above mentioned verses are as explosive as dynamite in the hearts and minds of true Muslims and motivate them to declare *Jihad*. No wonder that we see the revival of *Jihad* in our days; the attacks on the World Trade Center and the Pentagon are clear evidence. The call of Bin Laden to Muslims to declare *Jihad* is echoed throughout Muslim countries.

There are three benefits for *Jihad* in the Muslim's mind.

First: Promoting Islam

Second: Booty to enjoy in this life

Third: Martyrdom with its immediate promise to enter paradise and be married to beautiful women with wide lovely eyes

In Appendix III of the English translation of the Koran by Dr. Muhammad T. Al-Hillali and Dr. Muhammad M. Khan we read the following words concerning *Jihad*:

> *Jihad* is the great deed indeed and there is no deed whose reward or blessing is as that of it, and for this reason, it is the best thing that one can volunteer for. All the Muslim religious scholars unanimously agree that *Jihad* is superior to *Hajj* and *Umrah* (pilgrimage) and also superior to non-obligatory *Salat* (prayer) and *Saum* (fasting) as mentioned in the Qur'an [sic] and Prophet's *Sunnah*. It is obvious that the benefits of *Jihad* for us are extensive and comprehensive; it (*Jihad*) includes all kinds of worship both hidden and open, it also includes (a great) love for Allah and it shows one's sincerity to Him and it also shows one's trust in Him, and it indicates the handing over of one's soul and property to Him it (*Jihad*) shows one's patience, one's devotion to Islam, one's remembrance to Allah and there are other kinds of good deeds which are present in *Jihad* and are not present in any other act of worship.
> For these above mentioned degrees of grades of various kinds of worship one should race for *Jihad*. It is confirmed in the two authentic books (of *Hadith*). Narrated Abu Hurairah (may Allah be pleased with him): 'I heard Allah's Messenger saying: "By Him in Whose Hand my soul is! Were it not for some men amongst the believers who dislike to be left behind me, and whom I cannot provide with means of conveyance, I would certainly never remain behind any *Sariyyah* (army unity) going out for *Jihad* in Allah's Cause. By Him in Whose Hand my life is! I would love to be martyred in Allah's Cause and then come back to life and then be martyred and then come back to life again and then be martyred and then come back to life again

and then be martyred."'(Sahih Al-Bukhari, Vol 4, *Hadith* No. 54)

So the Prophet through his ways of life, his firmness, his courage, and his patience has deeply encouraged the *Mujahidin* for Allah's Cause.

He informed them the immediate and deferred reward of Jihad for them, and how different kinds of evils Allah repels with it; and what a great honour, power, dignity and high grade is obtained through it and he has placed *Jihad* at the top in Islam. The Prophet ways:

'Paradise has one hundred grades, the distance between each of the two grades is like the distance between the heaven and the earth, and these grades Allah has reserved for the *Mujahidin* who fight in His Cause' [as mentioned in the two authentic Books {Al-Bukhari and Muslim)]. [See Sahih Al-Bukhari, Vol 4, Hadith No. 48].

Likewise Allah's Messenger [Muhammad] said:
1) 'The souls of the martyrs are in the green birds dwelling in Paradise wherever they like.
2) That all their sins and faults are forgiven.
3) That each of them can intercede with Allah for seventy of his family members.
4) That he will come secure on the Day of Resurrection from the great terror.
5) That he will not feel the agonies and distress of death.
6) That he will not be horrified by the (great) Gathering (on the Day of Resurrection).
7) That he does not feel the pain of "the killing" except like that of a pinch.'

And how many agonies and distresses are there for a person who dies on his bed and a standing (praying) or a sleeping person in *Jihad* is better than a fasting or standing (praying) person not in *Jihad* and whosoever acted as a guard or escort in Allah's Cause, his eyes will never witness the Fire (Hell) and that a day spent while one is in *Jihad* for Allah's Cause is better than the world and whatsoever is in it.

(Appendix III, Al-Hillali and Khan)

Jihad takes a new turn nowadays besides *Jihad* with weapons, bombs, biological missiles, and different kinds of terrorism. A German writer, who wishes to remain anonymous, wrote:

A compromise between liberal efforts and fundamentalist goals is being made in the world mission of the Muslims. By infiltrating companies, banks and governments with extra finances from the production of oil, Muslims hope to increase the influence of Islam in the East and in the West. Arabic language schools, foreign workers and students, mosques on all continents and mixed marriages between Muslims and non-Muslims are viewed as further means of increasing the presence of Muslims in the 'House of War.' The Muslims with their growing numbers in Christian countries demand social and political rights, Islamic religious instruction in public schools and political recognition in questions of taxation, so that their religious community would become anchored not only socially but also legally. This financial, economic, social and educational 'holy war' is well on its way. And it is the Western countries who are knowingly or unknowingly supporting Muslim efforts through child support, unemployment help and other social benefits. At the same time the Muslim leaders try to put a stop to the integration of the

Muslims through the reformation of their faith as foreigners far from their homeland.

A glance at the world map shows that Islamic *Jihad* is the cause of unrest all over the world. *Jihad*'s focal point is to attack Jews and Christians. Not long ago sneak attacks and unforeseen scenarios continued to surprise the United States: the bombings of United States' military barracks in Saudi Arabia in 1996, of the United States' embassies in Kenya and Tanzania in 1998, and of the USS Cole navy ship in 2000.

The Arab leaders and Muslim imams say that Muslims who fight Jews are freedom fighters, not terrorists. On April 7, 2002, *The Washington Post* reported that the foreign ministers of the twenty-two member Arab league, who had an emergency meeting on April 6, 2002 in Cairo, Egypt, said that what President Bush considers terrorism is justified resistance against an occupying army, meaning Israel.

Zacarias Moussaoui, the co-conspirator of the September 11 hijackers, said in Federal Court in Alexandria, Virginia, on Monday, April 22, 2002, that America is facing determined enemies with a very clear goal, the destruction of the United States and the Jewish people and state, and, for good measure, the return of Spain to Muslim rule (*The Washington Post*, April 25, 2002).

Islamic fundamentalists are brutal not only in fighting Jews and Christians but also in fighting each other. More than 120,000 people were butchered in Algeria's Islamic insurgency which broke out in 1992 when the army canceled elections that a fundamentalist party was expected to win.

The late Dr. Samuel Zwemer recorded in his book, *The Disintegration of Islam*, the following statement:

> Some years ago Sheikh Abd-ul-Haqq of Baghdad, a Moslem of the old school, wrote an article on behalf of the Pan-Islamic League. It appeared in a French journal and was entitled, *The Final Word of Islam to Europe*:

'For us in the world there are only believers and unbelievers; love, charity, fraternity toward believers; contempt, disgust, hatred, and war against unbelievers. Amongst unbelievers the most hateful and criminal are those who, while recognizing God, attribute to Him earthly relationships, give Him a son, a mother. Learn then, European observers, that a Christian of no matter what position, from the simple fact that he is a Christian, is in our eyes a blind man fallen from all human dignity.'

This is the true spirit and attitude of Muslims toward Christians (*The Disintegration of Islam*, pp 190-191).

The Washington Post reported the story of Sayed Abdullah, a Muslim who was arrested and tortured by the Taliban soldiers because he owned two copies of the Bible, one in English and one in Dari, the main language of Afghanistan. Sayed was brutally tortured and imprisoned just because he owned these two copies. Bibles were strictly forbidden by the Taliban. When Sayed was released he was totally broken psychologically, emotionally and physically (*The Washington Post*, January 5, 2002).

After September 11 many young Muslims volunteered to go to Afghanistan for *Jihad*. One of them said, "I am going back for *Jihad* against America. They are going to attack, so we are going to fight."

In Palestine and such Muslim countries as Egypt, the school circulars are full of hatred toward Jews and incitement to kill them and rid the Middle East of their presence. In fact, we who are living in the United States are afraid of another attack like September 11 or worse.

The hatred of Jews motivated two young Palestinian girls, one of whom was the 18-year-old Ayat Al-Akhras, to become suicide bombers and kill many Israelis.

Muslims were quiet until the mid-twentieth century because western imperialism and colonial domination had suppressed Islam for a century. When Islamic countries gained their independence after World War II, *Jihad* surfaced again. With the wealth that came to some Islamic states from oil revenues, terrorists, supported generously by millions of petro dollars, began to wage their *Jihad* against Jews and Christians.

In spite of millions of dollars given as aid to some Islamic states like Egypt, many of the terrorists who attacked American targets were Egyptians. There was no gratitude for what America had done to save Kuwait and Saudi Arabia from Iraq or to help Egypt economically.

The war in the Middle East is not for land, it is a spiritual war between Allah of the Koran and God of the Bible. This is why Muslims destroy churches and burn synagogues when given the opportunity.

We have to consider that after the fall of man in the garden of Eden, mankind was divided into two kingdoms: the kingdom of the devil and the kingdom of God. Everyone is born by natural birth into the kingdom of the devil (John 8:44), but anyone can pass from the kingdom of the devil into the kingdom of God by believing that forgiveness is only through the redemptive blood of Jesus Christ.

There are also two religions: the man-made religion, which is based on the belief that forgiveness can be granted through good deeds, and God's religion, which depends absolutely on His grace.

Through his faith in the redemptive blood, Abel passed from the kingdom of the devil to the kingdom of God. Cain rejected the religion of God and chose instead to approach God through his good works. When his plan failed, he killed his brother Abel.

Man-made religion is bloody and brutal; It is inspired by the devil. This is Cain's religion and Cain's way (Jude 11).

Here is what we read in the Bible:

314

In this the children of God and the children of the devil are manifest: Whoever does not practice righteousness is not of God, nor he who does not love his brother. For this is the message that you heard from the beginning, that we should love one another not as Cain who was of the wicked one and murdered his brother. And why did he murder him? Because his works were evil and his brother's were righteous. (1 John 3:10-12 NKJ)

This is the great difference between God's religion and the devil's religion.

Jihad is also mentioned in the Bible, but it is a different kind of *Jihad*, with different kinds of weapons and a different kind of reward. The Apostle Paul wrote to the Christians in Corinth:

For though we walk in the flesh, we do not war according to the flesh. For the weapons of our warfare are not carnal but mighty in God for pulling down strongholds, casting down arguments and every high thing that exalts itself against the knowledge of God, bringing every thought into captivity to the obedience of Christ.... (2 Corinthians 10:3-5 NKJ)

What is the reward for this true holy war? Here is what the Apostle Paul says:

For I am already being poured out as a drink offering, and the time of my departure is at hand. I have fought the good fight, I have finished the race, I have kept the faith. Finally, there is laid up for me the crown of righteousness, which the Lord, the righteous Judge, will give to me on that day, and not to me only but also to all who have loved His appearing.
(2 Timothy 4:6-8 NKJ)

True Christians are not looking forward to paradise so they can be wed to 100 virgins with wide lovely eyes. They are looking forward to the second coming of Christ when they will be with Him and will be awarded the crown of righteousness.

Not long ago I received a letter from someone who wrote:

> Why do we Christians condemn Muslim terrorists while we read in the Old Testament that God commanded the children of Israel to exterminate the inhabitants of the land of Canaan?
>
> How would you justify the atrocities of the Crusades in the Holy Land?
>
> How would you explain the terrible crimes committed by the Roman Catholics during the inquisition era of the dark ages?
>
> What do you say about the extermination of the Indians in North America by the so-called Christians?
>
> What do you think about the Catholics and the Protestants killing each other in Northern Ireland?
>
> (Name Withheld)

First, let me emphasize that the true God of the Jews never commanded them to fight any country to promote Judaism, however, Allah of the Muslims commanded them to fight in his cause to promote Islam.

Second, when God made a blood covenant with Abraham to give him and his descendants the land of Canaan, He told him that his descendants would be strangers in a land that is not theirs, and would serve them and they would afflict them four hundred years. Then He said to him:

> But in the fourth generation they shall return here, *for the iniquity of the Amorites* is not yet complete.
>
> (Genesis 15:16 NKJ – author's emphasis)

The inhabitants of Canaan committed gross sins and abominations. They let their sons and daughters pass through fire to please their gods. They practiced witchcraft. They had relations with demons. Many of them were sorcerers. They practiced spiritism. (Deuteronomy 18:9-11) God said to the children of Israel, "Because of all these abominations the LORD your God drives them out from before you" (Deuteronomy 18:12 NKJ).

God gave the former inhabitants of Canaan four hundred years to repent. They did not repent, and God commanded that they should be annihilated so that their abominations would not spread among His people.

We have to remember that when the LORD saw that the wickedness of man was great on the earth and that every intent of the thoughts of his heart was only evil continually, He annihilated all mankind, except for Noah and his family, by the great flood (Genesis 6-7).

When God saw the terrible sins of Sodom and Gomorrah, He destroyed them with fire. God is a Holy God, a just God, and he must punish sinners if they do not repent. Remember, God Himself sent the flood and the fire on the wicked and destroyed them.

When a nation or a country becomes wicked, God has the means to deal with them. He does not need the Muslim army to inflict His judgement. When the children of Israel committed gross sins against God and became apostates, He punished them, and dispersed them all over the world. God deals according to His holiness and justice with his people Israel or with any other nation.

Third: The atrocities of the Crusaders were not commanded or approved by God. The land of Israel is not the land of the so-called Christian crusaders; it is the land of Israel given to Abraham by a covenant. The Crusaders had no right to it. The Crusades were against God's plan and God's Word.

Furthermore, the New Testament does not approve such war. Jesus said to Peter who wanted to defend him:

Put your sword in its place, for all who take the sword
will perish by the sword.   (Matthew 26:52 NKJ)

Here is what Chris Bassford wrote in *The Washington Post*
on October 27, 2001, concerning the Crusades:

> Bloody as they were, the Crusades were hardly an
> unprovoked act of aggression by the West but rather a
> counterattack   one must ask, after all, how the 'holy
> land' came to be in the possession of Islam in the first
> place.   The answer, of course, is that the Arabs
> conquered it through violent military action.   Indeed,
> for most of the past 1,400 years, it has been the West
> that was under assault by Islam, not the other way
> around.   The European counterattack against Muslim
> armies began on the territory of France, and it took
> centuries to retake Spain.   As late as 1689, Turkish
> Muslim armies were laying siege to Vienna, in the very
> heart of Europe.   It took two more centuries after that to
> free central Europe, the Balkans and Greece from
> foreign Muslim domination.
> When considering the balance of barbarities, one should
> consider examples such as what happened in 1571 to
> the defeated European commander of Cyprus, who -
> after being guaranteed safe passage - was skinned alive,
> the skin then being stuffed with straw and put on
> parade.   And, of course, one should remember that it
> wasn't the West that put an end to Arab glory - it was
> the Turks who turned the Arabs into second-class
> citizens within Islam.

What I have said could be applied to the case of the Indian
extermination and also to the fight between Catholics and
Protestants in Northern Ireland.   Christ said to His disciples:

You have heard that it was said, 'You shall love your neighbor and hate your enemy.' But I say to you, love your enemies, bless those who curse you, do good to those who hate you, and pray for those who spitefully use you and persecute you, that you may be sons of your Father in heaven. (Matthew 5:44 NKJ)

There are no similarities between *Jihad* in Islam and any atrocities committed by the so-called Christians. The first is commanded by the Koran, while the second is against the New Testament commandments.

Chapter Twenty Four

Major Differences Between Christianity and Islam

To understand Islam, you have to know the major differences between Christianity and Islam. That knowledge will enable you to discern between the true and false religion.

I have discussed some of these differences in previous chapters but will mention them here again so the reader might have a complete list.

First: Christianity and Islam have two different deities.

Certainly, there is a great difference between Allah of the Koran and the true God who revealed Himself in the Bible. Muhammad wanted to win Jews and Christians to his Islam, so he uttered the following words:

> And dispute ye not with the People of the Book (Jews and Christians), except in the best way, unless it be with those of them who do wrong but say, 'We believe in the Revelation which has come down to us and in that which came down to you. *Our God and your God is One* and it is to Him we submit.'
>
> (Surat Al-Ankabut 29:46 – Author's emphasis)

This verse in the Koran creates a big problem for Muslims. The Koran declares "Our God and Your God is One." So why do Jews and Christians need Islam at all? This is yet another contradiction in their Koran.

The fact is, Allah of the Koran is not the God of the Bible.

1. They have different names.

Allah is not God's name in the Hebrew Bible. The Hebrew name for God is JEHOVAH. Here is what the Book of Psalms says concerning the name of God:

> That men may know that Thou, whose name alone is JEHOVAH, art the Most High over all the earth.
>
> (Psalm 83:18)

The name Allah was known in pre-Islamic Arabia. Muhammad's father's name was Abd-Allah, which means "slave of Allah;" this is clear evidence that Allah was known before Muhammad.

Muhammad's ancestors were pagans. His great-grandfather Qussai was the guardian of the Kaabah where 360 idols were worshiped. Allah was one of the pagan gods not the true God.

In his book, *Islamic Invasion*, Dr. Robert Morey wrote that Allah was known as the moon god.

> According to Middle East scholar E. M. Wherry, whose translation of the Quran is still used today, in pre-Islamic times, Allah-worship, as well as Baal-worship, were both astral religions in that they involved the worship of the sun, the moon and the stars.
>
> In Arabia, the sun god was viewed as a female goddess and the moon as the male god. As has been pointed out by many scholars such as Alfred Guillaume,

322

the moon god was called by various names, one of which was Allah!

The name Allah was used as the personal name of the moon god versus other titles that could be given to him.   (p 48)

The crescent moon is a symbol used throughout Islamic countries. Even *Ramadhan*, the month of fasting, must be confirmed by the moon.

If someone would say that Muhammad took the name Allah from the Jews and Christians, we have to say that he gave to his Allah attributes contrary to those mentioned in the Bible. Muhammad declared that Allah was greater than the idols worshipped in Arabia. If Allah was the absolute sovereign, the words should have been, "Allah is the Greatest," not only greater.

It is a pity that the name JEHOVAH was translated in the Arabic Bible into the word Allah. The use of the name Allah in the Arabic Bible is a source of confusion regarding the different identity of the two deities.

2. They have different attributes.

In the Koran Allah has 99 beautiful names:

And the Most Beautiful Names belong to Allah, so call Him by them.   (Surat Al-Araf 7:180)

None of these beautiful names call Allah 'Father' or 'Love.' There is a reason behind the Koran's denial of the fatherhood of God or that He is Love. To declare that God is Father, we have to admit that He has to be an Eternal Father. The attributes of God are eternal, nothing can be added to them, nothing can be taken from them.

If God is the Eternal Father, then He must have an Eternal Son, for there is no Eternal Fatherhood without Eternal Sonship

And if God is love, at the same time He must demonstrate His love to mankind. In eternity the Father loved the Son. In his prayer to the Father, Christ said:

> Father, I desire that they also whom You gave Me may be with Me where I am, that they may behold My glory which You have given Me; for You loved Me before the foundation of the world. (John 17:24 NKJ)

Furthermore, in due time God proved His love to mankind:

> But God demonstrates His own love toward us, in that while we were still sinners, Christ died for us.
> (Romans 5:8 NKJ)

In the Bible God is the Father of Christ from eternity. He is the Father of angels by creation. He is the Father of those who believe in His Son Christ Jesus by adoption. Muhammad rejected this truth.

The Allah of the Koran has no son. Muslims do not experience the love of God because the only way to experience God's love is by the Holy Spirit:

> ... because the love of God has been poured out in our hearts by the Holy Spirit who was given to us.
> (Romans 5:5 NKJ)

Nor can Muslims pray, "Our Father in heaven, hallowed be your name" (Matthew 6:9 NKJ), because the only way to become a son of God is by believing in Christ Jesus: "For you are all sons of God through faith in Christ Jesus" (Galatians 3:26 NKJ).

3. The God of the Bible is the God of miracles.

Allah of the Koran did not give Muhammad even one miracle to authenticate his claim that he was a true prophet, nor did he do any miracle to authenticate Islam.

4. The God of the Bible does not abrogate or alter His word; He is immutable.

Here is what He says:

My covenant I will not break. Nor alter the word that has gone out of My lips.   (Psalm 89:34 NKJ)

Allah of the Koran changes and abrogates his words:

Wherever a verse (of the Koran) do We abrogate or cause to be forgotten, we bring a better one or similar to it. Know you not that Allah is able to do all things.
                                        (Surat Al-Baqarah 2:106)

There are still many more differences between the God of the Bible and the Allah of the Koran.

Second: Christianity and Islam have two different founders.

Christ is the Founder and the Foundation of the Christian Church, and therefore of true Christianity (Matthew 16:18 and 1 Corinthians 3:11).

Muhammad is the founder of Islam. It is very inappropriate to compare Christ, the Son of the blessed Virgin Mary, and Muhammad, the son of Aminah, the pagan woman, who was raised in a pagan society.

Christ lived a sinless life (John 8:46). Muhammad lived a sinful life.

The Koran commanded him to seek the forgiveness of Allah again and again (Surat Al-Nisa 4:106, Surat Ghafir 40:55, Surat Muhammad 47:19, Surat Al-Nasr 110:3, Surat Al-Fath 48:1,2).

Christ has power over Satan and demons (Mark 9:25, Luke 8:2). He also gave authority to His disciples to cast them out (Matthew 10:8, Luke 10:17). Muhammad lived under the sway of Satan and the fear of demons, and he even uttered Satanic verses.

Satan caused Muhammad to forget.
(Surat Al-Anam 6:68)

Satan used to whisper evil thoughts to Muhammad.
(Surat Al-Araf 7:200)

Muhammad was bewitched. Muhammad Farid Wagdy in his exposition of the Koran recorded:

It is said that a Jew bewitched Muhammad. He used to do a thing then think that he did not do it. Allah gave him Surat Al-Nas, the last surah of the Koran. When Muhammad recited this surah he was cured.

Muhammad uttered satanic verses. On one occasion, Muhammad wanted to win the Qurayish clan to Islam, so when he met with them Allah gave him the following verses:

Have you then considered Al-Lat, and Al-Uzza. And Manat. (Surat Al-Najm 53:19-20)

326

Al-Lat, and Al-Uzza and Manat were three pagan idols believed to be the offspring of the moon god and the sun goddess. The Qurayish tribe worshipped these pagan gods. Muhammad went on to say, "These beautiful goddesses, their intercession is accepted."

Ibn Abass says that Gabriel came to Muhammad and told him he had uttered satanic verses. Muhammad was very sad, so Gabriel gave him the following verse to comfort him:

> Never did we send a Messenger or a prophet before you but when he did recite the revelation, Satan threw (some falsehood) in it. But Allah abolishes that which Satan throws in. Then Allah establishes His Revelations. And Allah is All-Knower, All-Wise.
>
> (Surat Al-Hajj 22:52)

The fact is, Muhammad uttered satanic verses, so we have to ask, which verses in the Koran are from Allah and which are from Satan?

What a great difference between Christ who has power over Satan and demons, and Muhammad who was under the sway of Satan!

Christ performed many miracles; he healed the sick, made the lame walk and gave sight to those who were born blind (The four Gospels and Surat Al-Imran 3:49)

The Apostle John mentioned seven miracles in his gospel, then he concluded:

> And truly Jesus did many other signs in the presence of His disciples, which are not written in this book; but these are written that you may believe that Jesus is the

Christ, the Son of God, and that believing you may have life in His name. (John 20:30-31 NKJ)

Muhammad did not perform one miracle (Surat Al-Isra 17:93 and Surat Al-Ankabut 29:50). When the blind man, Ibn Um Maktoom came to Muhammad, he could not give him his sight, instead, he frowned and turned away. But when blind Bartimaeus, the son of Timaeus, asked for Christ's mercy, Christ stood and gave him back his sight (Mark 10:46-52).

The greatness of Christ is clearly seen when we compare Him with the powerless Muhammad.

Christ gives assurance of eternal life with God to those who trust Him.

Most assuredly, I say to you, he who hears My word and believes in Him who sent Me has everlasting life, and shall not come into judgment, but has passed from death into life. (John 5:24 NKJ)

Muhammad assures every Muslim that he or she will enter Hell:

So by your Lord, surely, We shall gather them together, and also the devils with them, then We shall bring them around Hell on their knees. There is not one of you but will enter it (Hell) [Author's translation]. This is with your Lord; a decree which must be accomplished.
(Surat Maryam 19:68,71)

I wonder how anyone wants to embrace a religion which emphatically assures its followers of such a destiny?

Third: Christianity and Islam have two different books: the Bible and the Koran.

The Bible was written by forty writers of different ranks and classes, over a period of fifteen hundred years, and has maintained amazing unity. This shows that the author is one: that is God Himself. Each book of the Bible has a specific message, and each book of the Bible speaks of the Messiah, Christ Jesus.

Men and women of God whose lives are recorded in the Bible are examples of those who learned to walk with God and are written for our admonition. We can learn to trust God fully from studying their lives. Fulfilled prophecies of the Bible challenge any intelligent person. The Bible warns us of trusting in the wrong things or people because such trust leads to misery and destruction.

The Koran was dictated to Muhammad by the spirit who squeezed him in the cave of Hira. While in Mecca Muhammad did not mention who that spirit was, but after he settled in Medina he claimed that the spirit was the angel Gabriel. Certainly that spirit disguised himself as Gabriel:

> And no wonder! For Satan himself transforms himself into an angel of light. (2 Corinthians 11:14 NKJ)

That spirit accompanied Muhammad for twenty-three years, fulfilled his desires and the desires of his associates by the revelations he gave to him. Muhammad repeated the stories written in the Bible with great distortion. Furthermore, the Koran also contains ancient fables.

The Koran recorded that Allah punished the Jews who broke the Sabbath by making them monkeys:

> And indeed you knew those amongst you who transgressed in the matter of the Sabbath. We said to them, 'Be you monkeys, despised and rejected.' So We make this punishment an example to their own and to

329

succeeding generations and a lesson to those who are pious. (Surat Al-Baqarah 2:65,66)

The Koran took the story of Joseph recorded in Genesis 39 and made it a comedy. The Koran says that Joseph's mistress sought to seduce him to sleep with her, but from there the Bible story is distorted in the Koran:

> And women in the city said: 'The wife of Al-Aziz is seeking to seduce her (slave) young man, indeed she loves him violently; verily, we see her in plain error.' So when she heard of their accusation, she sent for them and prepared a banquet for them; she gave each one of them a knife (to cut the foodstuff with), and she said [to Usuf (Joseph)]: 'Come out before them.' Then, when they saw him, they exalted him (at his beauty) and (in their astonishment) cut their hands. They said: 'How perfect is Allah (or Allah forbid)! No man is this! This is none other than a noble angel!' She said: 'This is he (the young man) about whom you did blame me, and I did seek to seduce him, but he refused. And now if he refuses to obey my order, he shall certainly be cast into prison, and will be one of those who are disgraced.'
> (Surat Yusuf 12:30-32)

The Koran also records a fable concerning four men, or five, or seven with their dog. No one knows the exact number but Allah. They went to a cave and remained asleep for 309 years (Surat Al-Kahf 18:9-26). Can you imagine a man or a dog which slept 309 years?

The beautiful story of the birth of Jesus recorded in Luke 2:1-20 and Matthew 2:1-12 is also distorted in the Koran. It claims that Jesus spoke while he was a baby in his cradle:

330

Then she pointed to him. They said: 'How can we talk to one who is a child in the cradle?' He [Isa (Jesus)] said: 'Verily, I am a slave of Allah, He has given me the Scripture and made me a Prophet; and He has made me blessed wheresoever I be, and has enjoined on me Salat (prayer), and Zakat, as long as I live.' 'And dutiful to my mother, and made me not arrogant, unblest. And Salam (peace) be upon me the day I was born, and the day I die, and the day I shall be raised alive!'   (Surat Maryam 19:29-33)

This is a fabricated story not mentioned in the New Testament. Jesus never spoke in the cradle.

Why should the Koran change the Bible stories?   The New Testament is the continuation of the Old Testament and therefore its writers did not change the Old Testament stories but only refer to them when needed.

The repetition of the Bible stories in such a distorted manner in the Koran indicates that the Koran cannot be the true word of God. Instead of being a continuation of the Bible and Christianity it considers itself a replacement of them.

Fourth: Christianity and Islam have two different ways to eternal life: the shed blood of the crucified Christ, or martyrdom in Allah's way.

The crucifixion of Christ is an irreconcilable crucial difference between Christianity and Islam.   Charles Haddon Spurgeon said, "Leave out the cross and you have killed the religion of Jesus. Atonement by the blood of Jesus is not an arm of Christian truth; it is the heart of it."

From Genesis, the first book of the Bible, to Revelation, the last book of the Bible, we see the crucified Christ as the only way to secure forgiveness and eternal life with God. In the book of Genesis we see Christ, the seed of the woman, the only one who

331

was born of a woman without a man, who was to bruise the head of Satan (Genesis 3:15). We also see a foreshadowed Christ in the ram provided by God to redeem Isaac, the son of Abraham (Genesis 22:13).

In the book of Exodus we see Christ crucified in the Passover lamb (Exodus 12:13), and through all the books of the Old Testament we see the crucified Christ. Chapter 53 of the book of the prophet Isaiah portrays the sufferings of the crucified Christ and how He would be buried in a rich man's tomb. That was written seven hundred years before the birth of Jesus Christ. The four gospels confirm that the prophecies written in that chapter were fulfilled to the letter.

David, who was the king of Israel as well as a prophet, prophesied Christ's crucifixion. This is what David wrote:

> For dogs have compassed me: the assembly of the wicked have enclosed me: they pierced my hands and my feet. (Psalm 22:16 NKJ)

David died an honorable death in his palace, but his son according to the flesh, Jesus Christ, died by crucifixion - the only death in which the hands and the feet are pierced.

All the offerings mentioned in the book of Leviticus were a type of Jesus Christ who was to be crucified. The crucified Christ was the burnt offering, the meat offering, the trespass offering, the peace offering, and the sin offering. God was preparing His people through these offerings, prophecies, symbols, and types for the crucifixion of His son Jesus Christ.

The fiery serpent made of brass and lifted up on a pole in the wilderness was also a symbol of Christ on the cross. It gave life to those who were bitten by fiery serpents if they looked at it in faith. Jesus referred to that symbol when He said:

> And as Moses lifted up the serpent in the wilderness, even so must the Son of Man be lifted up. That

whosoever believeth in him should not perish, but have
eternal life.   (John 3:14-15 NKJ)

We have to remember that the brazen serpent was in the
shape of the fiery serpent but with no poison in it. Jesus came in
the form of man yet was born without sin and lived a sinless life.

Christ sacrificed Himself and died on the cross to grant
forgiveness and eternal life to all who trust Him. Christ said to His
disciples:

> For even the Son of man did not come to be served, but
> to serve, and to give His life a ransom for many.
>   (Mark 10:45 NKJ)

> Greater love has no one than this, than to lay down
> one's life for his friends.   (John 15:13 NKJ)

On the other hand, Muhammad commanded Muslims to
fight and die as martyrs in the way of Allah that they may go to
paradise. The Attorney General of the United States, John
Ashcroft, was asked by writer Cal Thomas what the difference is
between Islam and Christianity. He replied:

> Islam is a religion in which Allah requires you to send
> your son to die for him. Christianity is a faith in which
> God sent His son to die for you.
>   (*The Washington Post*, February 20, 2002)

While redemption through the shed blood of Jesus Christ
on the cross of Calvary is the focal theme of the Bible, it is a
doctrine rejected by the Muslims.

The Apostle John, who was an eyewitness of the crucifixion of Christ recorded:

> Then came the soldiers, and brake the legs of the first, and of the other which was crucified with him. But when they came to Jesus, and saw that he was dead already, they brake not his legs: But one of the soldiers with a spear pierced his side, and forthwith came there out blood and water. And he that saw it bore record, and his record is true: and he knoweth that he saith true, that ye might believe. For these things were done, that the scripture should be fulfilled, 'A bone of him shall not be broken.' And again another scripture saith, 'They shall look on him whom they pierced.'
>
> (John 19:32-37)

Thomas, one of Jesus' disciples, put his finger in the pierced hands of the risen Christ, and cried out:

> My Lord and my God.   (John 20:28)

These words were not an exclamation but a confession.

The Apostle Peter declared to the Jews who lived at the time of the crucifixion of Christ:

> Ye men of Israel, hear these words; Jesus of Nazareth, a man approved of God among you by miracles and wonders and signs, which God did by him in the midst of you, as ye yourselves also know: Him being delivered by the determinate counsel and foreknowledge of God, ye have taken, and by wicked hands have crucified and slain: Whom God hath raised

up, having loosed the pains of death: because it was not possible that he should be holden of it.   (Acts 2:22-24)

More than five hundred people saw the risen Christ (I Corinthians 15:6).

The Koran Denies the Crucifixion of Christ

All of these solid proofs confirm the crucifixion of Jesus Christ. Yet, Muhammad, who lived six hundred years later; never lived in the land of Israel, and was illiterate and unable to read the prophecies of the true prophets, denied the crucifixion of Christ in his Koran.

That they said [in boast], 'We killed Christ Jesus the son of Mary, the Messenger of Allah,' but they killed him not, nor crucified him. Only a likeness of that was shown to them. And those who differ therein are full of doubts, with no [certain] knowledge.   But only conjecture to follow, for of a surety they killed him not.

(Surat Al-Nisa 4:157)

This verse in the Koran says that someone other than Jesus was crucified.   That is in total contrast with the Bible.   The four Gospels: Matthew, Mark, Luke and John are centered around the crucifixion of Christ.   If Christ was not crucified, then the New Testament, indeed Christianity as a whole, is null and void.

Even the Koran says Jesus predicted his death and his resurrection. The Koran records that Jesus said:

Peace on me the day I was born, and the day I die, and the day I shall be raised alive.

(Surat Maryam 19:33 MPT)

Yet, Muhammad denies it.

335

All of the events of the crucifixion and resurrection of Jesus Christ were "according to the scriptures" and fulfilled exactly as the Old Testament prophecies had recorded (I Corinthians 15:1-4). All of the witnesses of these events - many of whom were martyred because of their testimonies - are more than sufficient to confirm the truth about the crucifixion of Christ.

More importantly, the crucifixion of Christ was foreordained before the foundation of the world:

> . . . knowing that you were not redeemed with corruptible things, like silver and gold, from your aimless conduct received by tradition from your fathers, but with the precious blood of Christ, as a lamb without blemish and without spot. He indeed was foreordained before the foundation of the world, but was manifest in these last times for you. (I Peter 1:18-20 NKJ)

For Muhammad to deny the crucifixion of Christ is absurd. If Muhammad and his Koran deny the crucifixion of Christ, then we have to apply the words of the Apostle Peter to him:

> But there were false prophets also among the people, even as there shall be false teachers among you, who privily shall bring in damnable heresies, even denying the Lord that bought them, and bring upon themselves swift destruction. And many shall follow their pernicious ways; by reason of whom the way of truth shall be evil spoken of. (2 Peter 2:1-2)

What did Paul say about that?

> But even if we, or an angel from heaven, preach any other gospel to you than what we have preached to you, let him be accursed. (Galatians 1:8 NKJ)

Fifth: Christianity and Islam produce two different societies.

There is a huge difference between the kindness, cleanliness, liberty and the selflessness of Christian society, and the harshness, brutality, bondage and disrespect for human rights of Islamic society.

Christ laid the foundation of the Christian society. He commanded his disciples:

> Love your enemies, bless those who curse you, do good to those who hate you, and pray for those who spitefully use you and persecute you, that you may be the sons of your Father in heaven.   (Matthew 5:44 NKJ)

He commanded Peter, His disciple:

> Put your sword in its place, for all who take the sword will perish by the sword.   (Matthew 26:52 NKJ)

But Muhammad divided the world into two parts: *Dar Al-Islam*, the House of Islam, where Muslims rule, *and Dar Al-Harb*, the House of War where non-Muslims live. Muslims must fight against those who are in *Dar Al-Harb* until they become Muslims and Islam becomes a great empire. The Koran commands Muslims to strike non-Muslims over the neck and smite over all their fingers and toes (Surat Al-Anfal 118:12). The Koran says:

> The recompense of those who wage war against Allah and His Messenger and do mischief in the land is only that they shall be killed or crucified or their hands and their feet be cut off from opposite sides, or be exiled

from the land. That is their disgrace in this world, and a great torment is theirs in the hereafter.

(Surat Al-Maidah 5:33)

Prime examples of sadistic Islamic society are found in Saudi Arabia, Afghanistan, Sudan and Pakistan. These countries apply the *shariah* (Islamic law) to the letter. In Saudi Arabia, Muttawa, religious police, enforce a strict Koranic code. Muslims are chased by the religious police to go to the mosque to pray each Friday. They also ensure women are covered in black and opposite sexes do not mix in public.

On March 11, 2002, the Muttawa stopped girls from fleeing a fire at their school in the holy city of Mecca because they were not covered in their mandatory *abayas* (black cloak with veil). Fifteen girls perished. In Saudi Arabia a woman cannot drive a car because it is against the law. In Pakistan, anyone who dares to criticize Muhammad or the Koran must be jailed or even murdered under Pakistan's blasphemy law.

Even Muslims do not like Islamic laws. This is why the people in Afghanistan, according to a *Washington Post* report on December 7, 2001, after the Taliban regime was toppled, took to the streets of Kabul saying good-bye to Kabul's moral police and showing posters of Indian film stars and pin-up girls.

The first century after Muhammad's death was a bloody century with much infighting and assassination of rulers. To this day we see civil war and terrorism in Lebanon, Egypt, Sudan, Indonesia, Nigeria, and other Islamic countries. We know also of the massacre of Muslims in Algeria, the war between Iraq and Iran, and the invasion of Kuwait by Iraq.

The role model of the Christian society, however, is beautifully seen in the book of Acts in the New Testament. There we see women praying with the Apostles of Christ in the upper room in Jerusalem:

These all continued with one accord in prayer and supplication, with the women, and Mary the mother of Jesus, and with His brothers.   (Acts 1:14 NKJ)

There we see also the unity and selflessness of the early Christians:

Now all who believed were together, and had all things in common, and sold their possessions and goods, and divided them among all, as anyone had need. So continuing daily with one accord in the temple, and breaking bread from house to house, they ate their food with gladness and simplicity of heart, praising God and having favor with all the people.   (Acts 2:44-47 NKJ)

There were no assassinations, no bloodshed or competition for authority in the early church. The Apostle Peter did not kill the Apostle Paul, nor did Matthew kill Andrew. In addition, men and women were equals in Christ:

For as many of you as were baptized into Christ have put on Christ. There is neither Jew nor Greek, there is neither slave nor free, there is neither male or female; for you are all one in Christ Jesus.
(Galatians 3:27-28 NKJ)

The cleanliness and the kind doctors and nurses in Christian hospitals declare the contribution of Christianity to humanity. Kings, princes and presidents come to Western hospitals seeking medical help.

Deterioration in moral values of Western society today can not be blamed on the Bible but on the failure to apply biblical principles in the people's daily lives. When the Bible is rejected or disregarded by a society, corruption, filthiness, crime,

339

pornography, homosexuality, and lesbianism will overflow it (Romans 1:8-32).

The following true story will give you a vivid picture which shows the difference between the Muslim society and the Christian society. Mark Gabriel, who was a Muslim and became a Christian, attended a meeting which was sponsored by the Islamic Society at Georgetown University. The meeting was packed with American students. Here is the story of what happened during that meeting:

> The speaker was an ex-Baptist minister from Texas who became a Muslim and called himself Sheik Yusef. I listened to that man who entered the auditorium in Islamic traditional clothes of the terrorist groups in Egypt. He talked for almost an hour. He tried hard to convince those students that Islam is a religion of peace and brotherhood and is the answer to the world's problems.
>
> There was a time for questions after his talk. I raised my hand, he motioned me to speak and gave me the microphone. When I got hold of the microphone I asked him the following questions:
>
> 'How long has it been since you became a Muslim?'
> 'Eight years,' he replied.
> 'Have you encountered any kind of persecution here in the United States since you became a Muslim?'
> 'Not at all,' he answered.
> 'Did your church or other churches ask their members to go after you and kill you because you became an apostate from Christianity?'
> 'None of that happened,' he said.
> 'Are there any verses in the Bible that say an apostate Christian should be killed?'
> 'No, there are no verses in the Bible that talk about that,' he answered.
> At that point, the ex-Baptist pastor's face turned pale.

I then told the audience that I am a former professor at Al-Azhar University where I taught Islamic history and literature. Eight years ago I was converted from Islam to Christianity.

After a pause, I continued: 'Do you know what happened to me after receiving Christ as my Savior and Lord? I immediately lost my profession at the university. I was put in prison by the police of internal security who tortured me almost to death. The Islamic groups in Egypt and my own family tried to kill me.'

'You, Sheik Yusef, are not threatened, you are protected by the laws of the United States. You are free to travel and to speak in meetings like this one, but I am under threat, with no home or family. I am a victim of the Islamic *Sharia*. I might be killed any day to satisfy Muslim fundamentalists because in their opinion I am an apostate.

'But you, former Baptist pastor, you traded the freedom of Christianity with the bondage of Islam. I say that because the day you think of leaving Islam to come back to Christianity, you will be killed by the sword of Islam. The sword of Islam will not permit you to practice Christianity again, even here in the United States of America, because the one who will kill you will be granted entrance to paradise.'

(Full story found in *Islam and Terrorism* by Mark Gabriel)

The difference in Christianity and Islam are clearly seen in the societies they produce.

Sixth: Christianity and Islam promise two different eternal destinies: the Biblical Heaven and the Koran's Paradise.

Heaven as described in the Bible is a holy place. The Apostle Peter says:

> Nevertheless we, according to His promise, look for new heavens and a new earth in which righteousness dwells. (2 Peter 3:13 NKJ)

Those who are not washed by the blood of Christ will not enter heaven:

> But the cowardly (those who fear men rather than God), unbelieving, abominable, murderers, sexually immoral, sorcerers, idolaters, and all liars shall have their part in the lake which burns with fire and brimstone, which is the second death. (Revelation 21:8 NKJ)

Because those people will not enter heaven, heaven will be a pure and safe place.

More importantly, heaven will be the place where we will see God's face and enjoy being with the Triune God. Here is the picture of the biblical heaven, as revealed in the book of Revelation:

> And I saw a new heaven and a new earth, for the first heaven and the first earth had passed away. Also, there was no more sea. Then I, John, saw the holy city, New Jerusalem, coming down out of heaven from God, prepared as a bride adorned for her husband. And I heard a loud voice from heaven saying, 'Behold, the tabernacle of God is with men, and He will dwell with

them, and they shall be His people, and God Himself will be with them and be their God. And God will wipe away every tear from their eyes; there shall be no more death, nor sorrow, nor crying; and there shall be no more pain, for the former things have passed away.' Then He who sat on the throne said, 'Behold, I make all things new.' And He said to me, 'Write, for these words are true and faithful.' (Revelation 21:1-5 NKJ)

And he showed me a pure river of water of life, clear as crystal, proceeding from the throne of God and of the Lamb. In the middle of its street, and on either side of the river, was the tree of life, which bore twelve fruits, each tree yielding its fruit every month. And the leaves of the tree were for the healing of the nations. And there shall be no more curse, but the throne of God and of the Lamb shall be in it, and His servants shall serve Him. They shall see His face, and His name shall be on their foreheads. And there shall be no night there: They need no lamp nor light of the sun, for the Lord God gives them light. And they shall reign forever and ever. (Revelation 22:1-5 NKJ)

This is the description of the biblical heaven; God will dwell with men. Sin prevented us from seeing God's face for millennia, but in heaven we will see His glorious face. There shall be no more death, nor sorrow, nor crying, nor pain, nor curse. What a magnificent place!

Moreover, there shall be no more marriages in heaven. Here is what we read in the gospel of Matthew:

The same day the Sadducees, who say there is no resurrection, came to Him and asked Him, saying: 'Teacher, Moses said that if a man dies, having no children, his brother shall marry his wife and raise up

343

offspring for his brother. Now there were with us seven brothers. The first died after he had married, and, having no offspring, left his wife to his brother. Likewise the second also, and the third, even to the seventh. And last of all the woman died also. Therefore, in the resurrection, whose wife of the seven will she be? For they all had her.' Jesus answered and said to them, 'You are mistaken, not knowing the Scriptures nor the power of God. For in the resurrection they neither marry nor are given in marriage, but are like angels of God in heaven.'

(Matthew 22:23-30 NKJ)

Now let us look at the Muslims' paradise as pictured in the Koran. On this subject, the Koran declares double standards, one for earth and one for paradise. On earth, Muslim men are permitted to marry up to four women at one time (Surat Al-Nisa 4:3). However, in paradise he will marry one hundred virgins according to the Hadith.

Here is what the Koran says concerning marriage in paradise:

Verily the pious will be in Gardens (Paradise) and Delight. Enjoying in that which their Lord has bestowed on them, and (the fact that) their Lord saved them from the torment of the blazing Fire. 'Eat and drink with happiness because of what you used to do.' They will recline on thrones arranged in ranks. And We shall marry them to Hur (fair female) with wide lovely eyes. And those who believe and whose offspring follow them in Faith: to them shall We join their offspring, and We shall not decrease the reward of their deeds in anything. Every person is a pledge for that which he has earned. And We shall provide them with fruit and meat such as they desire.

(Surat Al-Tur 52:17-22)

There is also a double standard concerning wine. Wine is forbidden for Muslims here on earth; it is called an abomination of Satan:

O you who believe (Muslims) wine [literal translation] and gambling... are an abomination of Satan, so avoid that abomination in order that you may be successful.

(Surat Al-Maidah 5:90)

Wine, which is an abomination of Satan on earth, will be given plentifully to Muslims who will enter paradise. What is forbidden on earth and is an abomination of Satan will be permissible there. Here are more verses of the Koran concerning wine:

There they shall pass from hand to hand a (wine) cup, free from any vain talk between them and free from sin (because it will be lawful for them to drink). And there will go around boys to serve them as if they were preserved pearls.   (Surat Al-Tur 52:23-24)

Verily, for the pious there will be a success (Paradise); gardens and vineyards, and young full-breasted maidens of equal age, and a full cup (of wine)... A reward from your Lord, an ample calculated gift (according to the best of their good deeds).   (Surat Al-Naba 78:31-36)

This is the description of paradise in the Koran. Paradise is made up of gardens of sensual pleasure, full-breasted virgins with wide lovely eyes, rivers of wine delicious to those who drink and beautiful boys as preserved pearls. What a paradise!

The question is, why does the Koran describe those boys as preserved pearls and immortal (Surat Al-Waqiah 56:17)? Rather than discuss such perversion, I will leave the answer to the intelligent reader!

There is no mention of Allah or absence of sin and curse in the Islamic paradise. How could any man think about the Holy God while he is busy drinking wine and having sex with a hundred virgins? The words "holiness" or "be holy" are never mentioned in the Koran.

The gulf between the biblical heaven and the Muslims' paradise cannot be crossed.

Seventh: Christianity and Islam have two different sources: The true God and the spirit who squeezed Muhammad.

The Torah was given to Moses by God on Mount Sinai. The New Testament was given to its writers by the Holy Spirit: The Apostle Peter wrote:

> ... knowing this first, that no prophecy of Scripture is of any private interpretation, for prophecy never came by the will of man, but holy men of God spoke as they were moved by the Holy Spirit. (2 Peter 1:20-21 NKJ)

The Apostle Paul wrote:

> All Scripture is given by inspiration of God, and is profitable for doctrine, for reproof, for correction, for instruction in righteousness, that the man of God may be complete, thoroughly equipped for every good work.
> (2 Timothy 3:16-17 NKJ)

346

The Old and New Testaments came from God Himself. The Koran was revealed to Muhammad by the spirit who squeezed him at the cave of Hira, not by Allah himself.

These are the major differences between Christianity and Islam. It is evident that Islam does not satisfy the spiritual needs of mankind. Only Christianity offers the way for the salvation of man through the precious blood of Christ.

Now to Him who is able to keep you from stumbling,
And to present you faultless
Before the presence of His glory with exceeding joy,
To God our Savior,
Who alone is wise,
Be glory and majesty,
Dominion and power,
Both now and forever. Amen
(Jude 24-25 NKJ)

Appendix A

THE SECTS AND JURIDICAL SCHOOLS OF ISLAM

It is said that there are more than seventy sects in Islam. They are divided between the heterodoxy (heretical) and orthodoxy (traditional). I will mention the names of most of these sects but will elaborate only on a few.

In Islam there are two main sects: Sunnis and Shiites.

The Sunnis

The Sunnis comprise the main body of Islam. They are known as Ahl-al-Sunnah Wa-Al-Hadith, or "followers in the way and practices laid out by the prophet Muhammad, and believers in the Hadith" (sayings of Muhammad). The main religious authority to them is the Koran, the Sunnah (practices of Muhammad) and the Hadith. In Sunni Islam, the Imam (clergy leader) is only the leader of the Friday weekly prayers.

The Shiites

The term *shiah* means "a follower" and is used to denote the followers of Ali, who was the son-in-law of the prophet Muhammad and the fourth caliph.

The Shiites clung to Ali with worshipful affection, insisting that only he and his descendants had legitimate right to be caliphs. The distinctive feature then of the Shiites is shown in the role and authority of the Imam. Shiites believe that the Imam is the divinely appointed religious, social, and political leader who preserves the purity of Islam. Shiites believe that the true Imam, or Al-Mahdi, will appear to restore and create a pure Islamic nation.

The Shiites permit marriage for pleasure, that is marriage for a period of time for a specific amount of money agreed upon by a man and a woman. This kind of marriage ends without divorce. This marriage for pleasure may last for hours, or days, or even years. There is no limit to the number of women a man can marry for pleasure (Read the Arabic book, *Marriage for Pleasure*, by Dr. Farag Fouda).

Shiites represent the majority in Iran, where the Mullahs (religious leaders) reign. There are also Shiites in Iraq, Lebanon and other Islamic countries.

The Ismailis

Shiism opened the floodgates for a large number of sects, which came into being in subsequent centuries. The Ismailis or "seveners" honor the line of succession down to the sixth Imam, Jafar Al-Sadiq. They regard his eldest son, Ismail, as the seventh (whence the name "seveners") and last Imam. He too in the eyes of his followers is the Imam-Mahdi who becomes the hidden leader and whose return they await (*Islam*, p 175). The Ismailis have great admiration for their Imam.

A journalist who was in the Royal Hotel in the French city of Evian many years ago, where Aja Khan, the great Imam of the Ismailis was staying, noticed that Aja Khan was receiving a large amount of money from his followers. The journalist was shocked to learn that Aja Khan received this huge sum of money from his followers who wanted to show their love and respect for him, while he did things totally against Islam, like drinking alcoholic beverages, gambling, and marrying many foreign dancers and beautiful models.

One day, the journalist asked one of Aja Kan's associates to explain to him this puzzle. "There is nothing shocking in that," the associate answered. "We know all that the Imam does, we are in complete agreement with what he does because he tries all these gross sins so that he can teach and advise us with his own personal experiences."

The Assassins

The founder of this terrible sect is Hasan Ibn Al-Sabbah, a native of Persia. This sect spread terror everywhere for almost two centuries. The Mongols (people of Chinese origin who, under Genghis Khan, built one the world's greatest empires, stretching from China to the Danube and into Persia) attacked and destroyed their strongholds in 1256 on their way to destroy Baghdad, so the Assassins were exterminated.

The Wahhabis

The founder of the Wahhabis sect was Muhammad-Ibn Abdul-Wahhab who was born in a village in Nejd, [Saudi Arabia] in the year 1691 AD. Muhammad was an intelligent youth who, after going through a course of Arabic literature, studied under a teacher of Hafini school and returned to his native village and became a religious teacher.

He saw that Arabs neglected the Koran and the traditions. When he began to teach against their behavior, they opposed him, and he had to seek the protection of Muhammad Ibn-Saud, a chief of some importance, who converted to Wahhabism around the year 1742 AD, and who was a stern and uncompromising man. 'As soon as you seize a place,' he said to his soldiers, 'put the males to the sword. Plunder and pillage at your pleasure, but spare the women, and do not strike a blow at their modesty.'

The traveler Burckhardt says that the rule of the Wahhabis was to kill all their enemies whom they found in arms. On the day of battle the chief used to give each soldier a paper, a safe-conduct to the other world. This letter was addressed to the Treasurer of Paradise. It was enclosed in a bag which the warrior suspended to his neck. The soldiers were persuaded that the souls of those who died in battle would go straight to heaven without being examined by the angels Munkir and Nakir in the grave. The widows and orphans of all who fell were supported by the survivors.

Nothing could resist men who, fired with a burning zeal for what they deemed the truth, received a shore of the booty, if conquerors; who went direct to Paradise if they were slain. In course of time, Muhammad-Ibn-Saud married the daughter of Abn-Abdul-Wahhab, and founded the Wahhabi dynasty, which to this day rules at *Ryadh*   *(The Faith of Islam*, p 154)

Osama Bin Laden was raised in the Wahhabbi sect.

Rosalind Gwynne, of the Department of Religious Studies at the University of Tennessee, wrote a draft dated September 18, 2001, in which she attempted to prove that Osama Bin Laden does not apply the correct interpretation of the Koran but took the Koranic verses out of their historical settings to incite Muslims to begin *Jihad* against the United States as well as against the Saudi regime.

Rosalind depended on the Al-Qurtubi exposition of the Koran and claimed that Islam is far from Osama Bin Laden's interpretation. The fact is that the Koran's verses very clearly command Muslims to wage war against Jews and Christians.

Osama Bin Laden, in his call to the Muslims for *Jihad*, recited actual verses of the Koran. He called America's war against Iraq to protect Saudi Arabia and liberate Kuwait the "greatest act of aggression."

Bin Laden said:

The occupation of the land of the two holy places - the foundation of the house of Islam, the place of the revelation, the source of the message and the place of the noble Kaaba, the Qiblah (direction of prayer) of all Muslims - by the armies of the American Crusaders and their allies, were the greatest act of aggression.

Bin Laden believes that the American presence in the Saudi kingdom defiles the Holy Land of Islam because in his belief all Americans are Christians, and Christians are impure and filthy according to the Koran (Surat Al-Taubah 9:28).

Osama Bin Laden is pure Wahabi so Rosalind's argument is not valid.

The Darawishes

The Darawishes are looked upon with disfavor by the orthodox Islamics, but they flourish nevertheless. They have a lot of influence in Turkey. There are two hundred orders of Darawishes, each order having its own special mysteries and practices by which its members think they can obtain a knowledge of the secrets of the invisible world.

The Sufiis

The term *Sufi* means "purifying the human soul by continuous striving of the devout Muslim to identify himself with the cause of all being." The Suffiis are Islam's mystics. The chief idea in Suffiism is that the souls of men differ in degree but not in kind from the divine spirit of which they are emanations and to which they will return.

The great object of life to the Sufi is to ascend to pure love and to return to the divine essence. In order to reach this higher state of existence, the seeker must pass through the following states: (1) Worship Allah; (2) Love Allah; (3) Seclusion, meaning that the Sufi passes his time in meditation on the deeper doctrines of sufiism; (4) Knowledge, which means that through the former states he will become an *Arif* - "one who knows;" (5) Ecstasy, when the Sufi will experience mental excitement caused by continued meditation.

The Druzes

The Druzes were originated and named after Al-Darazi, a Fatimid, who was appointed by Caliph Al-Hakim in the year 1021 AD. to propogate the Ismaili doctrine.   Druzes believe in reincarnation as well as some other secret doctrines. For the most part they submitted completely to the will of Al-Hakim.

> The preaching of Al-Darazi centered on the notion that the intolerant Caliph Al-Hakim, notorious for his persecution of Jews, Christians and Orthodox Muslims, represented the last in a series of incarnations of the one and only God.   (*Islam*, p 179)

The Ahmadiyya

The Ahmadiyya sect is considered heretical by orthodox Islam. The founder of this sect is Gulah Ahmad, who is considered to be a prophet by the Ahmadiyyas. Because the Koran declares that Muhammad is the last prophet, that there is no prophet to come after him, the Ahmadiyya sect is rejected.

One of the main beliefs of this sect is that Jesus traveled to Northern India and that He died and was buried there.

Black Muslims in America

Early in this century, many African-Americans converted to Islam as a way to escape racism. There are many leaders who are known in the history of African-American Muslims: Nobel Drew

Ali, Elijah Muhammad, Malcolm X and Warith Al-Deen Muhammad. Malcolm X embraced orthodox Islam after his Hajj to Mecca, and then influenced Warith Al-Deen Muhammad. Warith Al-Deen Muhammad was Elijah Muhammad's son who, after the death of his father led the Nation of Islam into the mainstream of Islam.

The Nation of Islam, led by minister Louis Farrakan severed itself from Orthodox Islam and maintains a radical racist ideology. Other Islamic groups in America include the Islamic party, the Ansaru Allah and the Hanafi sect.

Other Sects

The Zaydis took their name from Zayd, the grandson of Hussayn, who following his grandfather's murder at Kerbala challenged the caliphate of the Umayyads. The Mutazila, the Carmathians, the Nusayris, and the Matawilah (those who profess love for Ali); they constitute a powerful element in Lebanon.

Dr. Samuel Zwener, in his book, *Disintegration of Islam*, came to the following conclusion:

> The revolt against Islam in its hard traditional form has generally been along one of three lines: Attempt to spiritualize its doctrines (Sufism); attempt to rid it of excrescencies, that is, to minimize the weight of tradition, as in the case of the Wahabis; and finally, especially in recent years, syncretism by the establishment of new sects, such as Babism, Bahaism, and the Ahmadiya movement. This might be called Moslem eclecticism. (p 64)

JURIDICAL SCHOOLS OF ISLAM

These schools are called *Madhahib* in Arabic and I will mention four of them briefly:

355

Hanafite

Hanafite was formed by Abu Hanifah (767 AD). This school reflects the views of the jurists of Iraq. It is less rigid in its doctrinal interpretations than the other three schools. We can call it the liberal school. This school rules Turkey, Lower Egypt, and India.

Malikite

Malikite comes second in history and was founded by Malik Ibn Anas of Medina in the year 795 AD. The Malikites preferred to depend more on the traditions associated with the companions of Muhammad than with the prophet himself on the grounds that these traditions could not have existed without knowledge of the prophet's Hadith and Sunnah. Adherents of this sect are strong in North Africa, especially Algeria.

Shafiite

This school was founded by Al-Shafii, who had been a disciple of Malik in the year 820 AD. Al-Shafii had great knowledge of the Koran and the Sunnah.

It was he who organized the *Shariah* under (1) the Koran, (2) Sunnah, (3) Ijma, and (4) Qiyas. Muslim theologians applied the principle of Ijma for the justification of religious beliefs or practices not mentioned in the Koran. It means agreement of theologians to legalize customs of the Jahiliyah period. Qiyas means the way a belief or practice gains official support on the grounds that it is similar to a practice or belief clearly mentioned in the Koran, Sunnah or Hadith.

It was Al-Shafii who elevated the authority of the Hadith to its position of pre-eminence. This school is strong in Lower Egypt, Syria, India and Indonesia.

Hanbalite

The founder of this school was Ahmad Ibn Hanbal (855 AD). It is known as the Hanbali. The Hanbalite school was not established by Ibn Hanbal himself but by his followers. It is strong in Iraq and Syria. This is the most conservative of the four schools.

The Hanbalis apply the literal wordings of the Koran and the Hadith with fanatical insistence on the fulfillment of the *Shariah* (Koran's law). Because Islam is a state religion, the Hambalis demand that the state should provide judges for them, who are called muftis, to enforce the *shariah*. Hanbalis do not compromise. This school has found new vitality in central Arabia from where it promotes its doctrines and motivates Muslims to return to fundamentalism.

BIBLIOGRAPHY

BIBLE VERSIONS

1. *The Holy Bible*: Authorized King James Version. Zondervan Publishing House.

2. *The Holy Bible*: The New King James Version. Thomas Nelson Publishers.

3. *The Holy Bible*: New International Version. Zondervan Bible Publishers.

KORAN VERSIONS

4. *The Glorious Qur'an: Text and Explanatory Translation*. By Muhammad Marmaduke Pickthall.

5. *The Holy Qu-ran: English Translation of the Meanings and Commentary*. Printed by order of King Fahd Ibn Abdul Aziz Al-Saud Printing Complex, PO Box 3561, Al-Madina, Al-Munawarah, Saudi Arabia.

6. *The Koran*. Translated with Notes, by N.J. Dawood, Penguin Books.

7. *The Koran*. Ivy Books, New York.

8. *The Noble Qur'an in the English Language*. Al-Hilali, Dr. Muhammad and Dr. Muhammad Muhsin Khan, Dar Alsalam-Al-Riyad, Saudi Arabia.

9. *The Qur'an: The First American Version*. Translation and Commentary by T.B. Irving, Amana Books, Brattleboro, Vermont .

10. *Quran: The Final Testament: Authorized English Version.* Translated from the original by Rashad Khalifa, Ph.D. Published by Islamic Productions, Tucson, Arizona.

ENGLISH BOOKS

11. *A Brief Illustrated Guide to Understanding Islam.* I. A. Ibramim, Darussalam, Houston, Texas, USA. Second Edition 1997.

12. *Answering Islam, The Crescent in the Light of the Cross.* Norman L. Geisler & Abdul Saleeb, Baker Books, 1994.

13. *Commentary on Proverbs.* Charles Bridges, The Banner of Truth Trust, Great Britain.

14. *The Dagger of Islam.* John Laffin.

15. *The Dhimmi, Jews and Christians Under Islam.* Bat Ye'or, Fairleigh Dickinson Unversity Press, London, 1985.

16. *The Disintegration of Islam.* Dr. Samuel M. Zwemer, Fleming H. Revell Company, London, 1916.

17. *The Divine Comedy.* Alighieri Dante.

18. *Epistles of John and Jude.* H. A. Ironside, Loizeaux Brothers, N.J. Seventeenth Printing 1979.

19. *The Faith of Islam.* Edward Sell, Fellow of the University of Madras. Kegan Paul, Trench, Trubner & Co., Ltd. Second Edition 1896.

20. *God's Last Messenger.* Dr. Labib Mikhail, Blessed Hope Ministry, 1998.

21. *The Historical Development of the Koran.* Rev. Canon Sell, People International, England.

22. *Is an Islamic World Empire Imminent?* Abd Al-Masih, Light of Life, Villach , Austria. First Edition 1994.

23. *Islam and Democracy, Fear of the Modern World.* Fatima Mernissi, Addison-Wesley Publishing Company, First paperback printing 1993.

24. *Islam and Dhimmitude, Where Civilizations Collide.* Bat Ye'or, printed in USA, 2002.

25. *Islam and Terrorism.* Mark A. Gabriel, published by Charisma House, Florida, USA, 2002.

26. *Islam, Beliefs and Observances.* Caesar E. Farah, PH.D., Fifth Edition 1994.

27. *Islam Debate.* McDowell, Josh and John Gilchrist, Campus Crusade for Christ, 1985.

28. *Islam Unveiled, The Pen vs. The Sword.* Abdullah Al-Araby, California.

29. *Islam Unveiled, The True Desert Storm.* Dr. Robert A. Morey, The Scholars Press, USA, 1996.

30. *Is the Koran Infallible?* Abdallah Abd al-Fadi, Light of Life, Villach, Austria.

31. *Jihad.* Paul Fregosi, published by Prometheus Books, USA, 1998.

32. *The Koran and The Bible in The Light of History and Science.* Dr. William Campbell, M.D., Middle East Resources.

33. *The Koran is Not the Word of God.* Sir Lionel Luckhoo, Luckhoo Ministries, Dallas, Texas.

34. *Knowing God.* J.I. Packer, Intervarsity Press, Downers Grove, Illinois.

35. *The Last of the Giants: Lifting the Veil on Islam and the End Times.* George Otis, Jr., Published by Fleming H. Revell Company, NY, USA.

36. *Mohammedanism.* Prof. H.A.R. Gibb, Oxford University Press, London, New York, Toronto.

37. *Muhammad in the Bible.* Prof. Abdu L-ahad Dawud, Pustaka Antara, Kuala Lumpur. Second Edition 1979.

38. *The 99 Beautiful Names of God for All the People of the Book.* David Bentley, William Carey Library, Pasadena, California, 1999.

39. *No God but God - Egypt and the Triumph of Islam.* Geneive Abdo, Oxford University Press 2000.

40. *Princess.* Jean P. Sason, Avon Books, New York.

41. Reader's Digest Illustrated Encyclopedic Dictionary.

42. *The Religion that is Raping America.* Dr. Moody Adams, The Moody Adams Evangelistic Association

43. *The Silence of God.* Sir Robert Anderson, Kregel Publications, USA, 1999.

44. *Towards Understanding Islam.* Abul A'la Mawdudi, Islamic Circle of North America, Tenth Edition 2001.

45. *23 Year Study of the Prophetic Career of Mohammad.* Allen, George and Uwin Ali Dashti. Translated from Persian by S. K. C. Bagli, London.

46. *Unveiling Islam.* Caner, Ergun Mehmet and Emir Fethi Caner, Kregel Publications.

47. *Who is Allah in Islam?* Abd-Al-Masih, Light of Life, Villach, Austria.

48. *Who Is This Allah?* G. J. O. Moshay, Dorchester House Publication.

49. *Why I Am Not A Muslim.* Ibn Warraq, Prometheus Books, New York, 1995.

ARABIC BOOKS

50. *Al-Gozoor Al-Tarikhia Lil-Shariah Al-Islamia.* Prof. Khali Abd-Alkareem, Sina Lil-Nashr, Cairo, Egypt. Seventeenth Printing 1989.

51. *Al-Hakika Al-Ghaiba.* Dr. Farag Foudah, Dar Al-Fikr Le-Aldrasat Wa-Al-Nashr, Cairo, Egypt. First Printing 1986.

52. *Al-Hezb Al-Hashimi Wa Tasses Al-Dawla Al-Islamiah.* Dr. Sayed Mahmoud Al-Limny, Sina Lil-Nashr, Cairo, Egypt. First Printing 1990.

53. *Al-Imam Al-Shafi WaTasses Al-Idoyologiia Al-Wasatia.* Dr. Nasr Hamed Abu-Zaid, Sina Lil-Nashr, Cairo, Egypt. First Printing 1992.

54. *Al-Kaaba Al-Musharafa Wa Al-Shaire Al-Mukadsa.* Al-Sayed Hamed Al-Sayed Ali, Maktbat Hamada Al-Hadesa. First Printing 1991.

55. *Al-Khaledoon Maa-ah Azamhom Muhammad Rasool Allah.* Anis Mansoor, Al-Maktab Al-Masri Al-Hadith, Cairo, Egypt. Sixth Printing.

56. *Alkhelapha Al-Islamia.* Chief Justice Muhammad Saeed El-Eshmawi, Madboly Alsagheir Library, Cairo, Egypt, 1996.

57. *Al-Mushaf Al-Mufasar.* Muhammad Farid Wagdy, Al-Shaab Press, Cairo, Egypt.

58. *Al-Mushaf Al-Shareef* (Arabic) *Research in its History and Texts.* Sheikh Abd-Elfatah Al-Kady, The Highest Council of Islamic Affairs, Cairo, Egypt.

59. *Al-Ostorah Wa-Alturath.* Sayed Mahmoud Al-kimney, Sena Lil-Nashr, Cairo, Egypt, 1993.

60. *Al-rasoul Fi Al-Koran.* Mahmoud Ibn Al-Shareef, Egyptian for Publication, 1967.

61. *Al-Serah Al-Nabawiah.* Abd Al-Malik Ibn Hesham, Dar Al-Jeel, Beirut, Lebanon. First Printing 1991 - 3 volumes.

62. *Al-Shafa-ah.* Dr. Mustafa Mahmoud, Kitab Al-Youm, Cairo, Egypt. July 1999.

63. *Al-Zawag Wa-Al-Alakaat Al-Gensia Fi Al-Islam.* Adel Abd-Almonim Abu-Alabaas, Maktabat Al-Koran, Cairo, Egypt, September 1987.

64. *Anbia Allah.* Ahmad Bahgat, Dar Alshorrok, Cairo, Egypt. Seventeenth Printing 1989.

65. *An-Nobowa Wa-Alanbia in Judaism, Christianity, and Islam.* Engineer Ahmad Ad-Elwahab, Dar Gharib Publishing, Cairo, Egypt.

66. *An-Nus Al-Moassas Wa-Mogtamoah.* Prof. Khalil Abd-Alkareem, Book One, First Printing, Dar Masr Al-Mahrosa, Cairo, Egypt, 2002.

67. *An-Nus Al-Moassas Wa-Mogtamoah.* Prof. Khalil Abd-Alkareem, Book Two, First Printing.

68. *Fatrat Al-Takween Fi Hayat Al Sadik Al-Amin* , Prof. Khalil Abd-Alkareem. Mereet Lil-Nashr, Cairo, Egypt, 2001.

69. *Fi Al-Shir Al-Jahily.* Dr. Taha Hussen, Dar Al-Kotob Almasria, Cairo, Egypt, 1926.

70. *Fi Zelal Al-Koran.* Sayed Kotb, Dar Al-Shorouk, Beirut, Lebanon. 27th Printing 1998 - 6 volumes.

71. *Howar Belkatl.* Muhammad Hassan Almounayer. Printed in Canada.

72. *Kalmat Al-Koran Tafseeron Wa-Baian Mustafa.* Sheikh Hassanien Muhammad Makhloof, 7th Edition, Alhalabi Publishing Company, Cairo, Egypt, 1967.

73. *Khawater Muslim Fi Al-Masalah Al-Gensia.* Muhammad Jalal Kishk, Maktabat Al-Turath Al-Islamy, Cairo, Egypt. Third Printing 1992.

74. *Kusson Wa Naby.* Abu Mossa Al-Harerri, Dar Le-Agl Almarefa, Lebanon, 1985.

75. *Nesaa Al-Napy.* Dr. Aisha Abd-Al-Rahman, Kitab Al-Hilal, December 1954.

76. *Saraya Rasoul Allah.* Abu Torab Al-Zahery, Tuham Publication, Geda, Saudi Arabia, First Printing 1984.

77. *Tafseer Al-Koran Al-Azeem.* Imam Al-Hafez Ibn Katheir, Dar Al-Jeel, Beirut, Lebanon, 4 volumes.

78. *Two Hundred Soaal Wa Gawab Fi Al-Akeeda Al-Islamia.* Sheik Hafez Ben Ahmad Hakamy, Dar Al-Itsam, Cairo, Egypt.

79. *Zawag Al-Mutah.* Dr. Farag Foudah, Al dar Al-Arabia, Cairo, Egypt. First Printing 1992.